# ROUTLEDGE LIBRARY EDITIONS: EMPLOYEE OWNERSHIP AND ECONOMIC DEMOCRACY

Volume 8

# TOWARDS A NEW INDUSTRIAL DEMOCRACY

# TOWARDS A NEW INDUSTRIAL DEMOCRACY

## Workers' Participation in Industry

MICHAEL POOLE

Routledge
Taylor & Francis Group

LONDON AND NEW YORK

First published in 1986 by Routledge & Kegan Paul

This edition first published in 2018
by Routledge
2 Park Square, Milton Park, Abingdon, Oxon OX14 4RN

and by Routledge
711 Third Avenue, New York, NY 10017

*Routledge is an imprint of the Taylor & Francis Group, an informa business*

*British Library Cataloguing in Publication Data*
A catalogue record for this book is available from the British Library

ISBN: 978-1-138-29962-7 (Set)
ISBN: 978-1-315-12163-5 (Set) (ebk)
ISBN: 978-1-138-30782-7 (Volume 8) (hbk)
ISBN: 978-1-315-14261-6 (Volume 8) (ebk)

**Publisher's Note**
The publisher has gone to great lengths to ensure the quality of this reprint but points out that some imperfections in the original copies may be apparent.

**Disclaimer**
The publisher has made every effort to trace copyright holders and would welcome correspondence from those they have been unable to trace.

# Towards a New Industrial Democracy

WORKERS' PARTICIPATION IN INDUSTRY

Michael Poole

Routledge & Kegan Paul
London and New York

First published in 1986 by
Routledge & Kegan Paul plc
11 New Fetter Lane, London EC4P 4EE

Published in the USA by
Routledge & Kegan Paul Inc.
in association with Methuen Inc.
29 West 35th Street, New York, NY 10001

Phototypeset in Linotron Sabon 10 on 12pt
by Input Typesetting Ltd, London
and printed in Great Britain
by Billing & Sons Ltd, Worcester

Library of Congress Cataloging in Publication Data

Poole, Michael.
Towards a new industrial democracy.
Rev. ed. of Workers' participation in industry. 1978.
Bibliography: p.
Includes indexes.
1. Management—Employee participation.  I Poole,
Michael.  Workers' participation.  I. Poole,
Michael.  Workers' participation in industry.
II. Title.
HD5650.P54   1986        658.3'152        85–30160

British Library CIP Data also available
ISBN  0–7102–0667–4 (c)
      0–7102–0916–9 (p)

For
Anne

# Contents

# Figures

# Tables

# Preface and acknowledgments

*Towards a New Industrial Democracy* is a book which has evolved from my earlier study, *Workers' Participation in Industry*. The original volume was first published in 1975 and a revised version appeared in 1978 to take account of notable developments of that period (and above all, the recommendations of the Bullock Committee of Inquiry on industrial democracy). For some time, however, it has been obvious to me that a further new approach is now necessary to accommodate: (1) the radically different political and economic conditions of the 1980s; (2) the emergent points of emphasis in current thinking and practice; (3) the findings of some impressive cross-national empirical researches; and (4) the relatively sophisticated theoretical analysis which has appeared during the last decade.

Such a substantial re-shaping clearly merited a distinctive title but, at the same time, I have sought to retain the underlying arguments, level of treatment and structure of chapters since these obviously proved to be a success in the earlier versions. And, indeed, it seemed appropriate to continue to accommodate the theme of the original inquiry by means of the subtitle. Once more, too, I have endeavoured within the compass of a single investigation to draw together material from a wide range of practices designed to extend the control of workers over decisions within their places of employment. Again, it is my considered view that, notwithstanding their disparate origins, these experiments have a certain unity and that the principles which bind them together are made intelligible by reference to deep-rooted causes in economic, political and social life. Furthermore, if a principal aim of this study is to maintain interest in and to create a sympathetic attitude towards developments in this direction, the primary focus remains explanatory.

Yet a word is also in order to convey to the reader some of the foremost changes which characterize the new study. To begin with, then, the book has been thoroughly updated and, in every chapter,

I have set out the main adaptations in policy, theory and experimentation that have occurred in industrial democracy in the 1980s. Secondly, I have re-analysed the role of managers here, since, in the new political and economic climate, these personnel have been responsible for a number of the current initiatives. Thirdly, in contrast with the earlier editions, I have viewed collective bargaining and other forms of trade union action as types of representative participation and have thus in no way set these out as an alternative to worker or employee-centred schemes. Fourthly, I have retained (and where possible extended) the comparative emphasis, paying special regard to developments in socialist countries and in the Third World. Fifthly, I have addressed ongoing theoretical debates, which focus on the respective claims of the so-called 'evolutionary' and 'cyclical' schools, by establishing a distinctive position and noting the importance of the segmentation of labour and the rise of new technologies for understanding the complex patterns of the 1980s. And, finally, I have continued to highlight issues of policy by extending the original concerns to embrace the financial participation of working people in the firms in which they are employed.

In this prefatory note, I should also like to avail myself of the opportunity to record my appreciation of the contributions of friends and colleagues. As always my greatest debt is to my wife, Anne, whose encouragement enabled the conflicting demands upon the author to be resolved in a way which left sufficient time for writing. The formative ideas at the root of this study owe much to Mr Bill Walker, since without his practical knowledge I should not have placed as much emphasis upon the power and organization of working people themselves for effective participation. Additional thoughts, which appear in both earlier and later versions, are derived from David Lee, Annette Kuhn and Bridget Pym. And, in the new edition, John Child, George Thomason, Malcolm Warner and Paul Blyton were very helpful in supplying references. Clare Walter of the UWIST Aberconway Library assisted me greatly in the preparation of the references. Moreover, for admirable speed and efficiency in typing (and for her endurance of some indifferent handwriting), I should particularly like to acknowledge my appreciation of the efforts of Sally Jarratt in bringing this book to fruition. In the latter stages, her vital skills were supplemented by those of Kath Hollister, Margaret Pritchard, Carol Andrewartha and Sarah Champ. Finally, however, it is incumbent upon me to add the usual rider that responsibility for the arguments advanced here is of course entirely my own.

It is also apposite at this point for acknowledgment to be made to the following copyright holders, not least because such good will is vital to the processes of scholarship. These are: Peter Abell (1983), 'The viability of industrial producer co-operation', in C. Crouch and F. A. Heller (eds), *International Yearbook of Organizational Democracy*, vol. 1, Chichester, Wiley, p. 93 (for Table 4.2); John Child (1969), *The Business Enterprise in Modern Industrial Society,* London, Collier Macmillan, p. 89 (for Table 2.2); Industrial Democracy in Europe International Research Group (IDE) (1981), *European Industrial Relations,* Oxford, Clarendon Press, p. 257 (for Table 3.5); Abraham Shuchman (1957), *Co-determination,* Washington, Public Affairs Press, p. 6 (for Table 2.3) and p. 8 (for Table 2.4); and Michael Terry (1983), 'Shop steward development and management strategies', in G. S. Bain (ed.), *Industrial Relations in Britain,* Oxford, Blackwell, p. 69 (for Table 4.3).

# 1 Point of departure

All workers participate in industry, by virtue of producing the substance of human material existence, but since the advent of the industrial revolution all but a few have had no effective voice either in the management of the firms in which they are employed or, at a higher level, in the framing of policies on the allocation of resources within the wider society. To be sure, by consequence of their task-based expertise, the subordinate majority have at times acquired a measure of control over the actual performance of work and this, together with other workgroup practices designed to extend their frontier of control over decisions at shop-floor level, has guaranteed the maintenance of rudimentary expressions of participation in many industrial milieux. But the mode of organization of work today is still incompatible with a condition in which all men and women are reconciled with themselves through productive activities, from which they derive a meaning and a purpose, and through which they can begin to regain *control* over human institutions and historical situations (Dawe, 1970:211).

By contrast, in pre-industrial societies, although the bulk of the population unquestionably suffered from the consequences of scientific and technical immaturity and, as a result, were by no means well adapted to their natural and physical habitat, the organization of activities was perforce highly decentralized, a situation which encouraged considerable local decision-making autonomy. But in industrial and post-industrial societies, although understanding of natural/scientific laws and control of the environment have proceeded apace with the result that material standards of living have been raised to heights undreamed of by earlier generations, this process has not been matched by a corresponding amelioration of the human social condition. On the contrary, with increasing concentration and centralization of decision-making processes at work, further exacerbated in some cases by many of the new technologies, people have become truly disenfranchised, being unable to determine the shape of their own economic existence and experiencing their lives as a series of traps (Mills, 1959: 3):

> They sense that within their everyday worlds, they cannot overcome their troubles, and in this feeling they are often quite correct. What ordinary men and women are directly aware of and what they try to do are bounded by the private orbits in which they live; their visions and their powers are limited to the close-up scenes of job, family, neighbourhood; in other milieux, they move vicariously and remain spectators. And the more aware they become, however vaguely, of ambitions and of threats which transcend their immediate locales, the more trapped they seem to feel.

Considerable alienation and individual passivity are inevitable consequences of lack of autonomy and are incompatible with the notion of people able to realize their 'full potential and to create a truly human order . . . freed from external constraint' (Dawe, 1970: 214). Indeed, to be deprived of any decisive influence within the social environment generates an intense and a seemingly inescapable experience of powerlessness and resort to 'world views' of an essentially passive, fatalistic and dependent kind.

But a determination to transform this situation has occasioned a worldwide search for appropriate means to create industrial democracy. Indeed, as a by-product of an enthusiasm for workers' participation and control, an appropriately persuasive case has been argued for the democratization of social institutions. This is upheld, first, by an appeal to selected values which are widely advocated in most industrial societies; second, by recourse to a body of ethical principles which strengthen this underlying reasoning, and, finally, by reference to abundant, carefully collected evidence, of the substantial socio-economic benefits of effective participation.

In the first place, then, the proponents of participation have been able to found their case on widespread commitment in industrial societies to democratic ideals, one necessary element of which is the inalienable right of the citizen to a voice in his or her own concerns. To be sure, the status accorded to participation in democratic thought is open to debate. Indeed, until recently, it appeared that the term had been successfully exorcized from the vocabulary of democracy by the so-called modern theorists for whom, following Schumpeter (1943), 'responsible' government was the essence of democracy. This orientation, incidentally, was in complete contrast to the position taken by those, including Bottomore (1964: 115), who claimed that 'modern democracy has most often . . . been defined as the participation of the mass of people in government', and, what is more, it ignored the retention of this meaning in popular political argument. But as a result of subsequent changes in thinking, participation again came to be represented in the mainstream of social and political thought with the creation of a genuinely participatory society (based in the first instance on participation in the work situation) being viewed as an essential foundation of any successful democratic system (Blumberg, 1968; Pateman, 1970; Poole, 1982b; Warner, 1984a).

A belief in the virtues of democratic control can thus be traced to certain fundamental human values which are commonly held and officially sanctioned in most industrial countries. In addition, participation has been hailed on theoretical grounds as the most appropriate solution to the problems of alienation in modern industrial societies, as the best method of facilitating the development of socially aware and public-spirited people, as a stepping-stone to the fulfilment of certain 'higher echelons' of needs which are deemed to be common to all men and women, and finally, as a means of overcoming major social disadvantages which are consequent upon non-democratic modes of decision-making.

Notwithstanding the controversy surrounding the concept, the conviction is thus widely shared that alienation, embodied in the estrangement of men and women from the products of their creation, is endemic in advanced industrial societies. To be sure, this tendency had been recognized in the early phases of the industrial revolution, but awareness of the problem has been particularly acute and widespread accompanying the far-reaching technological changes which are currently in train and the massive social dislocations accompanying mass unemployment. And increasingly, involvement in decision-making processes and greater control by workers over their work environment have been recognized as necessary, if partial, solutions to these monumental problems of our era.

The value of participation had, of course, been argued by a number of early political theorists as a means of optimizing individual freedom and self-determination within a collective context. Indeed, the very act of participation was seen to increase willingness to participate on future occasions, and the ultimate ideal to be furthered by active involvement was a society in which social awareness and public-spiritedness were the norm rather than the exception in human behaviour (Pateman, 1970; 1983).

These ideas have been reinforced by the contributions of social psychologists, including Maslow (1954), McGregor (1960) and Likert (1961), who argued that much of human motivation can be explained by the existence of a hierarchy of needs, the ultimate of which is 'self-actualization'. And although this analysis may be culturally specific (in other contexts 'collective actualization' might be a more appropriate term), it is reasonable to argue that, having satisfied their primary physiological, economic and social needs, people will intensify their search for self-expression, self-actualization and creativity within their work environment. It is also logical to hypothesize that, notwithstanding the intractable problems of unemployment, with the progressive evolution of industrial societies and the consequent gratification of primary requirements, certain emergent needs, which are satisfied in participatory environments, take on a new significance.

Furthermore, it has always been recognized that undesirable social consequences can ensue from the concentration of decision-making power. This, in its most general formulation, has been best expressed by Lord Acton ('power tends to corrupt, and absolute power corrupts absolutely'), but more specifically it has been argued that, under competitive conditions, these problems are magnified by the danger and, indeed, the likelihood of the unscrupulous reaching controlling positions. This is 'because of the way in which the processes of selection for positions of authority favour ruthless power seekers' since, with competition, 'those with too many scruples' are effectively excluded leaving the prizes to be won by the most ruthless and least humanitarian in the population (Andreski, 1954: 217–18).

This situation is exacerbated by the geographical mobility of the upwardly mobile, a process which has a number of important consequences. First, the highly mobile tend to place only limited value on stable friendship and kinship patterns; second, whenever there is a conflict between achievement and satisfactory human relationships almost inevitably the former is chosen; and finally, the association of the highly mobile with others and, by corollary, any commitment to humanitarian goals, is essentially calculative and associated with a 'capacity to give up existing social relationships and to form new but superficial (and more profitable) ones at a higher social level' (Musgrove, 1963: 218). It is a salutary thought, then, that the chances of selecting leaders with genuinely humanitarian sympathies become particularly remote in societies in which recruitment to elites is based on competitive mobility. Indeed, the need for genuine participation and active involvement by the majority becomes absolutely essential if untoward human and social consequences are not to ensue in these circumstances.

The impressive a priori case which may be advanced for the extension of participation has been amply supported on empirical grounds as well, though naturally not all the studies in question have been wholly consistent. The aims of the investigators, the research methods used, the samples selected and even, at times, the results, have been by no means identical but the overwhelming trend in the evidence has given substantial support for the case in favour of democratic control. Hence, after an exhaustive review of these findings, Blumberg (1968: 123) was able to argue that 'there is scarcely a study in the entire literature which fails to demonstrate that satisfaction in work is enhanced or that other generally acknowledged beneficial consequences accrue from a genuine increase in workers' decision-making power', and to make the further point that such a degree of unanimity in findings is rare in social scientific research.

Indeed, despite certain minor inconsistencies, it is possible to make a number of definitive judgments about the effects of various 'experiments' in participation. First, in so far as the ordinary worker is concerned, participation at shop-floor level has often had impressive results; second, representative systems involving participation in decisions of a policy nature have been by no means unsuccessful; and third, the attitudes of workers towards industrial participation tend to be positive though other satisfactions are still frequently placed higher on the list of priorities.

And at all events, the evolution of these ideas has provided a backcloth for a worldwide concern to experiment with practices designed to further industrial democracy. The most radical remain the workers' self-management systems, which have emerged in decentralized socialist economies such as Yugoslavia, and which involve a substantial degree of *de jure* workers' participation on the main decision-making bodies. Typical participative channels include workers' assemblies, workers' councils and direct forms of worker involvement through basic organizations of associated labour. Producer co-operatives have also attracted considerable interest in recent years and occur in a variety of political economies. In such enterprises, workers typically have ownership rights, participate in management and share in the distribution of the surplus. Moreover, while Móndragón is the most celebrated experiment here, producer co-operatives have attracted considerable attention in a wide range of Third World countries as well as in Western Europe and North America.

Meanwhile, in predominantly private enterprise economies, co-determination and works councils have featured prominently in the emergent company structure of the post-war period. Co-determination encompasses the right of workers' representatives to joint decision-making on actual enterprise boards and, while West Germany has provided the key experiment, such practices have for some time been obligatory in countries such as Austria, the Netherlands, Norway, Sweden and Spain. Moreover, works councils and similar institutions involve representative bodies in regular meetings with management and, indeed, amongst current participants in the EEC, Great Britain and Eire are the only countries where such practices are not yet mandatory. Third World nations with similar arrangements include India, Indonesia, Tanzania, Tunisia and Zambia (ILO, 1976; Poole, 1979).

The trade union channel has also been a time-honoured means for achieving a measure of influence by representatives of workers over decisions in their places of employment. The disjunctive or oppositional form is through collective bargaining and, arguably, this is still the most common form of participation in pluralist societies such as Australia, Canada, Great Britain, New Zealand and the USA. But in state socialist societies (e.g. USSR and many Eastern European countries) the arrangements are of an integrative form and, despite changes in recent years (Ruble, 1981), typically involve the rights of trade unions to determine various issues within a framework of harmoniously conceived interests of the various parties to the employment relationship.

There have also been a series of experiments at shop-floor level including autonomous workgroups, quality of work-life programmes, quality circles and an array of workers' initiatives to extend the frontier of their control over decision-making processes. More generally, too, the debates on participation have been extended recently to embrace the notions of financial and economic democracy to cover the respective rights of the workforce to a stake in ownership and in the broader processes of planning (Meidner, 1981; Brannen, 1983a).

In an endeavour to create a more systematic approach to these procedures, a series of important proposals have also stemmed from the institutions of the European Community. Indeed, in

January 1974, the Council declared increased participation of employees in the life of their companies to be a central goal of community policy. The upshot is that there are currently a series of interlocking initiatives, covering diverse areas of participation, modes of involvement and types of undertaking.

The first of these stems from a directive in February 1975 and covers the case of collective redundancies. The second, the important Vredeling Proposal, is on information disclosure and embraces procedures for informing and consulting employees. The third, the so-called fifth directive, submitted to the council in October 1972, is designed to ensure that employees are represented in the governing bodies of large-scale public companies. However, the original proposal here for a two-tier supervisory and management board in all undertakings with fifty or more employees and with workers' participation on the higher tier has been modified by the European Parliament to cover four options (the original proposals backed by statute, a unitary board with employee representation, the creation of a further, separate, employee representation body, and collective agreements). Finally, there are the far-reaching proposals for a system of employee participation for the *European* company. These have three interconnected parts (European works councils, collective agreements and a major role for employee representatives on supervisory boards in the appointment, supervision and dismissal of management). However, the last stipulation has been latterly amended to embrace a structure which consists of one-third representatives of shareholders, a further one-third comprising the representatives of employees and the final third consisting of members co-opted by the first two groups (for a detailed review see Pipkorn, 1984).

For their part, the main political parties in Great Britain have gradually taken up distinctive positions on industrial democracy and their respective policies must surely at some time be reflected in at least a nominal transformation of the rights of workers to participate in the decision-making processes in the companies in which they are employed.

On the face of it, the British Labour Party has been broadly committed to industrial democracy for a longer period than any of its rivals, since Clause 4 of the party's constitution calls not only for the common ownership of the means of production, distribution and exchange, but also for 'the best obtainable system of popular administration and control of each industry or service'. But until the 1960s its enthusiasm for industrial democracy had been circumspect and confined largely to extensions of bargaining and consultative machinery in nationalized industries. However, a more positive commitment could be detected in the publication, in 1974, of the Green Paper, *The Community and the Company*, which established the basis for comprehensive legislation in this area. Moreover, the concern of the Labour Party to ensure joint control by unions and management at all levels of decision-making, using existing trade-union machinery and shop stewards' organizations, formed the reference point for the central proposals of the Bullock Committee. Indeed, the home policy committee of the Labour Party gave this report its full backing, placing emphasis on the desirability of worker directors sitting on the main policy board of the company with powers over pricing, sales, export policies, productivity, product development, personnel and employment and the appointment and supervision of senior management. Moreover, in 1976, the Industrial Common Ownership Act came into force designed to extend co-operative manufacturing in small-scale enterprises.

To reaffirm this commitment, the Labour Party produced a further major report to the 1982 Trades Union Congress and Labour Party Conference, entitled *Economic Planning and Industrial Democracy: The Framework for Full Employment*, in which a strong consultative and participative element was envisaged as being integral to a planning system for the economy as a whole. In detail, the role of collective bargaining and other forms of ownership such as co-operatives were seen as of only partial relevance to the solution of current problems, with 'widespread and rapid progress' requiring 'the availability of new statutory rights to information, consultation and representation' (TUC-Labour Party Liaison Committee, 1982:24). Specifically, extensive legally based provisions on disclosure of information are now proposed (including statutory backing to the right of access by unions in one country to the Head Office of a multi-national), together with the establishment of Joint Union Committees (comprising both full-time officers and lay members) with rights to *representation* at all levels of decision-making in the enterprise up to, and including, board level.

But industrial democracy is undoubtedly a central plank of the industrial relations policy of the Alliance parties as well even though the mechanisms differ substantially from those envisaged in Labour's proposals. Indeed, the Liberal Party has been a supporter of employee participation for over fifty years, *The*

*Liberal Yellow Book* in 1928 calling for a series of measures including 'participation in framing of factory rules and protection against arbitrary dismissal, representation of workers on a supervisory board and profit sharing' (Liberal Party, 1985:2). And currently, the Liberals envisage a comprehensive system of employee participation (on the shop floor, on works councils and on company boards) and are of the view that works councils and departmental meetings are 'the foundations of industrial democracy' (Liberal Party, 1973: 8; 1985). They, too, like their Labour Party counterparts, favour the fifty/fifty representation of employees and shareholders on a supervisory board, but differ from Labour on the question of union membership. Under the Liberals' plan, the employee representatives on supervisory boards would be elected through the works council and, in principle at least, it would be irrelevant whether or not those selected were in fact trade unionists. Indeed, they are opposed to Bullock-type proposals which they regard as an abuse of union power and would particularly like to see the establishment of a two-tier board system, for, in their view, the single board 'has failed to promote adequate direction to British industry and has equally failed to provide democratic control over directors' (Liberal Party, 1973:8; 1985).

The Liberal Party has also consistently supported profit-sharing and employee share-ownership schemes, the essential purpose of their measures for financial participation being to involve as many employees as possible as 'full partners in their enterprise'. Moreover, the provisions in the 1978 Finance Act (in which specific tax relief is given to employers who participate in an Inland Revenue 'approved scheme' used to acquire shares on the employees' behalf) were a direct consequence of Liberal initiatives during the period of the Liberal-Labour (Lib-Lab) pact.

Moreover, the Social Democratic Party (n.d.) has extensive proposals for industrial democracy, set out in its fourth *Policy Document on Industrial Relations*, that are based on five main principles: (1) the right of all individual employees to participate; (2) the involvement of trade unions when these are well established in organizations; (3) participation at all levels in the enterprise based initially on works councils; (4) co-operation of all parties (owners, managers and employees) in shaping the arrangements; and (5) rights to full disclosure of information subject to certain safeguards in commercially sensitive areas. Indeed, if elected, these recommendations for participation would be encompassed in legislation through an Industrial Democracy Act, and supported by a Code of Practice and an Industrial Democracy Agency. More specifically, the SDP envisages various options for participation to include: (1) directors elected by employees at top-level representative councils; (2) direct participation by employees with management about the content of jobs (including a grant-aided job-design scheme and training to promote 'quality circles'); and (3) collective share-ownership or profit-sharing schemes. There are also comprehensive recommendations on incentives and support services for the promotion of employee-owned enterprises and co-operatives (including a range of personal and corporate tax incentives, assistance to the unemployed to invest in new co-operatives, a comprehensive management advice service for employee-owned enterprises, workforces in firms going to liquidation or being privatized to be given the first option to buy out the organization and a broad-ranging employee and share-ownership scheme).

By contrast, the position of the Conservative Party is that a number of forms of voluntary employee involvement (not least, those involving a financial stake in the company) should be encouraged, with its essential policies being generally traced to the view of Winston Churchill that (see Daly, (n.d.)):

> Our Conservative aim is to build a property owning democracy, independent and interdependent. In this we include profit-sharing schemes in suitable industries and intimate consultation between employers and wage-earners. In fact, we seek as far as possible to make the status of the wage-earner that of a partner rather than that of an irresponsible employee.

For a number of years, the position has been adopted in Conservative circles that opponents of participation endeavour to maintain 'rights and privileges which have no part in a progressive industrial society'. But again, this political party has typically espoused flexibility and enabling legislation, while opposing Bullock-type proposals on the grounds that they would endanger worthwhile ventures which are currently evolving and transfer collective bargaining from the shop floor to the board room (Abbott, 1973; Cassidy, 1973; Daly, n.d.).

Yet, leaving aside some important further stimuli to participation (and especially employee share-ownership) contained in the 1980 Finance Act, the most far-reaching legislation during a period of Conservative Government has stemmed largely fortuitously from an amendment in the House of Lords currently incorporated in Section 1 of the Employment Act, 1982. Taking effect from 1

January 1983, this section has made it a statutory requirement that, in every directors' report (in companies with more than 250 employees), a statement must be included describing the action taken during the year to introduce, maintain and develop arrangements aimed at (Hansard, 1985: 537–8):

(i) providing employees systematically with information of concern to them as employees;
(ii) consulting employees or their representatives on a regular basis so that the views of employees can be taken into account in making decisions which are likely to affect their interests;
(iii) encouraging the involvement of employees in the company's performance through an employees' share scheme or by some other means;
(iv) achieving a common awareness on the part of all employees of the financial and economic factors affecting the performance of the company.

But if the case for participation is so impressive and the breadth of political support is so extensive, why, it may reasonably be asked, has not industrial democracy proceeded further? Why do the bulk of symptoms of alienation, exacerbated by high unemployment and rapid technological change, show only limited signs of abatement, if any at all? Why has the passage of legislation in countries such as the UK been so fitful and halting? Why has there not been further progress on the European initiatives? And, above all, why is it that, in arguably the most impressive comparative empirical research on this subject, the conclusion was reached that, in Western Europe, so far as actual employee *influence* is concerned, 'the picture overall is one of centralised top management control' (IDE, 1979: 282; 1981b)?

In reply the contention here is that the critical role of power in industrial life has simply been ignored or at best treated circumspectly by those who are most active in the industrial democracy cause and whose reasoning has been either naive or Utopian. Appropriately, then, the study which follows is explanatory. Concentrating on participation as a dependent rather than as an independent variable, it is hoped that there will be a rather more reliable guide than has hitherto been available to the proposals most likely to achieve viable democratic institutions in the workplace in the long term. To this end, in Chapter 2, the nature of power and its relation to the issues of participation and control is clarified. The central proposition to be developed is that workers' participation and control are shaped by certain underlying or latent power forces and a climate of values which may or may not be conducive to evolution along these lines. Evidence from all manner of schemes for participation by workers in industry will then be cited in support of this contention. The order of treatment of selected examples of the various practices is dependent on the source from which they emerge, namely, managers, workers, trade union officials or government. But it is in the identification of basic explanatory elements that the main value of this study lies. And the upshot should be a vital contribution to our understanding of the workings of industrial relations, and a pointer to those changes which are fundamental if political, economic and social institutions are to be adapted for the betterment of mankind.

# 2 Power in industrial relations

## Introduction

In any significant debate concerning the form and content of workers' participation in decision-making, broader issues inevitably arise about the exercise of power in industry and society at large. Indeed, as early as 1912, Graham Wallas (1912: 245–57), in his address at the annual meeting of the Sociological Society on the question of syndicalism, made the point that:

> industry was now organized on a scale and with an intensity without precedent in the history of the world, and perhaps the most important question before the Sociological Society was what forces or body of men (and women) should control this vast organization.

As a sequel to this, it is not surprising that such issues as the nature of power in industry and the modes of control in organizations have emerged frequently in the subsequent literature. It is appropriate in this chapter, therefore, to say something – if only rather briefly – about the principal meanings of power and to relate the more specific debates about workers' participation and control firmly into this broader theoretical canvas.

The main argument in this chapter is that participation and control are important *manifestations* of fundamental processes involved in the *exercise* of power in society. To be sure, the more ardent apostles of participation have usually regarded it as an especially critical component of power, principally because in their view it is through participation in decision-making (and especially in an industrial context) that basic lessons about human subjectivity can be learned, and also, by virtue of being so central, it can significantly affect other questions in social life such as what is to be produced in society and on the basis of which principles the fruits of labour should be distributed. However, without in any way wishing to challenge significantly the validity of such assertions, participation is regarded here as only one manifestation of power, albeit an important one. Moreover – and this is fundamental to our enquiry – participation is viewed as very much the offspring of deeper, *latent* power processes which operate in society and the *values* about participation which obtain at any given point in time in particular societies and organizations.

### Power in industry

At root, most definitions of *power* can be traced to Weber's (1968: 53) conception to refer to 'the probability that one actor within a social relationship will be in a position to carry out his [or her] will despite resistance, regardless of the basis on which the probability rests'. Moreover, other vital terms in the power vocabulary include *authority* (legitimated, i.e. positively accepted power or domination), *domination* ('the probability that certain specific commands (or all commands) will be obeyed by a given group of persons' (Weber, 1968: 212)), *influence* (the capacity to achieve ends related to one's aims or objectives regardless of actual formal position in an administrative hierarchy) and *control* (the capacity to shape or determine events consistent with certain specified objectives).

But amongst those who have taken systematic account of the concept of power in industrial life there has been a major division between those who view its exercise in an essentially positive light (non-zero-sum theorists) (e.g. Parsons, 1960) and those who have emphasized its more negative consequences (zero-sum theorists) (e.g. Mills, 1956; 1958). The principal case of non-zero-sum theorists is that power can be best understood as a 'circulating medium', similar to money in the economic system, which can have major social and economic benefits. In particular, it facilitates the co-ordination and integration of the capacities, talents and work of very large numbers of people and, in so doing, gives those societies, institutions and groups which are prepared to maximize this potential immense evolutionary advantages in the struggle between different social orders and social systems. Again, turning more specifically to the principal organizational developments of modern industrial societies, non-zero-sum theorists have suggested that these permit what Parsons (1967: 240) has referred to as the 'miracle of loaves and fishes' – that is to say, particular circulations of power occurring in modern organizations have major and even potentially unforeseen positive social effects. Thus, for example, present-day manufacturing industry, by generating immense productive capacities from what must be regarded historically as a proportionately small part of the population of a given society, has enabled about a quarter of the world's population to have a standard of living undreamed of by earlier generations of men and women.

By way of contrast, zero-sum theorists have emphasized entirely different problems and issues. To be sure, they have acknowledged that modern organizations have the capacity to create great productive wealth but, in its distribution at least, it must in their view obey the laws of a zero-sum game where the gains of one party or group inevitably involve losses for another. Moreover, any accretions in material wealth (which may in any event be temporary) have to be weighed against certain further social consequences brought about by immense concentrations of power. Thus, in characteristically graphic manner, C. Wright Mills (1959: 29–41) was to argue that, in the modern era, 'if men (and women) do not make history, they tend increasingly to become the utensils of history makers'. In other words, the passivity of the majority of the human population as far as crucial decisions affecting the future of mankind are concerned is the very consequence of those movements in history which non-zero-sum theorists are most ready to welcome. Again, zero-sum theorists would never regard power as a potentially value-neutral circulating medium. Rather, on their assumptions, the directions taken by particular organizations either must obey certain external laws which are thereby alien to mankind or must reflect the values and decisions of those in key controlling positions. And, on either view, not only do the majority exercise only limited impact on their own futures but also fundamental structural conflicts are generated in society between those who occupy dominant positions and those over whom power is exercised.

## Dimensions of power: manifest and latent

But while non-zero-sum and zero-sum power theorists have both come to grips with certain fundamental problems associated with the exercise of power in social and industrial life, they have seldom developed adequate definitions of the concept, nor have they really related these problems very closely to the wider issues of participation and control. It is apposite at this point, therefore, to review briefly the principal dimensions of the concept since, as we shall see, this helps to clarify not only our own position on the question of workers' participation and control but also many of the previous theoretical discussions on this subject.

## Manifest power

A great many interpretations of power have focused on its more obvious *manifestations* in given social relationships and social structures. At root, most may be traced to Weber's (1968) classic definition and variously embrace such dimensions as formal positions within particular societies or organizations, the scope and range of issues controlled or influenced and, finally, success or otherwise in a given power conflict. Moreover, advocates of workers' participation in decision-making have usually had in mind a conception of power based on two of its principal manifestations: namely, the formal patterns of control within organizations; and the scope and range of issues over which particular parties have some influence. Indeed, workers' participation is viewed as the principal means of obtaining greater control by workers over several aspects of their working lives and in so doing augmenting their power *vis-à-vis* that of management. Thus, to begin with, in terms of the formal patterns of control within organizations a number of levels have been identified which broadly correspond with the formal patterns of decision-making within the firm and wider society (see Table 2.1).

### Table 2.1: **Levels of participation**

1 'On the job' decision-making by individuals
2 Workgroup or workteam
3 Sectional or departmental levels
4 Plant or undertaking
5 Enterprise
6 Industry
7 Economy

The first level concerns *individual 'on the job' decision-making* where the worker is viewed as having some right to organize his or her activities within certain discretionary limits. Technological factors, however, are very important at this level, as we shall see, for, in general, the higher the degree of skill of the worker the less easy it is to measure directly his or her work activities and the greater will tend to be the freedom from managerial supervision.

By contrast, in a technology where the level of skill required of an individual worker is not of any great magnitude, the easier it is for management to control the worker's activities and to introduce such schemes as measured day work and productivity bargains, which are specifically designed to reduce the worker's own initiative and autonomy.

The second level comprises the *workgroup* or *workteam*. Again the decisions here may cover production questions and, indeed, are likely to do so whenever group activities are involved in the actual production process itself. However, at this level there are a number of further possible decision-making areas which may involve the workers actively but which, as a rule, management has sought to determine unilaterally and to define as its 'prerogatives'. These may include hiring and firing, starting and stopping times, the distribution of wages, hours of work, overtime working and so on.

Table 2.2: **Forms of workers' participation and control: policy and execution**

| focal level | goals and means ('democratic') | means only ('conservative') |
|---|---|---|
| Whole organization | A | B |
| Small group | D | C |

Based on Child (1969: 89).

It would in general be reasonable to argue that the higher the level of decision-making the less likely it has been for workers to have any major influence on the outcome of events, and the more vigorously managerial 'prerogatives' have been defended. Between the levels of plant and workgroup there are a number of *sectional and departmental levels* which have thus proved difficult for workers to penetrate. Moreover, moving to the highest decision-making levels there are again a number of potential and logically separable foci of decision-making, namely *plant* (or undertaking), *enterprise, industry* and *economy*.

As far as these ultimate levels are concerned, it has not been unusual to make the distinction between processes of industrial *government* and those of industrial *management*. This is necessary in order to differentiate broad policy-making bodies from their executive organs; to distinguish, in other words, between decision-making processes about the aims or ends of particular organizations, and the means of achieving them (Chamberlain, 1951: 121). And although it is not always easy to achieve such a separation in practice, this is theoretically useful in separating ends and means, and also, with a consideration of levels, it informs such classifications of participation as that developed by Child (1969) (see Table 2.2).

Type A here includes most forms of workers' self-management and control as well as co-determination experiments; type D involves some of the many attempts at workgroup autonomy; types B and particularly C, however, derive largely from the human relations tradition and are really techniques for ensuring that certain general decisions (which are not open for negotiation or debate) are carried out in practice (Child, 1969: 89–92).

But not only can participation clearly entail a number of distinct decision-making levels, but also the *scope* of actual influence by workers over any given issue may vary enormously from the most minimal forms of information to outright control. In order to account for these variations, several writers have developed continua of workers' participation, probably the most sophisticated of which remains that of Shuchman (1957) who distinguished between 'co-operation' and 'co-determination'. The former, relating to those schemes in which workers influence decisions but are not responsible for them, contrasts with the situation of the second in which workers have actual control and authority over particular decisions (see Table 2.3).

Table 2.3: **The scope of issues involved in workers' participation and control**

| co-operation | co-determination |
|---|---|
| 1　Right to information | 1　Right to veto |
| 2　Right to protest | 　　(a) temporary |
| 3　Right to suggestion | 　　(b) permanent |
| | 2　Right to 'co-decision' |
| | 3　Right to decision |
| 4　Right to consultation | |

Based on Shuchman (1957: 6).

Clearly a continuum of this kind has important merits; it helps the analyst to avoid *lengthy* definitional problems which have been only too apparent in the literature on this subject, while still incorporating the distinction between influence over decisions by working people and their actual involvement in the formulation and execution of a given decision itself. Again, it encompasses a wide range of possible models of participation including the right of either temporary or permanent veto as well as the more familiar gradation from information, through consultation, co-determination and finally control. None the less, without wishing to be unnecessarily pedantic about meaning, there has been a growing consensus in this context that situations where management effectively exerts control cannot be synonymous with fully fledged participation in decision-making and, similarly, that participation must itself be incompatible with genuine workers' control. Thus Verba (1961), not unreasonably, has found fault with a collection of schemes on the grounds that they offer merely '*pseudo-participation*' and involve no genuine control, even of a partial kind, by workers in the actual processes of decision-making (see also Pateman, 1970; 1983). There are, for example, certain supervisory styles which are usually labelled as participative, in which in fact the final decision-making prerogative rests entirely in the hands of the supervisor. And, while these devices may well be conducive to more harmonious industrial relations and to increases in industrial efficiency, this is peripheral to the question of whether the role of workers is decisive rather than purely marginal in the formulation of policies which are significant to them. Moreover, and this is a subject to which we shall return when the issue of industrial ownership is raised, there is a great deal of difference between workers, say, jointly controlling with management a given process of decision-making within the private sector of the economy and actually controlling it within the framework of publicly owned industry. Moreover, many theories of workers' control have presupposed the creating of *acephalous* organizational forms in which management *roles* cease to exist in any meaningful sense.

It is evident, then, that certain problems of definition are unavoidable in any analysis of the scope of workers' participation. To some extent the same applies when we come to highlight the *range* of issues involved here; there are thus numerous potential areas over which workers may – and indeed do – have a measure of decision-making control, from technical 'on-the-job' problems, to questions covering welfare and safety, wages and working conditions, and wider production, commercial and economic issues. These can be clarified conceptually and the classification used most often here is, again, based on the work of Shuchman (1957) who endeavoured to relate these areas of workers' participation to the levels in which they are confined. Unfortunately, he focused entirely on 'enterprise' and 'supra-enterprise' contexts and in so doing omitted individual, workgroup and departmental levels, those very areas which involve the ordinary worker most and in which his or her most notable contributions might be made. However, this does not entirely detract from the importance or the utility of his contribution which may be summarized as in Table 2.4.

Table 2.4:  **The range of issues involved in workers' participation and control**

| enterprise | supra-enterprise |
|---|---|
| 1  Personnel | 1  Manpower |
| 2  Social | 2  Social welfare |
| 3  Economic | 3  Economic |
|    (a) technical | |
|    (b) 'business' | |

Based on Shuchman (1957: 8).

Thus at enterprise level, the main areas of workers' participation may focus on; first, *personnel decisions*, such as the hiring, firing, promotion and transfer of workers; second, *social decisions*, including such matters as health and safety, the form and administration of pension funds and so on; and third, a range of *economic questions* including (a) *technical aspects*, such as new methods of production and the introduction of new machinery; and (b) *'business' issues* which refer more to marketing and financial questions; the latter usually involving the uppermost decision-making layers within the enterprise. But of special interest in Shuchman's classification is that supra-enterprise considerations supplement plant-related issues and this underpins the rights of workers in *policy-formation at regional and national levels*. The momentous consequences of this involvement have been emphasized in the Report of the Club of Rome (Meadows *et al.*, 1972: 18–19):

There can be disappointments and dangers in limiting one's view to an area that is too small. There are many examples of a person striving with all his might to solve some immediate, local problem, only to find his efforts defeated by events occurring in a larger context. A farmer's carefully maintained fields can be destroyed by international war. Local officials' plans can be overturned by a national policy. A country's economic development can be thwarted by a lack of world demand for its products. Indeed there is increasing concern today that most personal and national objectives may ultimately be frustrated by long-term, global trends.

Thus, it is clearly not enough to restrict workers' participation and control to more limited objectives, since, although these may be most meaningful to the individual worker, their outcome may, in fact, be decided by more general trends over which he or she has almost no control. Again, these general issues do not necessarily involve global questions; they may include 'manpower' policies, and notably those relating to the transfer and mobility of workers from one geographical area to the next, social welfare programmes, and of course the business of control over the economy as a whole. And once again, such issues, which are usually left out of discussions concerned specifically with workers' participation at enterprise or plant level, set major limitations on the ultimate possibility of effective domestic and local participation.

In recent years, too, a series of developments (notably, the breakdown of rigid demarcations between home and work, the role of 'unpaid' (usually female) labour in all societies and the notions of worksharing) have widened the debate on participation to include different *zones* or *segments* in which productive activities are undertaken. Above all, there is a concern to include not only participation in political life but, more especially, the connection of this involvement with personal and family life. As Pateman (1983: 118) has argued:

> If women are to be equal members of democratic workplaces, if they are to be full citizens, then radical changes are required at home as well as in the public world. Men and women have to share equally the responsibilities and gratifications of domestic life, especially in child-rearing, if women are to take their rightful place in democratized workplaces. Conversely, if men are to take an equal part in the domestic division of labour, democracy in the workplace has to include a complete re-thinking of our notions of 'work' and how it is organized. Almost all writers of democratization have, so far, concentrated on the problems of the class structure of liberal societies, and thus 'democracy', whether in the workplace or the state, has been constructed upon the foundation of a fundamental form of domination. The patriarchal structure of our organizations and institutions has to be confronted together with the class structure if 'democracy' is truly to mean the active participation of *all* the people.

Workers' participation in decision-making therefore involves a number of distinctive levels of potential operation, a considerable variation in the scope of actual control of workers over any given decision, and a range of areas and zones in which participation can, in fact, take place. Thus, from a classificatory point of view, any study which purported to highlight variations in workers' participation experienced within given organizations or societies would have to take some account of all these variables.

### Latent power

And yet, notwithstanding the problems of measurement, there are many power theorists who have not been content to restrict the concept to its more obvious and concrete manifestations in social life. These so-called *latent power theorists* have sought not only to define the concept in a different way but also to focus primarily on the power *bases* or *sources* at the disposal of particular parties. That is to say, they have endeavoured to obtain some guide to the *underlying power* of particular groups and to their *potential* for achieving given ends, if necessary at the expense of those of conflicting groups.

Indeed, it is the general view of latent theorists that no group or class has the capacity to exercise power unless it first develops certain power bases or sources which are potentially available to it, and they have been anxious to ensure that the actual exercise of force should never be confused with the concept of power. Bierstedt (1950: 733), in particular, as a well-known representative of this school, has argued that power 'is the predisposition or prior capacity which makes the application of force possible ... the ability to employ force, not its actual employment, the ability to apply sanctions, not their actual application'. Nor should such arguments be regarded merely as exercises in semantics, for they have helped to open up a separate dimension of power which, as we shall see, is a principal component in the controversy on power in industry and society and in the more specific argument over workers' participation and control.

Of all the classical sociological theorists it was Marx (1946), above all, who was the main exponent of the latent approach, for although he was highly sensitive to the role of force in social transformation and of the importance of consciousness in social action, a great deal of his work was designed to uncover the latent power bases of particular social classes. And in this respect, of course, he argued that the power of given classes rested primarily on the nature of, and developments in, the underlying material forces of production (consisting primarily of technical and economic factors) and of the social relationships with which these are associated.

Table 2.5: **Control of resources, sanctions and participation**

| Dependence of: | Positive sanctions | Negative sanctions |
|---|---|---|
| E on U | U can (co-) sponsor productivity drive, stimulate other co-operative endeavours, etc. | U can threaten with or initiate strikes, slowdowns, etc. |
| U on E | E can grant material or other demands of workers and their organizations. | E can resist demands or withdraw privileges of workers and their organizations; E can also threaten with or initiate lock-outs, reprisals, etc. |
| U and E on G | Legislation or policies wanted or approved of by U and/or E can be enacted by G; G can also bestow financial benefits on the constituents of U and/or E. | Legislation or policies not wanted or disapproved of by U and/or E can be enacted by G; G can also withhold or withdraw benefits from the constituents of U and/or E. |
| G on U and E | E and/or U can contribute to a positive image of G as guardian of the general welfare; U can render political support. | E and/or U can contribute to a negative image of G as guardian of the general welfare; U can withdraw or withhold political support. |

E = Decision-making organ or organization of employers' association or management.
U = Decision-making organ or organization of unions or workers.
G = The government in office or third parties.
Based on Industrial Democracy in Europe (IDE) (1981a: 257).

More specifically, too, latent theorists have been associated with so-called *resource* approaches to the interpretation and measurement of power, viewing effective participation in decision-making as the outcome of the possession and marshalling of key resources by groups who may or may not be in conflict with each other. In essence, the theory here commences with the notion of the *interdependence* of the main actors in any industrial relations system, with the degree of dependence varying according to the extent to which one grouping is able to *control resources of vital interest to another*. So far as most industrial relations systems are concerned the principal groups are generally agreed to be employers and management; unions and working people themselves; and governmental or third party agencies (see, e.g., Dunlop, 1958; Clegg, 1979; Poole, 1981b). And, at any given point in time, as is indicated in Table 2.5, the main parties have a series of positive and negative sanctions (based on the specific resources at their disposal) with which to affect outcomes, including the degree of participation actually experienced (see IDE, 1981a: 256–9).

In detail, then, labour is a vital resource for the functioning of any productive concern and any control by workers or their independently organized associations here can certainly be deployed, in principle, to further participative decision-making. But the considerable powers of management over organizational resources and of employers over the granting of employment itself naturally comprises a fundamental oppositional check to any rapid developments in this direction. Moreover, through legislation, governments also have a considerable capacity to influence the basic employment relationship and workers' participation in decision-making, though again so long as employers and trade unions are independently organized, this relationship is inevitably reciprocal.

## Values

But values are also central here, and reflect the possibility of people actually shaping their own environment in the light of their powers of reason, rather than this being largely determined by forces of social evolution over which they have limited control. They also highlight the problems of subjectivity within the social sciences, since, if men and women can be clearly distinguished from phenomena in the physical and natural world by their possession of independent powers of reason (which give them a measure of free will to 'make their own history'), subjective elements must always be central rather than peripheral to social-scientific investigations and this, in turn, must sharply differentiate the basic methodologies of the natural and social sciences. Moreover, turning more specifically to the question of values as a component of power, these must be significant in this context, since it is precisely the human powers encapsulated in values and consciousness which enable the capacity for participation to be realized.

It is scarcely surprising, then, that the role of values and ideologies as components of social action has provided a focal point for theoretical discussions on the question of power in industrial relations. Indeed, the main emphasis here has been on the effects of values in legitimizing the authority of a dominant group or class or in permitting any subordinate group to challenge successfully the hegemony of the dominant grouping. Thus, the question of consciousness was fundamental in the work of Marx (1951), who not only saw it as decisive in converting a class in itself to a class for itself, but who also, with respect to trade unions, criticized a great deal of working-class action for its limited scope which resulted in trade-union power being largely latent and trade-union action being confined to 'resistance against the encroachments of capital', rather than to the search for simultaneous changes in the existing system of production and production relations. For Dahrendorf (1959), too, it was only when the occupants of subordinate roles in specific organizations became aware or conscious of their particular interests and hence developed clear 'political' structures that loosely cohering quasi-groups became fully fledged interest groups capable of taking effective action. Again, for Parsons (1960), the commonly shared values of the members of a given social system not only formed the crucial basis of its solidarity but also underpinned his by now familiar non-zero-sum conception of power.

Nevertheless, it was Weber (1968), of course, who provided the best-developed contribution to the debate on values as a component of social power. To be sure, he was concerned largely with the role of values in *maintaining* given patterns of domination and in bestowing to these a measure of *stability, persistence* and *endurance*, and a rather more general account would have considered how values lead to effective challenges by any subordinate grouping to the rule of a dominant class. But, at the same time, it is difficult to minimize Weber's contribution to this question.

Now Weber's views on patterns of domination were firmly grounded in his conception of power. He thus regarded domination as only one aspect of the exercise of power or influence over other persons. Moreover, he was keen to point out that 'not every case of domination makes use of economic means, still less does it always have economic objectives' (Weber, 1968: 212) to ensure compliance, though it generally required the existence of a so-called 'administrative staff' who could 'normally be trusted to execute the general policy as well as the specific commands'. But every form of domination also necessitated 'a minimum of voluntary compliance' on the part of subordinates which depended on their perceived *interest* in carrying out specific directives or decisions. The most obvious bases of such an interest would be economic, affectual or ideal in character, but as Weber (1968: 213) pointed out – and this was crucial to his general position on the question of *legitimate* domination:

> Experience shows that in no instance does domination voluntarily limit itself to material or affectual or ideal motives as a basis for its continuance. In addition every such system attempts to establish and to cultivate the belief in its legitimacy.

Moreover, it was precisely the principal variations in 'claims to legitimacy' which provided the basis for classifying different aspects of domination structures (Weber, 1968: 213):

> But according to the kind of legitimacy which is claimed, the type of obedience, the kind of administrative staff developed to guarantee it, and the mode of exercising authority, will all differ fundamentally. Equally fundamental is the variation in *effect*.

And then, finally, Weber (1968: 215) arrived at the most familiar part of his thesis, that there are three pure types of legitimate domination (authority), the validity of their claims being based on (1) rational grounds, (2) traditional grounds, and (3) charismatic grounds.

In a subsequent section we shall see how two of these grounds in particular have been developed by management as a means of supporting their domination over the lives of others in work contexts. Moreover, we shall observe that workers' participation and control does offer a major challenge to managerial hegemony and to the kinds of arguments which have normally been deployed to protect the existing systems of social control in industry. But there are certain problems in Weber's contribution to the debate on values as integral components of power which merit further consideration at this point.

The most obvious – as we have mentioned earlier – is that the foundations of Weber's argument lie in the role of values as a means of supporting or maintaining given patterns of control; he does not give any guide to the origins and nature of rather different values and ideologies which favour the interests of subordinate groups. A great deal of information is thus provided on the methods used by dominant groups to cultivate a belief in the legitimacy of their rule, but there is virtually nothing on the genesis of counter-values and ideologies which serve to challenge existing control structures. Moreover, the language he employs tends to be *dichotomous* in nature. That is to say, structures of domination, whatever their basis of legitimacy, tend to be of an inherently order-giving, order-receiving form: there is therefore little room in the model for any participation or control by subordinates over the decision-making processes in any organization. And while historically this may represent the most common social pattern, this in no sense implies its inevitability, or that power in social life must invariably be possessed by one class, party or group. On the contrary, even if in most formal patterns of domination it is easy to identify superordinate and subordinate roles and to classify the incumbents of these roles on the basis of whether they issue commands, directives or decisions or receive them, there is usually *some* reciprocal influence by the subordinate not only on the outcome of particular decisions but also on their genesis. Moreover, it is this reciprocity that Wrong (1968: 673) has in mind when he argues convincingly that:

> People exercise mutual influence and control over one another's behaviour in all social interaction – in fact, that is what we *mean* by social interaction. Power relations are asymmetrical in that the power holder exercises greater control over the behaviour of the power subject than the reverse, but reciprocity of influence – the defining criterion of the social relationship itself – is never entirely destroyed except in those forms of physical violence which, although directed against a human being, treat him (or her) as little more than a physical object.

Thus, although we would in no way wish to suggest that power equality has ever been the main pattern of distribution, it is equally erroneous to imply the inevitability of dichotomous decision-making processes.

Finally, with respect to the broader question of values as an aspect of social power, it is easy to develop a rather one-sided idealist analysis in which ideas are stripped from their origins, in particular structural contexts, and in which the interplay between other bases of power and values becomes a secondary theme. But as we shall see it is precisely when the question of values and processes of legitimation are linked with wider questions of the underlying power of particular classes and groups that the greatest explanatory advantages with respect to the questions of workers' participation and control are to be gained.


## An explanatory framework

So far, then, in our theoretical analysis, various meanings and dimensions of power have been evaluated, with workers' participation and control being understood as specific manifestations of power *exercise*. But as we have also argued, these practices are linked, in turn, with underlying or *latent* power *resources* and a series of *values* which either buttress particular power distributions or facilitate their successful challenge. At this point, it is appropriate: (1) to specify the relationships between participation, latent power and values in more detail; and (2) to identify a series of conditions which lead to diversity in these primary explanatory variables. This preludes an assessment of long-term changes including the isolation of both evolutionary and cyclical patterns.


## The central argument

The basic explanatory propositions of this study are contained in the framework in Figure 2.1 and convey the elemental argument that *workers' participation and control are reflections of the latent power of particular industrial classes, parties or groups and the value 'climate' which may or may not be favourable to participation experiments.* These values thus mediate between certain *structural factors* associated with latent power and their realization in the form of workers' participation and control. It will also be seen that the principal structural factors associated with the latent power of the main industrial classes, parties or groups are *economic factors,* such as the levels of employment, the profit margins of particular companies, the levels of competition, the degree of industrial concentration and periods of economic 'disintegration'; *technological factors,* such as the approximation of the technology of a company to a given point on the 'technical scale', the degree of complexity and education involved in any given task and the effects of the micro-electronic revolution; and finally, various forms of *government action* such as legislation on 'labour' issues, its intervention in the workings of the economic system and so on. *In*

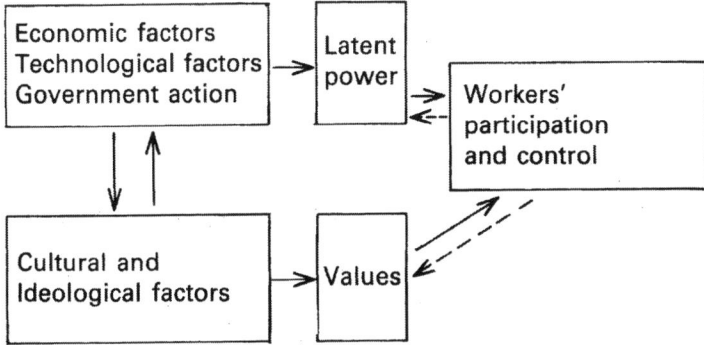

Figure 2.1: **The basic explanatory framework**

*short, latent power is shaped by economic factors, technological factors and government action.* Finally, more specific values may be underpinned by broader, subjective, *cultural* and *ideological* considerations, such as religious, managerialist, socialist, democratic, libertarian and humanitarian ideals. And values concerning participation and control are influenced not only by such general cultural and ideological predispositions, but also by the existing levels and development of workers' participation and control (these refer to the dynamic components of participation); *latent* elements of power such as educational resources and the levels of 'needs' already fulfilled by subordinate classes, parties and groups as a result of this power; and finally, *government action* which may be conducive to participation experiments and their acceptance within a given society. *In other words, values about participation and control are shaped by the existing levels of workers' participation and control, latent power, government action and ideologies.* These arguments should be developed more fully at this point.

Proposition 1 Workers' participation and control are reflections of latent power and values

It is our main aim to demonstrate, therefore, that developments in workers' participation and control, their ebb and flow in particular historical periods, their variations in significance in specific industries and factories and even their main international variations, can *largely be attributed to differences in the latent or underlying strength of the main industrial classes, parties and groups, although the question of values is a central part of the equation.* When, that is, the underlying power of workers as a whole, of their specific organizations, or at the still more local level of particular work-groups, has for some cause or other been enhanced this has usually been expressed *at the manifest level of power* in given developments in participation and control. As we shall see the possibilities of variation are multiple, and recalling our previous discussions on the meaning of participation, the levels at which workers have had an influence over decisions have differed greatly as have the range and scope of control over particular areas, but any lasting development along these lines has, we suggest, been dependent on certain external factors which have enhanced the power of workers (or particular groups among them) *vis-à-vis* management. Yet these changes in latent power, while necessary conditions, are not the sole impetus for extending the scope of workers' influence. There have been many occasions, indeed, when the latent power of workers would appear to merit their greater participation in decision-making but this has not taken place, or has occurred only circumspectly, because particular values – whether of workers or management – have been indispensable intermediary influences. But by the same token, as we shall see, values *on their own* are not the crucial determinants and cannot explain the development of *effective* participation and control without the question of latent power being taken into account. For participation schemes which have been instigated as a result of value considerations alone have been at worst short-lived or at best shaped very much as a reflection of the interests of the initiators concerned.

Proposition 2 Latent power is shaped by economic factors, technological factors and government action

The first proposition, however, conveys nothing about the overall explanatory framework it is intended to develop here and, left on its own, would remain largely descriptive. The main components of both latent power and values have, therefore, to be outlined at this point as well.

In so far as latent power is concerned, the strength of workers *vis-à-vis* management is closely affected by a number of economic factors. To begin with, periods of full employment doubtless signal an increase in the latent power of working people. Their numbers, of course, grow in such circumstances, but, in addition, the development of effective opposition is fostered in the absence of any serious threat from non-unionized and unemployed labour. Moreover, resources are likely to be enhanced in these conditions; with the growth in the pecuniary power of unions it is possible to support correspondingly more officials from union funds; victimization and other arbitrary acts of management are less likely to occur than in periods of depression and this enables highly talented and educated workers to represent their members at local level without any great fear of loss of livelihood; and finally, locally based representatives have sufficient time, free from any such threats, to gain valuable experience in union affairs.

But other economic factors have an important influence on the potential or latent power of workers. A number of market criteria – and notably, the profit margins of particular companies, the degree of competition experienced in a given industry, and whether an industry is an expanding or a contracting one – may all affect the underlying strength of particular sections of working people. After all, bargaining, not just on wage questions, but also on a wide range of other issues, must be facilitated, for instance, in a highly profitable section of industry which is comparatively free of external competition, and in the mainstream of a growing sector of the economy.

Moreover, the increasing scale of industrial operations is also of importance in this respect for concentration is associated with increasing bureaucratization and the consequent elimination of paternalistic practices which may operate in smaller firms to the detriment of unionization. There are, indeed, several reasons why industrial concentration favours union growth, the most obvious being that large aggregates of workers are prone to perceive common interests *vis-à-vis* their employers, and this facilitates joint action and, hence, union organization. Similarly, promotion within the firm increasingly depends on technical criteria and less on 'affectual' ties and, therefore, those workers who perceive their opportunities for individual advancement to be inescapably limited, tend to see union organization as their only effective means of improving their wages and conditions. Management, too, may gradually wish to deal with their employees on a relatively more systematic and regular basis and this enhances the prospects of their recognizing particular unions. And finally, union agents are likely to seek recruitment in highly concentrated firms, partly because here the 'objective' conditions for unionization are in any event favourable, but also because their costs per worker recruited will be somewhat lower by comparison with an equivalent recruitment programme among a much more scattered workforce (see

Bain, 1970). Again, while having an indirect effect on workers' latent power, concentration may directly favour participation since, as Banks (1970: 290) has argued: 'The very magnitude of the social problems involved in large-scale collective co-ordination has resulted in some participation by workers with managers in the conduct of day-to-day production affairs.'

Although, on balance, periods of depression (such as the one we have witnessed in the 1980s) will tend to reduce the latent power of workers, this may not be the case during violent economic upheaval and, in particular, in times of actual economic disintegration. For, after all, in such periods of chaos, the legitimacy of a whole social order may be brought into question and workers, having of necessity to be concerned with day-to-day survival, may take control over production processes at all levels, this having been particularly evident during the present century on the cessation of wars.

But technical factors also impinge on the opportunities for workers' participation by affecting the latent power of workers *vis-à-vis* management. It was Sayles (1958) who pointed out, of course, that the latent power of workgroups, as well as the social characteristics of their members, could be profoundly influenced by the technical organization of work itself. Indeed, contributions such as this from the so-called 'technical implications' school have become familiar in industrial sociology. The main exponents of this view have not only sought to relate variations in workers' latent power to different technological structures but have been at pains to demonstrate the variety of managerial characteristics and forms of managerial organization which stem from these very differences in underlying technology (Woodward, 1965). More specifically, for instance, with respect to the question of alienation and the influence of work processes on the chances of workers having a significant degree of control over task-based decision-making, it is usual to posit that an inverted 'U' curve may be observed as the technical scale is ascended (Blauner, 1964). In craft-type industries, the diversity of work and the high levels of skill among workers not only have certain direct implications with regard to the discretionary power of workers over task-based decision-making, but also, while craft workers are able to control the supply of labour into their occupations, such workers are difficult to replace, and this furnishes them with an important additional resource of power which is not shared by their less-skilled colleagues. By contrast, in the intermediary ranges of the technical scale – and especially in assembly-line industries – the prospects of workers having any significant measure of 'on-the-job' control are slight, the opportunities for direct mensuration of work are maximal, and workers are reduced to more negative forms of influence over their tasks, such as absenteeism, labour turnover and industrial sabotage. On the other hand, because, increasingly, the proportion of costs attributable to 'labour' tends to decline and those of capital machinery to escalate with every advance in technology, the economic damage that workers can inflict by direct action multiplies accordingly. Finally, in more fully automated industries, where workers' productive functions have been taken over by machinery, the need for 'intellectual' labour and for highly skilled maintenance craftsmen is accelerated so that, once again, technology can be seen substantially to affect power relations between management and workforce. To begin with, because of their high levels of skill, it is difficult for managements to monitor all workers' tasks directly and, although they may be able to negotiate productivity deals to ensure greater task flexibility, they cannot easily control the on-the-job, decision-making environment of the individual operative. At the same time, 'labour' costs as a proportion of total costs tend to be small, while with the unrelenting demand for highly trained 'labour', the development of fully automated industries could provide the technical basis for integrating intellectual and manual working people, Equally, of course, however, there could emerge a marked segmentation of labour (see Gordon, Edwards and Reich, 1983), with a tiny aristocracy of highly skilled workers alongside the growth of an impoverished proletariat, unable to find any employment in basic manufacturing industries at all. But, whatever the outcome of these developments, there will undoubtedly be major repercussions of the far-reaching changes in micro-electronics and other advanced technologies which characterize the present era (see Sorge *et al.*, 1983; Warner, 1984b).

And yet, neither economic nor technological variables exhaust all possible latent factors, for certain wider political questions are salient in this context as well. We are not referring at this point, of course, to the many governmental enactments on the specific question of workers' participation and control, since these very much reflect what is possible within the constraints of given socio-economic and political systems. But governments can certainly be more or less influential in affecting the latent power of the main industrial classes. For instance, with respect to the organizational strength of workers, government action may be of positive benefit:

first, by guaranteeing minimal rights of workers to belong to trade unions; second, by putting pressure on employers to recognize trade unions; and, finally, by its own policies with regard to unionization in the publicly owned sector of the economy. Bain (1970) has thus argued with respect to white-collar unionization that government action has been critical in ensuring the ultimate success of workers in certain major recruitment battles. Indeed, because nationalization acts have given positive encouragement to union formation, there is a considerable disparity in organizational strength between white-collar workers in the private and publicly owned sectors of the economy. It is evident, therefore, that political action can affect the latent power of the labour movement to a not inconsequential degree and this can be observed especially clearly by a consideration of negative aspects of governmental intervention. Totalitarian regimes, for instance, have generally sought to eradicate trade unionism, or to control it closely, or, at the very least, to inhibit 'free' collective bargaining, and this has clearly constrained even the most rudimentary forms of workers' action at local levels. But, of course, these actions are not confined to such regimes. In almost all Western industrial societies the influence of government on the wages and salaries front has been increasing, with the result that many pay 'battles' have been between government and workers rather than employers and trade unions. Moreover, recent employment legislation in Great Britain represents a major legislative attempt to reduce the powers of trade unions and to outlaw many practices which are not only important trade union tactics but also integral to their *latent* strength.

Proposition 3 Values concerning workers' participation and control are shaped by the existing levels of participation, latent power, government action and ideologies

If we turn finally to the role of values as regards developments of workers' participation and control, these, too, may be traced to a number of antecedent conditions.

There are to begin with the probable dynamic consequences of the establishment of given participation and control programmes; indeed, it is worth pointing out that there is a *reciprocal* influence between values and workers' participation, with the result that the development of a given participation programme may not only serve to reduce the level of opposition to future extensions in participation by virtue of making it a 'normal' practice for resolving problems, but it may also increase the desire for, and efficiency of, participation from the standpoint of members of subordinate groups.

Similarly, although as we have argued values may intervene between particular latent power distributions and their reflection in participation and control practices they, too, may be modified by latent power. More especially, since the latent power of workers may be expected also to lead to rises in their material standard of living, this may have further consequences for their general attitudes and values, as Maslow (1954) postulated. 'Higher echelons of needs' thus not only lead to the desire for more interesting and fulfilling work but also, more importantly in this context, to the search for greater participation and control over decisions which affect one's livelihood. And yet, this hierarchy may be substantially affected by further values – and notably materialist ones – which tend to restrict demands to a lower level of 'needs' and also, of course, by the consequences of periods of substantial unemployment.

It is our view that government action has often been most effective in advancing participation when it has altered the latent power of the main industrial classes, but the merits of the deliberate promotion of participation may be considerable if taken in the context of its impact on values. That is to say, government action may help to set a threshold of expectations with regard to participation which thereby forms an anticipated minimum of interpersonal conduct not only within factory contexts but also in other organizations and in society at large.

Finally, values towards participation are profoundly influenced by more general cultural predispositions and ideologies about human social organizations and the nature of man. On the negative side, whenever the predominant ethos of society has been authoritarian and whenever the main assumption of the leaders of given organizations has been based on their belief in men and women's essential evil rather than good, the prospects of enhancing human freedom by way of participation – where the people as a whole are able to control their own destinies within the context of a genuinely 'human' social order – have been inescapably limited and circumscribed. But other cultural factors and ideologies have had positive effects: indeed, participation has been a mainspring for many broadly humanitarian philosophies, whether socialist, democratic, libertarian, humanistic, religious or whatever.

In order to make sense of these variations, the main cultural predispositions which are linked with participation may be specified to include: moral codes (especially in the employment relationship), the degree of legalism or voluntarism, regionalism, religious values and a wider emphasis on social integration and accommodation. More specifically, too, relevant ideologies embrace: modern capitalism, managerialism, corporatism, liberal pluralism and social democracy, democratic socialism, centralized communism, decentralized communism and syndicalism, anarchism and guild socialism (for a detailed review see Poole, 1981a).

## Evolutionary trends and cyclical movements

But variations in the underlying power resources at the disposal of the industrial relations parties and diversity in values are also linked with changes in the *extent* of workers' participation and control experienced over time. Broadly speaking (and despite the many qualifications which will subsequently be made), latent movements in power alluded to so far, coupled with supportive values, have been sufficiently durable to ensure a substantial degree of *institutionalization* of machinery for industrial democracy, particularly in Western Europe. But periods of *innovation* and *heightened workers' influence* over decisions are far more cyclical in incidence and are *associated with epochs of intensification of industrial conflict*.

There will be an attempt to provide empirical support for these arguments later in the volume but, from a theoretical standpoint, it is important to note here that structural movements in modern societies (especially advances in technology and the growth of complex and interdependent roles in modern industry), changes in values (including an increasing concern for social justice, and the challenge to traditional types of domination associated with the so-called 'democratic current') and a redistribution of power in favour of working people and their associations have led to durable institutional procedures for industrial democracy. (For a development of this case, see Brannen *et al.*, 1976; Poole, 1982b.) Certainly, so far as Western Europe is concerned, the extensive institutional practices which now prevail have few obvious historical parallels. Moreover, amongst developing nations, machinery for industrial democracy is far more likely to be encompassed in general programmes of economic and industrial advance than was the case in either the west or the east at a roughly equivalent phase of development (see Dore, 1973).

Yet, it is important to note that the more the focus of attention shifts from an analysis of institutional forms to explaining the *origins* of institutions, the *effectiveness* of particular institutional programmes, the *types* of participative practice which are emphasized at any given point in time and, above all, the *extent*, *scope* and *range* of actual workers' influence itself, the more persuasive is a cyclical interpretation of the main historical movements. To be sure, the term *favourable conjunctures* in many respects more accurately reflects the considerable degree of discontinuity over time. For after all, even though periods of rapid advance have often been followed by retrenchment and even the abandonment of particular practices, the pattern has occurred in a way which does not easily fit the more rhythmic sequences of a cyclical movement. But this in no way invalidates the case that the historical record is by no means one of a linear evolutionary expansion across the whole range of participative experiences. Indeed, epochs of advance are, as we have argued, linked with: (a) a rise in the underlying or latent power of the workforce and a favourable 'climate of values'; and (b) the intensification of industrial conflict. Moreover, in this latter respect, there is no doubt that periods of crisis (such as wartime or post-war reconstruction) or of domestic economic and industrial upheavals ' are favourable to the emergence of programmes for industrial democracy (partly because of changing power balances, but also on account of radical shifts in values and a concern for the re-institutionalization of conflict). And finally, diversity in values (partly explained by new phases of economic and social development) may be associated with the emergence of distinctive types of participative machinery in each successive conjuncture (see Cronin, 1979; Poole, 1982b; Ramsay, 1983).

# 3 Proposals by management

The thrust of the argument so far is that advances in industrial democracy are most likely when a rise in the underlying power of workers and their representatives is supported by favourable values. Changes in the balance of power (and attempts to accommodate resultant conflicts) are basic to participation. By contrast preferences for democratic leadership styles, better organizational communications and so on are seen to be of lesser explanatory consequence. At this point, we subject our central explanatory propositions to a more rigorous empirical scrutiny. This takes place during the course of an examination of a rich array of types of workers' participation.

## A framework for analysis

Although, as we have argued, the distribution of power in industry and society underlies effective participation, insofar as managerial roles are concerned, a series of wider constraints on action, as well as distinctive ideologies, must be outlined prior to a more detailed appraisal of managerial practices themselves. The principal elements are summarized in Figure 3.1, where it will be seen that several general structural constraints and subjective meanings have been isolated and that, in the analytical framework, account is also taken of the power of the other parties to the employment relationship, the problem of control (the subject of extensive further examination later in this chapter), the values of managers towards participation, and finally the outcomes in terms of managerially initiated practices.

## Structural constraints

Taking first of all, then, the constraints of structure, there is no doubt that managerial initiatives are affected by a number of economic conditions. Certainly the higher levels of unemployment

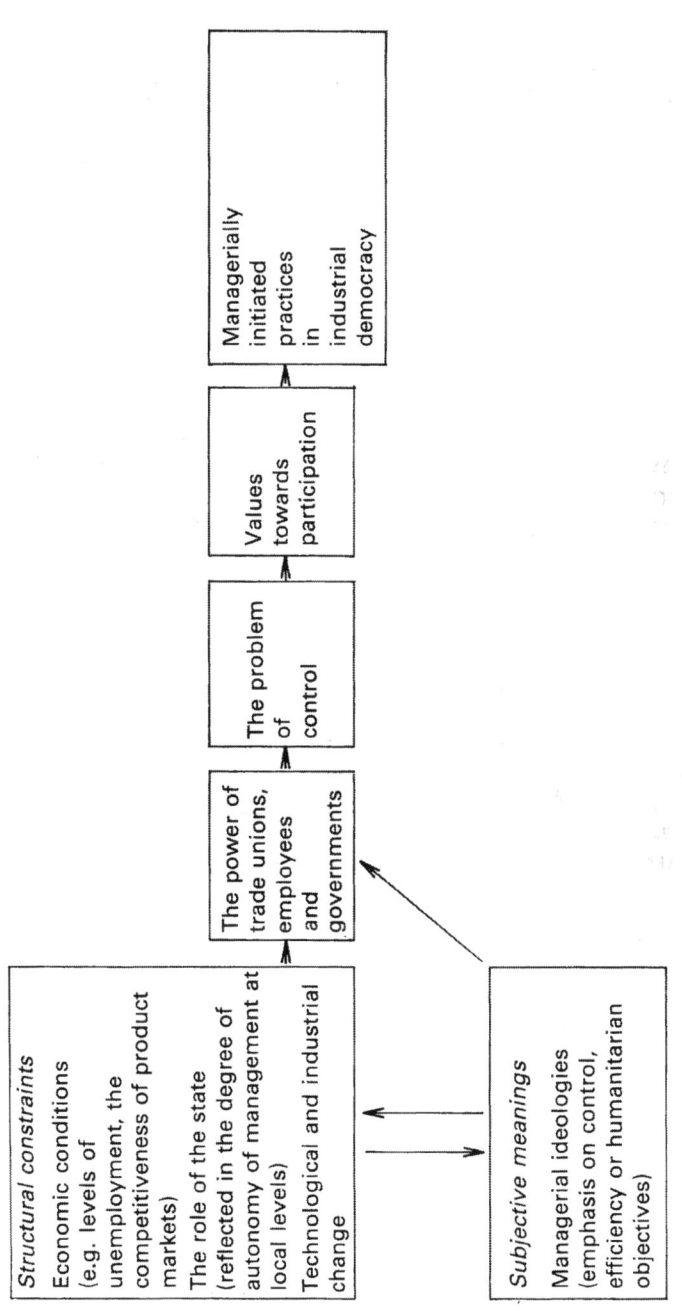

Figure 3.1: **A framework for analysing managerial initiatives**

experienced in the 1980s have relieved an earlier tightness in the labour market and this has ensured that, instead of reacting to trade union and worker pressure, managers have been able to mount a number of proposals and practices in recent years. By contrast, however, competitiveness in product markets has less advantageous consequences from a managerial standpoint. To be sure, it can stimulate programmes (such as quality circles) which are consistent with environmental pressures of this type, but it can also force managers to seek to regain control over the workforce at the point of production by reverting to authoritarian decision-making styles.

Moreover, the role of the state is particularly critical in understanding managerial initiatives in furthering employee participation. This is because extensive governmental controls over the economy and industry circumscribe managerial autonomy at local levels and restrict the possibilities of developing participatory schemes other than those anchored in the legislature. This is a case which applies to both socialist and capitalist societies (indeed, in the former, the reliance on central planning or markets respectively has far-reaching implications for managerial practices) (see Poole, 1980 for a review).

But periods of technological and industrial change are also central to the initiatives of management. Organic and flexible patterns of decision-making are particularly likely to occur in such circumstances. This tendency, too, applies especially to the new technologies for a number of key workers are elevated in the power structure of the enterprise and typically enjoy considerable 'responsible autonomy'.

### Subjective meanings: managerial ideologies and the problem of control

A more lengthy treatment, however, is necessary to outline broader changes in managerial ideologies and in patterns of control within the enterprise, since these are basic to power and values in this area.

Ever since the publication of Bendix's (1956) classic treatise, *Work and Authority in Industry*, it has been understood that there is a fundamental difference between entrepreneurial and managerial ideologies. The first arose during the early phases of industrialism and represented the struggle of a rising class of entrepreneurs to establish an industrial way of life in a hostile environment. The ideals of this expanding group were those of individualism, enterprise, initiative and profitability. The second accompanied 'the multiplication of technical and administrative tasks' and was associated with attempts to ensure *rational domination of personnel and functions in the large-scale enterprise.* The rather different emphasis was now on a shared 'universe of discourse' reflected in a unitary conception of authority in the organization (Fox, 1971; 1985), the rise of so-called 'organizational' men and women, and the view that managers were indispensable to the effective administration of business enterprises regardless of the wider political environment. And, above all, whereas entrepreneurial ideologies elevated self-interest to legitimate a 'quest for advantage, social prestige and political participation', managerial ideologies enshrined a concept of organization which not only sanctioned control by managers over decision-making, but also was 'designed to enlist the areas in which "subordinates exercise their judgment" for managerial ends' (Bendix, 1956: 251).

The emergence of distinctive managerial ideologies was also related to a progressive differentiation of organizational functions associated with the separation of control from ownership at the top of the larger-scale corporation. Indeed, the so-called 'managerialist' thesis contains three assumptions of great significance: first, that a divorce of ownership from control of the means of production was rapidly taking place in all advanced industrial countries; second, that in view of this the new controllers of industry would become largely non-propertied, technically proficient and highly professional; and third, that a very different distribution of social rewards would now be forthcoming. The legitimacy of managerial domination was thus gradually transferred from traditional (property ownership) to legal-rational grounds, resting on the expertise of key industrial administrators. In consequence, too, a belief was fostered that industry would be controlled by those most fitted in terms of natural and acquired abilities. Achievement rather than family connection would be the basis for acquiring managerial posts in the first place, industry would reach undreamed-of levels of efficiency and therefore any attempt to curb managerial powers would be socially and economically short-sighted.

At this point in the thesis there were some differences of opinion as to the additional effects of these developments, two principal variants being recognized here. In one view, a non-zero-sum power situation would obtain and management would therefore exercise its decision-making powers in a socially responsible way to the resultant benefit of all members of the population. But in the other, which rested more on a zero-sum power conception, any accretions in managerial power brought about by such developments would inevitably take place to the detriment not only of older entrepreneurial classes but also of all other classes. Again, the more meritocratic societies became, the greater would be this tendency, since lower social classes would be robbed of effective and talented leaders.

And at all events the progressive advance of managerial ideologies and the emergence of designated functions of control have undoubtedly proved to be major obstacles to the development of industrial democracy. Indeed, these are far more antithetical to genuine workers' participation than the entrepreneurial ideologies of traditional organizations that have regard only for profit-making criteria. After all, it can usually be shown that profit and efficiency are enhanced by workers' participation in decision-making. However, in as much as modern managers have internalized an ideology which defends their decision-making authority on the basis of expertise in a controlling function, they will be unwilling to threaten this by encouraging participative and democratic practices. Indeed it is to be expected that the more a given manager approximates or considers himself or herself to approximate to the stereotype encapsulated by the managerialist thesis, the more vehemently will be his or her opposition to workers' participation and control. Conversely, it will be the profit-oriented managers who should be most supportive of limited experiments in participatory democracy.

To be sure, as Clarke, Fatchett and Roberts (1972: 179) have suggested, it may well be that new criteria, relatively more consistent with workers' participation in decision-making, will ultimately be found in managerial circles:

> Looking to the future the desirable form of the industrial enterprise would seem to be one in which that autonomy, which in the nineteenth century was considered justified by ownership and which in the first half of the twentieth century was seen as a right exercised by managers because they were the appointees of the owners who were the sole judge of their ability, as well as the sole source of their right to manage, will increasingly be seen to spring from an objective and accepted

appraisal of functional requirements in which all concerned are recognized to have a legitimate interest.

But, at all events, what is important to note, in so far as managerial attitudes to workers' participation in decision-making is concerned, is that the main managerial ideology of the twentieth century has worked strongly against radical initiatives in industrial democracy.

Indeed, the most common and generally preferred solution to any expansion of the latent power of working people has historically been for management to develop paternalistic practices for which the 'human relations movement' provided the main rationale and personnel management the most obvious institutional form. The growth of humanitarian policies may be viewed as a direct response to changing economic, political and technical circumstances which altered the balance of latent power between the main industrial relations classes. Thus, during the post-Second World War period – and especially in the 1950s – there were actual labour shortages in most advanced industrial countries and as a result the recruitment and retention of an adequate labour force was imperative to management. This, therefore, provided a fertile ground not only for the development of a number of welfare practices, such as sickness and pensions schemes, but also for the growth of personnel departments at workplace level to deal with the problems of individual workers. Morever, the easy availability of employment undoubtedly increased the bargaining power of workers and this was manifested principally in the emergence of domestic bargaining arrangements based on the shop-steward system.

The post-war period, too, saw the growing intervention by government in labour-management relations and this, in turn, led to a host of legal measures which required more systematic attention by employers to 'human relations' practices than was the case in the inter-war years. Again, although the economic and technical changes of the 1980s have led to an erosion of job opportunities in traditional manufacturing industries (and in some cases there has been substantial de-skilling), other developments have continued to further the latent power of working people. Thus, as a result of technical integration of production processes in large-scale companies, many workers have found themselves in particularly strategic positions to inflict major economic costs on their respective employers, while the growing scale and concentration of industry are undoubtedly favourable to union growth and to collective action by the employees of these large combines. And, with the increased demand for highly skilled workers as the 'technical scale' is ascended, skill shortages have remained in certain segments of the labour market and this again has the effect of ensuring that, in such milieux, the balance of latent power is still to the benefit of the workers concerned.

Of course, none of the arguments above should be taken to imply that workers are in any sense stronger than their employers (indeed, on balance, the depression of the 1980s has seen an appreciable weakening of labour). But the main point here is that for most of the post-Second World War period certain forces were in operation which served to advance the position of working people and that the most common managerial response to this situation was not to encourage workers' participation in decision-making but rather to develop paternalistic human relations and personnel policies.

This again is linked with the fact that even when managements recognize conflicting interests at workplace level, they still *prefer* to hold on to a 'unitary conception of the organization', i.e. 'to favour the view which sees it as having but one proper source of authority and one focus of loyalty' (Fox, 1971: 126). After all, such a conception is part of an ideology which serves three purposes: 'It is at once a method of self-reassurance, an instrument of persuasion, and a technique of seeking legitimation of authority' (Fox, 1971: 126). And, to the extent that it is a fair judgment, there are clearly important grounds here for managements who seek to retain such a view of the authority structure of the enterprise to make social welfare policies *a function of management* and thereby to deprive workers of effective autonomy to control such issues themselves.

As a consquence, too, it is scarcely surprising that the bulk of schemes for employee participation initiated by management have been restricted in terms of the scope, level and range of issues involved. Typically, there is a preference for *task-* rather than *power*-centred forms of employee involvement and an inclination towards *consultative* rather than *participative* institutions. As Clarke and his colleagues (1972: 134) have argued,

on the whole, employers and their spokesmen have evinced deep mistrust as to the value of participation, particularly in integrative forms, such as the appointment of workers' directors, though they reflect a widespread belief in prior consultation with workers on matters which concern them.

And certainly such a view is endorsed by empirical findings on managerial attitudes to industrial democracy, where although the provision of more information to employees and the extension of consultative practices (both formal and informal) have found favour, the majority of managers are still opposed to extensions in collective bargaining and to worker directors (Poole, *et al.*, 1981: 87). Moreover, in the light of such preferences, it is scarcely surprising that employers' and managers' organizations have consistently opposed comprehensive reforms in this area, such as those advocated by the Bullock Committee.

In general, therefore, managements have only sought to institute broader programmes when the power of workers has been sufficiently strong, or when they have been obliged to do so as a consequence of government legislation, or when they have internalized certain general ideologies different from the main ones examined so far in this chapter – chief among these being humanist, religious or an overriding commitment to industrial efficiency.

There is also some evidence to suggest that *radical* managerial initiatives are cyclical in character. To be sure, even when labour is weaker, developments in information-sharing and consultation may still take place, since these are entirely consistent with modern managerial ideologies. But more comprehensive power-sharing is only likely under rather different circumstances in which, as Flanders (1967: 32) trenchantly observed, managements are forced to seek to 'regain control by sharing it'. As Ramsay (1983: 204) has argued:

> managements have been attracted to the idea of participation when their control over labour has been perceived to be under pressure in some way. This perception has coincided with periods of experience of a growing challenge from labour to the legitimacy of capital and its agents. In Britain these challenges have coincided this century with the impact and aftermath of two world wars, and with the rise of shop-floor union organization at the same time as squeezed profit margins in the 1960s and 1970s. In each case mounting pressure, including demands for 'industrial democracy' from sections of the labour movement, helped to precipitate management's response.

Otherwise, managements have been typically drawn into root and branch reforms only under the impact of facilitative or mandatory governmental legislation (IDE, 1981b).

Of course, there has always been a minority of employers who have objected on broadly humanitarian grounds to the predominant modes of the social organization of work in industry, but because of the importance of market rather than ethical criteria in determining economic success, the evolution of industrial organization is punctuated by the graveyards of some of the boldest, most imaginative, and humanitarian attempts to develop rather different work relationships. Not infrequently, the secular humanism implied here has been buttressed by certain religious convictions – and this has been especially true of Quaker employers. More commonly, however, an overriding concern with industrial efficiency has been the principal ideological stimulus behind the acceptance of new forms of organization of work. Participation has been seen to facilitate this in the following ways: it enables the skills and abilities of workers to be effectively tapped, it reduces workers' resistance to technological change, it spurs management to increase efficiency, it raises the level of workers' satisfaction and thereby makes for a more contented workforce, and finally it is viewed as an important means for improving industrial relations. Naturally, assumptions such as these are open to investigation, but our concern here is the ideological basis for changing assessments of the utility of employee participation and its relationship with different power distributions and the values of the participants themselves.

## Types of managerial initiative

Turning, then, to actual empirical cases, in this chapter and those which follow, the principal types of participation have been classified on the basis of the *initiators* of the different programmes. For other purposes, it might be preferable to use taxonomies based on geographical location or internal structural properties (Poole, 1979). But, in our case, an approach is necessary which links with the themes of power and values, the uppermost explanatory concerns of our study. And, of course, to focus on initiators is valuable in this respect because it obviously requires a certain measure of *power* to bring any specific scheme into effect, and also for the reason that the *values* of given classes, parties and groups can be easily recognized by this method. However, in so far as forms of participation initiated by management are concerned, it is also particularly important to make the further distinction between *direct* participation on the one hand and *indirect* or *representative* participation on the other, for, by so doing, different levels of decision-making within the managerial hierarchy may be fairly readily identified. These distinctions thus form the basis of the classifications in Table 3.1.

Table 3.1: **Forms of participation initiated by management**

**Direct participation**

1 Piecemeal attempts by management to raise production and efficiency while reducing conflict and increasing workers' satisfaction on the basis of workgroup participation, 'total participation' exercises, quality circles
2 Disclosure of information
3 Job rotation, job enlargement and job enrichment: quality of work-life programmes
4 Suggestions schemes, employee shareholding and other profit-sharing schemes, co-partnership and 'commonwealth' ventures

**Indirect participation**

1 Joint consultative committees
2 Specific committees covering productivity, welfare and safety, the administration of various trusts, funds and occupational pension schemes
3 Productivity bargaining and job evaluation

### Direct participation

Turning more specifically now to the managerially initiated programmes for involving working people in decision-making, we shall begin our analysis with an examination of the most important forms of direct participation. These involve practices in which all the members of a given workgroup, or workteam, are able to influence decision-making processes; they do not therefore have to rely on their representative alone. However, not surprisingly, as we shall see, the majority of these practices are restricted to very low levels of decision-making and, further, they are largely confined to issues of an 'on-the-job' character. Therefore, even if they may have had important effects in so far as industrial 'efficiency' is concerned, it is doubtful whether they imply any significant erosion of managerial 'prerogatives' and, as a result, to many critics they are examples of 'pseudo-participation'.

## Piecemeal attempts to raise efficiency by means of workgroup participation, quality circles

Ever since the Hawthorne experiments began to have an impact on managerial and academic thinking during the 1930s, it has been understood that workgroups can have a particularly important influence on industrial efficiency. On the one hand they may develop various practices which prevent competition between members and thereby restrict individual output to a common group norm; on the other hand, the workgroup itself may figure as a powerful vehicle for enhancing output and productivity. Moreover, for the latter situation to obtain, a critically important component is the development of 'workshop democracy'. Thus, in the classical relay assembly test-room experiment – in which output of the group was observed to rise progressively week by week despite major changes in the physical environment of work – the most important social factor appeared to be the almost total disappearance of externally imposed discipline and supervision. As Blumberg (1968: 34) has argued, 'In brief, the entire system of industrial authority which these workers had been accustomed to labouring under was transformed during the experiment, as the test-room workers developed into an almost self-governing body.' Therefore, although, to be sure, the level of decision-making implicated here was largely confined to the workgroup, the relevance of autonomy to workers' satisfaction and raising industrial efficiency had begun to be recognized.

Following the Hawthorne experiments there have, of course, been many extensive and detailed studies of workgroup behaviour although the majority have been related in only a rather peripheral way to the issues of power and participation. But there have at the same time been some attempts to bring these themes into closer apposition. Thus, in the USA, the Scanlon Plan provided for developments in participation based on working groups as a stimulus to industrial efficiency (Lesieur, 1958) and two further studies are noteworthy at this point because they highlight the more general explanatory themes of our own study exceptionally well.

The earliest and best-known attempt to measure the effects of participation on workers' output and satisfaction was carried out by Coch and French (1959) in an American clothing factory in which production methods were changing in order to cater for civilian rather than military markets after the end of the Second World War. The details of the study are too well known to merit a lengthy treatment here, but its most important aspects were as follows. In the main experiments, three groups of workers were set up: first, a control group for whom there was *no participation* in decisions relating to the prospective changes; second, an experimental *participation through representation* group; and third, certain experimental, *total participation* groups, in which all members were involved in designing the changeover in production. The results of this study have formed the basis of many of the most optimistic projections as to the consequences of participation by workgroups. Thus, in the control group, for whom no participation in the changes was possible (Coch and French, 1959: 329):

> Resistance developed almost immediately after the change occurred. Marked expressions of aggression against management occurred, such as conflicts with the methods engineer, expressions of hostility against the supervisor, deliberate restriction of production, and lack of co-operation with the supervisor. There were 17% quits in the first 40 days. Grievances were filed about the piece rate, but when the rate was checked, it was found to be a little 'loose'.

But the situation in the other groups was markedly different. The attitude of the representative group was 'co-operative and permissive', the group adapted well to the changes and their output soon reached a level higher than that obtaining before the experiments were set up. There was only one recorded act of aggression from this group and no one left the workteam as a result of the changeover. Moreover, the total participation groups adapted most speedily of all to the changes, their 'efficiency ratings' showed sustained progress 'to a level about 14% higher than the prechange level'. There were no indications of aggression to management and supervision and, again, no labour turnover within the group (Coch and French, 1959: 329–32). Thus, the positive effects of participation on output, satisfaction and labour-management relations appeared to be confirmed.

However, notwithstanding the more obvious criticisms of these experiments in so far as the distribution of power in industry is concerned – and notably, that participation took place at a very low level, that the decisions which the workers influenced focused on means towards ends already established by management, and that these decisions were largely confined to task-based problems – there are certain further points of interest which should be raised here. To begin with, such forms of 'participation' are of course likely to be preferred to higher-level programmes by management because they demand so little change in the traditional authority structure of the firm and therefore fit reasonably well into the so-called 'unitary conception' of authority within the enterprise. Indeed, in view of the positive effects of these experiments, it is somewhat surprising that they are not already the most common means for dealing with managerial problems of this type.

But what is particularly intriguing in the study by Coch and French is that the workers concerned should have shown so little resistance not to the changeover in production but to the specific forms of managerial initiative involved in this experiment, and the principal reason for this was almost certainly the low levels of latent power obtaining among these employees. Such a conclusion is certainly justified if we consider the equally well known attempt to replicate this study in a Norwegian factory (French, Israel and As, 1960). Once again, the details of the experiment are not especially important for our purposes, but it is of fundamental significance that the researchers had *to refine their theory of participation* by demonstrating that increased participation affected production, labour-management relations, and job satisfaction (French, Israel and As, 1960: 17) only to the extent that four conditioning variables were present: (a) the decisions were important, (b) the content of decisions was relevant to the dependent variable, (c) the participation was considered legitimate, and (d) there was no resistance to change (i.e. no negative reaction to the *methods* of managing the change).

Fundamental to the outcome of these experiments was the level of unionization of the workpeople in each factory, as French, Israel and As (1960: 18) pointed out:

> The Norwegian workers had a stronger tradition of being organized in a union than had workers in the American factory. This in turn can produce an attitude that the legitimate pattern of participation is through union representatives rather than direct participation.

But we would wish to take this argument somewhat further by postulating that the higher level of organizational power of workers in the Norwegian factory almost certainly necessitated the introduction of the four conditioning variables. That is to say, it was precisely the power of these workers that enabled them to insist that the decisions they took were important, that they were relevant to the dependent variable concerned (e.g. job satisfaction), and that prompted them to regard certain forms of participation as *illegitimate* (because they were perceived either as manipulative or to clash with their own representation). Finally for this reason, too, the Norwegian workers were able and willing to resist certain *methods* of managing the change.

Moreover, to the extent that these interpretations are valid, there are certain general conclusions to be drawn concerning the relationship between power and participation. To begin with, although it clearly requires a modicum of latent power, together with appropriate values, to establish a given participation programme in the first instance, the latent power and values *of the other party* are clearly critical in affecting the degree of success recorded in any particular scheme. Thus, whereas in the American factory very modest erosions of managerial prerogatives were sufficient to ensure major changes in workers' attitudes and behaviour, this was clearly less true in the Norwegian works. And second, it would appear that not only does the latent power of workers substantially affect their demands for taking decisions on matters which are important to them, but this also forms a basis for developing certain values towards participation in which a distinction is made between certain managerially initiated programmes which *may* be regarded as illegitimate and those, based on their union organizations, which are recognized as the most appropriate means for handling problems. Values towards participation are therefore affected by latent power. And finally, if our assessment is correct, this also suggests that the success of small-scale, managerially initiated programmes depends to a great extent on the latent power and values of the workers. When workers are poorly organized, the best results from a managerial point of view are likely to ensue, since major benefits may be expected to accrue from small changes in the authority structure of the firm; but by way of contrast, certain programmes may be rejected outright by workers in highly unionized firms, unless they are conducted through the union channels which are regarded by the workers as the legitimate means for handling labour-relations issues. And, in any event, workers in such highly unionized firms may characteristically demand rather more control over decision-making processes than management might wish to concede.

This judgment tends to be ratified further by the experience of certain 'total involvement' exercises carried out during periods of dramatic technical change. A particularly well-researched example is the case of Imperial Chemical Industries at its Gloucester nylon-spinning plant where not only were shop-floor discussion groups set up to involve all the workers in the changes, but also a joint management-union working party including the shop stewards was established together with a joint negotiating party to sanction any proposals and suggestions emerging from the groups and the working party (Cotgrove, Dunham and Vamplew, 1971; see also Pettigrew, 1985). Clearly, therefore, a much broader framework of participation was appropriate on account of the strength of workplace union organization.

Furthermore, although top management may welcome such changes on the grounds that they are concerned largely with means for implementing managerial policy decisions, the consequences may be particularly severe for lower and middle management in terms of both decision-making authority and ideology. Indeed, in the ICI study by Cotgrove and his colleagues, enthusiasm for the scheme among supervisory personnel was much less marked than among top management, workers and shop stewards. Thus, although efficiency and 'happiness' among workers were undoubtedly encouraged by such developments (Cotgrove, Dunham and Vamplew, 1971: 111–12):

> The adoption of a supervisory style based on participation was
> not easy. For all supervisors, it meant a threat to their status
> and security; for some, the fundamental changes in behaviour
> required were more than they could manage. Some had left,
> and others had experienced severe strain in adjusting to the
> demands of the new style, with its shift in emphasis from
> authority and directives to participatory leadership.

But the 1970s and early 1980s witnessed further attempts by management to enlist the commitment of the workforce through workgroup participation (most notably in the Ford Motor Company). However, interest in this latter period particularly developed in so-called *quality circles*. These consist of small groups of workers 'who meet regularly to solve problems and find ways of improving aspects of their work' (Department of Employment, 1983: 102–4). As Warner (1984b: 90–1) has pointed out, they involve an attempt by managements 'to achieve an error free level of performance by appealing to the workers' sense of craftsmanship'. Though the idea itself originally developed in the USA, it is of course especially associated with Japan where 10 million workers are members of quality circles (Hayes, 1981; Warner, 1984b). But there was a rapid worldwide spread of quality circles in the 1980s and, in September 1982, in Britain, the National Society of Quality Circles was formed. Earlier, too, in the USA, in 1973 a group from Lockheed Missiles of California re-imported the idea from Japan and there is now an American organization, the International Association of Quality Circles (Department of Employment, 1983: 104). These participatory organs have a number of characteristics which commend themselves to managers (the task-based level of operation, the unitary conception and the direct rather than representative nature of employee involvement). But, to explain the rise of this particular phenomenon in the 1980s, worldwide product competition was undoubtedly a factor. However, micro-processor technology, which tends to require 'more, not less, need for quality, involvement and employee participation in decision-making' (Department of Employment, 1983: 104), also fuelled this movement and had obvious implications for the power of workgroups at task-level.

## Disclosure of information

Historically, managements have been most favourably disposed to introducing employee involvement programmes in times of economic buoyancy and labour unrest. But, the recent record suggests that this tendency is by no means inevitable and, in certain cases (and notably disclosure of information), favourable legislation has been an important further stimulus. To be sure, managers operating from a unitary frame of reference should be willing – regardless of economic circumstances – to impart information to employees to encourage organizational loyalty and commitment. However, they will be unwilling to share information in this way (without wider pressures for change), if it becomes a power resource for trade unions to be deployed in collective bargaining.

The origins of disclosure of information in Britain are by no means easy to trace, but the antecedents are almost certainly linked with early profit-sharing schemes and formal joint consultation within works councils (see Hussey and Marsh, 1983). More recently, too, a number of surveys have revealed highly positive attitudes among managers to developments in information-sharing (the weakest single form of participation in terms of scope of workers' influence) (Poole *et al.*, 1981; Marsh, 1982). But the appreciable growth of disclosure of information in the 1970s was almost certainly triggered by favourable legislation.

To begin with, then, the Industrial Relations Act, 1971, provided that employers 'of more than 350 persons' should make an annual written statement to all employees and placed upon them a duty 'to disclose to representatives of recognised registered unions all information within their possession relating to their undertakings', in order not to impede trade unions in carrying out collective bargaining and to be in accordance with good industrial relations practice (Hussey and Marsh, 1983: xvii). Following the repeal of this Act, a number of the disclosure clauses were reintroduced and extended in subsequent legislation. Notably, the Employment Protection Act, 1975, included some significant changes on enforcement (allowing trade unions, for example, to make complaints to the Central Arbitration Committee), while the Industry Act of the same year made a number of provisions for information sharing within planning agreements. But although there is now no legal obligation on employers to make annual statements to employees, the practice has continued to flourish.

Indeed, despite a falling off in the number of companies newly adopting employee reporting at the end of the 1970s, in a survey by Marsh and Hussey (1979), 42 per cent of firms reported this practice (80 per cent of those with more than 1,000 employees) (see also Hussey and Marsh, 1983). To be sure, it is clear from data from the Department of Employment/Policy Studies Institute/ Social Science Research Council Survey that there are discrepancies in managers' and trade unionists' accounts of the information actually given (consistently, on pay and conditions of service, manpower requirements and the financial position of the company, managements were found to take the more favourable view of what had actually been provided) (Daniel and Millward, 1983: 149). Moreover, there is little doubt that codes on disclosure of information have had only a circumscribed impact upon actual practice (Willman and Gospel, 1983). But disclosure of information was an important element in the changing policies of managements in the 1970s and it is also clear that supportive legislation significantly encouraged its general expansion. Moreover, partly because it is a relatively weak form of participation, like joint consultation, it remained important in the 1980s, despite the disquiet which was sometimes voiced by employees and their representatives on the actual amount of information they received. Again, in the 1980s, disclosure of information received a further impetus as a consequence of the rise of the new technologies and the emergent problems which managements faced in ensuring that these were successfully implemented (see Briefs, Ciborra and Schneider, 1983; NEDO, 1983; Ruskin College, 1984).

## Job rotation, job enlargement and job enrichment; quality of work-life programmes

In the 1970s especially there were many other attempts by management to overcome some of the emergent problems it faced as a consequence of the growth in the latent power of working people. Four of these will be examined at this point: job rotation, which refers to the practice of changing workers from one job to another; job enlargement, which involves some extension of the range of jobs undertaken by a particular operator; job enrichment (otherwise known as job restructuring or job redesign), which entails giving far greater responsibility to workers and enabling them to take decisions that were formerly the prerogative of supervisors; and the more extensive changes envisaged in quality of work-life programmes.

For the great majority of employees, of course, work has always been an alienating experience: indeed, this has been so marked that the concept of work has come to be interpreted in explicitly alienative terms. Moroever, certain technical developments have, if anything, considerably aggravated this problem with the result that, in the so-called middle range of the technical scale (epitomized by the assembly line), even management will acknowledge that working conditions are of an extremely unsatisfying nature. To be sure, many of the workers who are actually in such employment may be untypical of working people as a whole and, in particular, they may have marked 'instrumental orientations' which enable them – so long as they are satisfied with their rates of pay – to accept more readily than their colleagues the major disincentives of their work environment (Goldthorpe *et al.*, 1968). But, in any event, monetary rewards only partially ameliorate this problem. After all, symptoms of alienation have multiplied in the great majority of industrial countries in the post-Second World War period; rates of absenteeism, labour turnover, sickness and accidents have typically shown a marked deterioration, while many small strikes and stoppages are almost certainly attributable to alienative environments, a few being explicitly so. Moreover, colourful examples of alienation have been provided by the numerous acts of industrial sabotage and restrictive practices. Again, most symptoms of alienation follow a distinctive weekly cycle in which the rate is highest on Mondays but declines progressively as the week advances, a pattern to be expected in alienative environments since, during the early part of the week, the workers' perception of the disrewards of work are likely to be particularly intense. However, this experience would be expected to subside somewhat as the prospect of enjoying 'free time' over the weekend becomes less distant.

Of course, from a managerial point of view, these indices of alienation were to reach unacceptable proportions. In the early 1970s, in the electronics industry, labour turnover alone was calculated to cost about £13 million a year and was generally adduced to the dreary and depressing nature of the work (Daniel and McIntosh, 1972). It is scarcely surprising, then, that efficiency-oriented managements vigorously sought means to minimize these problems and began to accept that the erosion of certain decision-making prerogatives was an acceptable price to pay if this offered some solution.

As it happens, job rotation and job enlargement have comparatively little impact on the hierarchy of authority in the firm. Indeed, under certain circumstances, they may be interpreted by workers as effecting a diminution in their job interest and autonomy since, when rotation, for example, is imposed by management, informal workgroup norms which help to reduce the worst consequences of alienation for the individual worker may also break down. To be sure, as Daniel and McIntosh have argued, these problems can be avoided (Daniel and McIntosh, 1972: 49):

> As far as job rotation and enlargement are concerned,
> management must create the conditions where this can
> naturally come about, through the style of supervision, the level
> of manning and the physical layout of the work area, rather
> than by imposing preconceived systems of rotation and
> enlargement on the workgroup. Though the intention may be
> to increase the workers' job interest and autonomy the effect
> is likely to reduce them because of closer supervision and loss
> of social satisfactions through the break-up of established group
> relationships.

Indeed, because under certain circumstances job rotation and enlargement may involve a slight but scarcely perceptible increase in a worker's ability to take decisions of a technical nature to the detriment of his or her control over a number of social decisions, they may involve no net gain in the power of the employee whatsoever. It is only job enrichment, therefore, which significantly affects the decision-making powers of working people and this accordingly merits more thorough consideration at this point (see Kelly and Clegg (eds), 1982; Warner, 1984b).

There have now been a number of detailed investigations of job enrichment schemes and in most cases the positive benefits in so far as productivity, flexibility, work satisfaction and industrial relations are concerned have been amply demonstrated. The three best documented programmes have been those at ICI, the American Telephone and Telegraph Company and at Philips. Paul and Robertson (1970) have reported that jobs were restructured at ICI in order that given workgroups might achieve more responsibility and autonomy. Particularly spectacular results were forthcoming from among the salesmen whose sales not only increased substantially but whose level of job satisfaction showed major gains as well, but in all groups the effects of these experiments were positive in terms of industrial efficiency (Ford, 1969). Considerable improvements in efficiency were also consequent upon the restructuring of decision-making in a subsidiary of the American Telephone and Telegraph Company. Here, following the reorganization, orders were almost invariably completed on time, the quality of work improved considerably, and, in so far as few grievances can be taken as an index of greater job satisfaction, there were also important gains in this direction. Furthermore, the experiments at Philips are of interest, principally because here an attempt was being made to combat chronic labour shortages. Once again, therefore, an improvement in the relative strength of workers *vis-à-vis* management may have important repercussions for day-to-day relations in the workplace. Indeed, the Philips management introduced several changes in production methods, the most significant for our purposes being the comparatively autonomous production teams which were set up, enjoying considerable decision-making powers which were once the prerogative of middle management and supervisory staff. Again, there were substantial benefits recorded on the efficiency dimension: quality and output increased, while labour turnover and absenteeism declined and the workers' attitudes to management became far less antagonistic (Philips, 1968).

But, by and large, job enrichment programmes of this nature

clearly suggest a zero-sum game in so far as decision-making powers at shop-floor level are concerned. Thus, the greater the power which accrues to working people in this respect, the less is available for middle management and first-line supervisors even though the power of top management may remain largely unaffected. Thus, among their colleagues, middle management and supervisors have been found to be most hostile to these changes and, in view of the conclusions of Daniel and McIntosh (1972: 49), this is hardly surprising:

> The one essential characteristic of any really effective change in the direction of job enrichment is the delegation of greater responsibility to individual workers and workgroups, so that some shop-floor decision-making passes from supervisors to the workgroup. But this immediately changes the position of the supervisor and there will be uncertainty for all at this level. This does not necessarily mean that fewer first-line managers or foremen will be needed or that their span of control will be increased but rather that the numbers at intermediary levels, such as assistant foremen, will be reduced or even eliminated. The jobs of those remaining will be very substantially changed. Indeed they may well feel that their last remaining vestige of status and responsibility has been stripped from them.

Indeed, the problems faced by supervisory and junior managerial personnel have been amply documented in the studies of job enrichment and work restructuring in Scandinavia as well as the USA and Britain. In Norway, for example, drawing upon the researches of the Tavistock Institute and developing the concept of 'autonomous groups' of workers relatively free of supervisory restrictions, Thorsrud, in particular, has translated some of these ideas into practice in a number of indigenous factories (see Thorsrud, 1980; Warner, 1984b). Moreover, these have gone beyond the 'job enrichment' programmes in the USA by linking them not only to the socio-psychological theories of Herzberg and his colleagues (1959) but also to democratic-egalitarian philosophies in which both workgroup and higher administrative levels are viewed as requiring a more open, participative decision-making structure.

In Sweden, too, enthusiasm for autonomous working groups has been noticeable. At Saab-Scania, for example, assembly lines have been effectively abolished by the division of the plant into separate construction areas where workers vary the pace and share out the work amongst themselves. These changes were undoubtedly stimulated by the unwillingness of employees to accept monotonous jobs as expectations had risen accompanying a period of unbroken affluence. Again, at Volvo, absenteeism of 14 per cent and labour turnover of 30–40 per cent had been commonplace and, in response, management removed the fixed-speed line and divided work amongst autonomous teams. But although the successful introduction of job restructuring depends upon the involvement of supervisors, ultimately, according to Jenkins (1974: chapter 13), it can lead to a substantial reduction in the numbers of supervisors, managers and specialists.

Meanwhile, in the United States and in policy circles in the EEC, the 1970s witnessed considerable interest in changing the quality of working life (see Davis and Cherns (eds), 1975a; 1975b). And, indeed, as Walton (1975) has observed, a typical strategy of this type encompassed the notions of adequate and fair compensation for work, safe and healthy working conditions, immediate opportunity to use and develop human capacities, opportunities for continued growth and security, social integration in the work organization, constitutionalism in the work organization, work and total life space (i.e. a balanced role of work and leisure) and the social relevance of work to life. Again, Peel (1979: 120), from the vantage point of once being Director of Industrial Relations for the Commission of the European Communities, identified the following guidelines in a comprehensive quality of work-life programme: clean and safe working conditions; continuity of employment; the right to organize into trade unions; fair and equitable pay relationships; the provision of employee benefits; personnel systems in which individual workers are considered to be human assets; participation in management; a workplace climate which encourages 'openness, a sense of community, and personal equality'; the right to free speech, privacy and dissent; and a balance between work and lifestyle.

But there is no doubt that, as the 1980s progressed, imaginative schemes of this type were to be a casualty of massive unemployment and the reduction of pressure on management by organized labour and governments in this area (see Willman and Winch, 1985). To be sure, in a number of new technology industries and in independent primary jobs generally where skills and abilities remained scarce, interest in these programmes of reform was to continue. For the most part, however, the shifting balance of power towards managements, and the increasing attention paid to production and marketing rather than to human resourcing issues, appreciably reduced the commitment to enrich and enhance the quality of the working lives of ordinary men and women.

Yet it is important to emphasize that the effects of the economic recession were uneven and, in relation to the new technologies, were accompanied by a pronounced *segmentation of labour*. That is to say, whereas on the one hand there was considerable evidence of de-skilling and an increase in secondary labour and secondary labour markets (involving jobs which are typically poorly paid, with few prospects and little job security); on the other hand, some activities were being created in the so-called *independent primary sector* (jobs with high pay, considerable worker autonomy and good prospects) in which an emphasis on quality of work-life remained a signal feature (see Loveridge and Mok, 1979; Gordon, Edwards and Reich, 1983; Rubery, Tarling and Wilkinson, 1984).

Indeed, the effects of the new technologies on employee participation are undoubtedly complex (for the consequences for trade unions, see Chapter 5). In firms in which new technologies are being introduced, there is often the tendency for managements (as in BL Cars) to choose automation rather than work redesign (see Willman and Winch, 1985: 55). But, above all, the consequences are typically to create a greater polarization between *independent* and *subordinate primary activities* (the first involving an appreciable enhancement of worker autonomy and control and the latter a considerable de-skilling). In this sense, then, the effects of the new technologies on participation are *indeterminate* and, as Warner (1982b; 1984c) has proposed, may 'permit a range of organizational and manpower solutions'. Hence, while in some cases control can be centralized and worker involvement decreased, in others there will be 'greater chances for decentralisation of decision-making and/or greater involvement of employees in this process' (Warner, 1984c: 162). And certainly the research by Sorge *et al.* (1983), in which the effects of Computer Numerically Controlled (CNC) machine-tools on organizational and related manpower variables was assessed, strongly supported the view that 'the new technology may *de facto* decentralise both decision-making and skill-making, even if it does lead to a reduced work-force' (Warner, 1984c: 163).

Moreover, in the new technology industries themselves, there is considerable evidence that managements have developed sophisticated 'human resourcing' strategies to recruit and retain the highly skilled and educated personnel to fill the many independent primary activities which have been created. Certainly, in Silicon Valley companies, personnel specialists have sought to bring together a wide range of employee participation practices (including both quality of work-life and profit-sharing), while remaining resolutely opposed to trade unions and endorsing a range of Japanese-style integration policies (see Poole, 1984). In short, in the segments of the labour market where demand for employees remained buoyant, even in the 1980s, there was considerable pressure on a number of managements to continue to develop imaginative quality of work-life programmes.

## Suggestions schemes, employee shareholding and other profit-sharing schemes, co-partnership and 'commonwealth' ventures

Turning now to our final category of direct participation initiated by management, this again involves a progression from rather limited accretions in workers' decision-making powers to programmes of a much more ambitious character. Taking *suggestions schemes* first of all, then, these only allow for a measure of participation by individual workers in facilitating rather specific technical changes at shop-floor level or in altering work practices which carry the risk of accidents or sickness. They are, however, a fairly familiar landmark in the British industrial relations landscape; indeed, in their study of workers' participation in management in Great Britain, Clarke, Fatchett and Roberts (1972: 164) discovered that 40 per cent of the companies they contacted had suggestions schemes and that, in large firms, they were especially common. In certain rare cases in which technical changes instituted as a result of suggestions schemes have induced substantial savings for particular managements, not inconsiderable financial rewards have been given to the individual workers concerned. None the less, it is far more common for awards to be quite small and, indeed, to be only nominal where suggestions relate to improvements in safety and health. Moreover, the decision to make an award or otherwise is usually taken by the departmental manager acting on the advice of a number of technical specialists, and although this decision may be subject to further negotiation with a worker's shop steward or joint consultative committee representative, ultimate authority over issues such as these resides clearly in managerial hands.

Suggestions schemes have a bearing, too, on relations at work-group level, on trade union negotiations and on the decision-making power and authority of foremen and other lower managerial personnel. The complaint is often heard, for example, that suggestions schemes are potentially damaging to morale within the workgroup. Indeed, at worst, suggestions schemes can encourage competitiion between members of particular workgroups and lead to substantial differentials in financial rewards. Nevertheless, these consequences may be overdramatized: indeed, in a case study by Gorfin (1969) of the operation of a suggestions scheme not only did workers generally approve of the scheme itself – particularly because they viewed it as a recognition that the man or woman working on a given piece of machinery not infrequently knew rather more about the job than the supervisor – but also, they made charitable remarks about their colleagues who had actually received awards. Indeed, dissatisfaction about the operation of the scheme was more evident among those who had actually made suggestions than among those who had never participated in the scheme at all (Gorfin, 1969: 378).

Again, because the effects of suggestions schemes are seldom dramatic, it is easy to overstate trade union objections to them. However, they clearly imply some by-passing of union channels since they create a system of *individual* rather than *collective* rewards and also because, unless the amount of money involved is itself a source of conflict, union officials and shop stewards are rarely implicated. Thus, although the majority of active unionists may still be broadly favourable to schemes of this kind, there is almost certainly some loss of union authority – albeit unremarkable – on questions of remuneration.

But perhaps the most interesting consequences of suggestions schemes are for the power and authority of lower managerial personnel. As Gorfin (1969) has pointed out, the successful participation of those below the supervisor can mean that the perceived difference between his skills and those of shop-floor workers becomes progressively narrower, and indeed, in those cases where rewards are really substantial, the position of the supervisor may suffer a marked deterioration. Moreover, this is clearly exacerbated whenever supervisors are expected to be technically more proficient than workers on the shop floor and especially when their authority is based largely on such criteria. There is a close parallel here with certain of the effects of job-enrichment programmes in so far as the power and authority of those in supervisory ranks are concerned, though because suggestions schemes are less extensive their consequences are accordingly less pervasive.

Moving at this point to yet another attempt by management to offer financial inducements for greater productivity and output while at the same time involving workers more closely in the affairs of the firm, it is again rather doubtful whether the majority of *employee shareholding* and *profit-sharing schemes* have in fact quite the decisive impact for working people assumed by their most ardent supporters. Indeed, certain practices of this kind differ little from traditional bonus incentives. They do, however, contrast with suggestions schemes in at least four main ways: the rewards are collective in nature; the whole workforce rather than a considerably smaller proportion of employees are involved; dividends are paid regularly, usually on an annual basis; and, not infrequently, individual employee shareholders have actual voting rights and can on the face of it, therefore, influence managerial policy.

Employee shareholding is in fact far more common than is generally appreciated, though until the results of a Department of Employment investigation are published, we await adequate information on the recent British experience. In a survey carried out in 1954, the Ministry of Labour found that about 500 companies practised some form of profit-sharing. Moreover, in an early study by Copeman (1958), a rich variety of forms of employee shareholding was discovered and Copeman consequently thought it fitting to identify at least nine types of scheme. But the most usual were the straightforward use of profit-sharing; the employee investing some savings in the company in return for an extra-high yield on this investment; the creation of an employee share trust which denied the employee full shareholding rights; and access to ordinary stock which the employee could purchase at a price below market value.

Yet there are clear indications of an appreciable expansion of employee shareholding in the late 1970s and early 1980s. In Britain, the main stimulus has been the Finance Acts of 1978 and 1980, which introduced special tax advantages for new profit-sharing schemes that satisfied a number of conditions. And certainly Daniel and Millward (1983: 210–11) found that half the schemes covered in their survey had been introduced in the three years prior to their investigation and noted that these were most common when: (1) firms were doing well financially, (2) product demand was rising, (3) the size of the workforce was increasing, and (4) managements 'gave a favourable rating to the financial performance of the establishment'.

This departure is also symptomatic of a trend in other leading Western countries where, in addition to legislative initiatives on employee financial participation, there have been wide-ranging public discussions (as well as a variety of facilitative measures) in this area. Indeed, in the United States, profit-sharing arrangements have been instituted in more than 300,000 firms, covering about 9 million employees. In France, such practices are mandatory for all companies with more than 100 employees. In the Federal Republic of Germany, profit-sharing for individual companies has been known for many decades, with the 'Gleitze Plan' introducing the idea of comprehensive wage-earner funds (with several characteristics in common with current Swedish practice). Furthermore, the Commission for the European Communities has indicated its support for employee participation in productive capital formation (for details see Meidner, 1981; Remus, 1983).

However, the expansion of profit-sharing and share-ownership schemes in recent years requires some explanation, since the earliest practices were introduced on a cyclical basis in periods of buoyant economic conditions and high levels of industrial conflict (see Ramsay, 1977). The first wave of profit-sharing was thus between 1865 and 1873, with further revivals in 1889–92, 1908–9, and 1912–14 (Ramsay, 1977: 84). And, as Church (1971: 10) has pointed out:

> If one examines the . . . history of profit sharing down to World War I, it is possible to identify a direct relationship between the introduction of profit sharing . . . with a high level of employment and labour unrest.

To explain the growth in employee shareholding and profit-sharing in the late 1970s and early 1980s thus requires a rather different explanation linked with: (1) the role of governments in passing facilitative legislation; and (2) the backcloth of favourable values linked with notions of a property-owning democracy and a 'unitary' framework of industrial relations in which employee financial participation rather than, say, power-sharing at board level via trade union channels has been emphasized. Moreover, to some extent consistent with previous experience, management in commercial firms experiencing conditions of appreciable growth have proved to be the most willing to develop schemes of this type, whereas their colleagues in manufacturing industry witnessing sharp falls in product demand and in employment have been far less prone to use the opportunities in existing legislation to advance employee shareholding.

But *co-partnership* represents an advance on employee shareholding, being a more genuine attempt by management to divest some of its decision-making prerogatives. Moreover, the genesis of such programmes is a very different managerial ideology from those we have examined so far in this chapter. Thus, while in the main we have identified efficiency-conscious employers who have relinquished certain of their decision-making rights (and especially those of their colleagues at supervisory level) in exchange for greater co-operation from workers during periods of technical change, for higher output and productivity, and for improved labour-management relations, co-partnership programmes have only arisen when key directors have been guided by broader ideologies – sometimes of a religious kind – to sacrifice rather more of their personal authority.

By way of illustration it is useful here to concentrate on one firm, the John Lewis Partnership, in which the efforts of one such man, the son of the founder of the firm, were fundamental in shaping the nature of the resulting experiment (Flanders, Pomeranz and Woodward, 1968). The main aim of this organization is to bestow the benefits of ownership on all employees and to ensure the sharing of knowledge, gain and power. Great emphasis has been placed on an extensive internal press which conveys items of information to the membership. The sharing of gain is facilitated largely by profit-sharing, the most important form being the partnership bonus which is wholly additional to normal pay. And finally the sharing of power is made possible by means of a rather complicated system of representation. Thus, while the direct participation of all employees takes place in terms of the sharing of profits, representative institutions have also been developed. The main elected body is the central council which consists of about 140 members, and although the chairman can appoint up to one-third of the council, in general the proportion is usually rather less than this, partly because a great many managers are, in any event, elected on to the council. There are, in addition, several standing committees of the central council, including general purposes, ways and means, central claims, pay and allowances and unassured pensions. Moreover, these central arrangements are supported by a system of branch councils which are far less managerial in composition.

Such a fundamental change in formal organizational structure could not have been expected without the guidance of a coherent and influential ideology. Indeed, in the Partnership, this has been developed in a number of important publications (Lewis, 1948;

1954) and is based on the premise of common ownership. Moreover, the ideology itself is so pervasive and its impact on managerial values so significant that the commitment of key managerial personnel can be observed to be commonly of a moral rather than of a calculative kind.

But while the Partnership itself is an outstanding commercial success, and the majority of its employees consider their working conditions to be significantly better than is usual in industry as a whole, there are some doubts as to whether rank-and-file workers have been very much affected by this ideology, and above all, so far as our general theme is concerned, whether they have genuine participation *in practice* in the decision-making processes of the Partnership. To be sure, the opportunities may be there, but whether these are taken up or not by individual workers depends on other important considerations and, indeed, as Flanders, Pomeranz and Woodward (1968: 129) have pointed out:

> Our attitude survey suggested that, for most rank and file workers, the general ethos of employment relations within the Partnership is not essentially different from that which prevails in employing organizations of a more usual kind. The facts of common ownership and accountability, and the ideology associated with them, are not powerful enough to break through the barrier of custom and beliefs which surround employment relationships in our society at large.

Again, as these authors have argued, the emphasis of the ideology is very much on 'government of the people' rather than 'government by the people', and the result is, of course, that there is a danger of paternalism here. Again, although many employees would prefer to work under conditions of benevolent paternalism than of arbitrary managerial authoritarianism, this can work against the development of 'pressure-group' democracy from below. So that, while Flanders and his colleagues judged it to be unreasonable to accuse the Partnership of any actual hostility to unionism, developments of this kind can have the effect of acting as a disincentive to employees setting up independent organizations.

Moreover, in so far as managerial ideologies are concerned, the requirement that management must be accountable to the Partnership as a whole, in one view, may be a source of managerial strength. For if a manager can survive a more open environment, in which his or her authority is never buttressed by arbitrary decision-making powers over employees, personal confidence in his or her own abilities may become correspondingly greater. Flanders and his co-investigators (1968), writing of an emphasis on the high quality of managers, noted, too, the development of 'superiority complexes' among a number of senior personnel, although to be sure, these feelings may themselves have served as mechanisms for the partial resolution of the conflict inherent in a manager who exercises power in an organization committed to power-sharing.

Nevertheless, the difference between the moral commitment of management to the principles of the partnership and the more calculative orientation of the majority of employees does suggest certain implicit limitations in any participation programme, however well-intentioned and far-reaching it may be, that is based on value considerations alone. To be sure, it is clear that powerful ideologies among key members of organizations can lead to major changes in values towards participation and consequently to fundamental alterations in the formal structure of decision-making within the firm. But unless this is backed by the second element in our equation, namely the latent power of employees, its effects are likely to be rather more paternalistic than participative in character.

In principle at least, *commonwealth* schemes go somewhat further than co-partnership systems by ensuring both common ownership and the more direct participation of the workforce in decision-making processes of a policy kind. But the differences between such programmes may be exaggerated and, certainly, both clearly depend on the adherence to strongly held convictions by their instigators. From the time when Robert Owen first set up his New Lanark community in 1816, there have been many isolated attempts to establish in industry principles of ownership and control which depart from the predominantly capitalist type. Nevertheless, being obliged to operate within an alien economic environment, many of these experiments have been short-lived. For, after all, unless the members of any given commonwealth operate within the terms of a market economy and, by so doing, of course, severely modify the principles on which their new work relationships are founded, it is very difficult to survive competitive pressures, however well-intentioned the experiment and enthusiastic its participants (Blum, 1968).

A great many commonwealth experiments owe their origins to fervent religious beliefs although it is true that the predominant religious creeds of North America and Western Europe have been of little assistance to the cause of democratic work relationships. Protestantism, above all, has had a profound impact on industrialization and industrial development, but its special emphasis on individual achievement and self-help has worked very much against the development of collective and co-operative industrial relations. Moreover, since the established Church has normally been content 'to render unto Caesar' and by so doing, by default, to accept and not infrequently to support the existing structure of ownership and control within industry, the general relationship (if one exists at all) between religious doctrine and secular behaviour has scarcely been favourable to workers' participation. But if this is the general pattern, there have also been many Christian social reformers who have called for changes 'in industrial ownership which will give workers the right to share in some measure in the fruit of their labour and to exercise some measure of control over the enterprises for which they work', and the contribution of a number of Quaker employers has been especially noteworthy in this respect. In other words, on certain occasions, religious ethics have been sufficiently strong to affect substantially the general climate of opinion at workplace level and to stimulate key managers to introduce major structural reforms in the nature of ownership and control.

The Scott-Bader commonwealth is a particularly cogent example, for, according to Blum (1968), it owed its existence to the 'deeply religious inspiration' of Ernest Bader, a convinced Quaker and pacifist, whose beliefs led to the formation of specific attitudes about the nature of work relationships. By the same token the objections he raised to many of the fundamentals of the capitalist organization of work were, as related by Blum (1968: 20), as far-reaching as those of any socialist:

The reduction of all products, people and of nature itself to marketable objects; capital accounting rather than merely monetary accounting became dominant and the principles of sound finance ruled over all human considerations; the transformation of all flesh, mind, heart and soul into prices and costs; the subordination of one group under another group thus making people means for the purposes of other people; the neglect of the ethics of interpersonal relationships and hence the separation of people from each other and from any humanly meaningful purpose – rule of impersonal market forces over all and of personal authority over most people; finally a division of labour without balance and consideration of human values.

Poverty amidst plenty, communal impoverishment and public squalor amidst private affluence resulted from such a situation. Being was transformed into saleable commodities and true Becoming was stunted.

Against such a backcloth and to avoid the problem of 'participation in the administration of evil', Bader sought to establish a different order in which ownership and control were viewed as equally important. The commonwealth envisaged in 1951 incorporated common ownership, the development of new channels of participation, the divestment of the right to dispose of profit, the gradual transference of power to members of the commonwealth and a division of power into legislative, executive and judicial organs. The main legislative body was the *general meeting* and all members of the commonwealth could participate in administrative and judicial areas as well. Nevertheless, notwithstanding the provisions in the constitution for direct participation by employees, the founder members retained 10 per cent of shares and ultimate veto rights. Again, although there were many further opportunities to participate – especially in departmental meetings – it was clear that 'people with managerial responsibility or people from the laboratory participated more actively than factory and maintenance people' (Blum, 1968: 20). And this was particularly important in view of the fact that the greater security enjoyed by members of the commonwealth, by comparison with their colleagues in industry at large, militated against unionization. Moreover, in the interviews with rank-and-file employees, it was clear that the main advantages of the commonwealth were seen in terms of job security and only secondarily in the opportunities it provided for workers' participation in decision-making.

In 1963, however, Bader, who had initially opposed the idea of the commonwealth members having the right to appoint directors, was prepared to divest his authority further so that ultimate power would rest with members of the commonwealth and a wider body of trustees. This does suggest that, given a sufficiently strongly held conviction in the idea, it is not impossible to promote a major transformation in the formal organization of work. But the outstanding obstacle to ventures of this kind is always their existence as 'islands in the sea of capitalism', for the danger lies in the neglect of technical-market criteria which can in turn herald a premature decline and closure of an otherwise valuable scheme. Moreover, to the extent that such a demise is not forthcoming, as in the successful Scott-Bader commonwealth, this implies some commensurate abrogation of principle. Blum (1968: 172), indeed, recognizes this: 'The central value of the organization – a concept of productivity defined in technical-market terms – continues to exist but the implementation of the new purposes will at least make a dent in this concept.' And this is a conspicuous departure from the early intention to effect a transformation in capitalist values and modes of organization in industry.

Furthermore, in so far as the ordinary members of the commonwealth are concerned, their ability to participate effectively may have been restricted by an absence of their own independent organizations. The tendency for members of the higher grades of commonwealth staff to participate particularly efficaciously in decision-making processes, and for the majority of 'employees' to view the benefits of the commonwealth in terms of job security, would seem to provide some indications of this. In addition, as was the case with the John Lewis Partnership, the great enthusiasm for the project among senior management did contrast somewhat with the perceptions of the commonwealth among the rank and file.

Nevertheless, although this would seem to confirm that it is only when there is some consonance between latent power and values that truly effective participation can take place, supporters of the commonwealth could claim that certain dynamic aspects of participation are facilitated by schemes of this kind and that these substantially outweigh any losses for working people of their own independent organizational power. In particular, it may be reasonably argued that a management which freely conceded participatory rights, without an embittered power struggle, will in no way wish to frustrate the democratic process in practice; on the contrary, it will do everything to sustain and foster it. Then again, it may be pointed out that 'political efficacy' is enhanced through active involvement and that therefore it is better to set up participatory programmes of this kind and to reap the benefits of the 'dynamic effects of participation' rather than to await a time when workers are both strong enough and sufficiently concerned to seek active involvement themselves. In support of such claims, it is worth mentioning that Blum (1968: Chapter 16) did indeed argue that certain *holistic* aspects of participation could be increasingly recognized in the commonwealth. Thus, participation in the actual processes of decision-making was seen as one essential aspect of participation, but also important were relations with fellow workers, the wider work environment, the organization of work, the purposes for which this is organized, and the means used to achieve the goals of the organization (Blum, 1968: 203). In short, participation in a commonwealth venture may encourage a much broader subjective consciousness on the part of the employee and a fuller understanding of his or her own work role in relation to the wider purposes of the organization as a whole.

If this case were to be conceded *in toto*, it would of course provide the first serious challenge to our explanatory model of the genesis of effective participatory and control practices, since it would infer that 'idealistic' factors alone can account for the emergence of particular programmes, albeit rather untypical ones. Nevertheless, although cumulative effects can be expected from any developed participation programme (and this is accounted for in our model) there is still in our view sufficient evidence that participation is greatly affected by formal status within the occupational and administrative hierarchy to maintain our original confidence in the utility of our own theoretical analysis.

### Indirect or representative participation

But at times, managements have turned to less direct forms of workers' participation which are equally applicable to our investigation into the exercise of power in industry at large. Moreover, since somewhat higher decision-making levels are entailed here than in direct participation, most managements can be seen to have sought even greater restrictions on the scope and range of issues discussed. Thus, they have generally been keen to ensure that ultimate powers of decision remain in managerial hands and have not infrequently demanded an embargo on a number of sensitive issues, notably on commercial, business and wages questions.

### Joint consultative committees

Taking first of all, then, joint consultative committees, the great advantage of all forms of consultation from the managerial viewpoint is that they are defined in such a way as to involve no major reduction of management's decision-making powers. In principle, they are limited to the inclusion of workers in discussions over issues which affect them, prior to a decision being made by management alone. Employees therefore *influence* but in no way *determine* managerial policy and practice. Of course, none of this should be taken to suggest that the line between consultation and decision-making can be so easily drawn, or that workers share these managerial definitions and assumptions, or again, that, if they are strong enough, workers cannot effectively ensure that decisions are taken only along certain lines. But it is to argue that, whereas for the majority of managers radical forms of participation have been generally rejected because they demand some sharing of decision-making powers, joint consultation is more favourably viewed, at least in principle, because it in no way disturbs a unitary conception of the authority structure of the enterprise or severely curtails management's right to decide.

This has typically applied, then, to the case of joint consultative committees which have been a characteristic feature of formal management-worker discussions in a great many British companies. Indeed, in several instances management has drawn a clear distinction between consultation and decision-making, the former involving frank and open discussions within advisory committees and the latter being the prerogative of management alone. Of course, these points of demarcation may be blurred in practice, and in any event are not adhered to by workers' representatives on such committees, but their existence seems to demonstrate that, on balance, the values of management are in general antithetical to fully fledged participation especially at higher levels.

The history of joint consultation in Great Britain is by now well documented and it would be superfluous to attempt any lengthy review here. The following points are worth making, however. First, most formal consultative schemes are instigated by management: indeed, an investigation by the National Institute of Industrial Psychology (1952) revealed that nearly three-quarters of the joint consultative schemes had been set up by management alone. Second, there is nevertheless a great variety of types of committee ranging from the purely advisory with agendas deliberately designed to avoid discussions of wages and related issues, to those in which shop stewards' organizations form the nucleus of workers' representatives and in which almost any matter may be brought up and concluded. Moreover, the nomenclature of such committees also varies, although works councils or joint consultative committees are commonly used. Third, joint consultative committees have been particularly prominent during periods when the organizational power of workers has been well developed and the climate of opinion favourable to co-operation rather than conflict. Thus, although a number of firms can trace their joint consultative machinery back to the nineteenth century, the most notable advances have followed the Whitley Committee recommendations in 1917 when the First World War was being fought; similarly, the growth of production, consultative and advisory committees was stimulated by the Second World War. It is worth mentioning, too, that unionism also flourished during these periods of international conflict, partly as a function of full employment but also because of the need for governments to court the union movement in a period of crisis. Joint consultation, however, suffered a major decline in the 'inter-war' period and, although post-Second World War conditions were favourable to the development of latent power among working people, and in particular to the extension of their rights to participation, the most important channel to emerge was the shop-steward system, since this was more suited to deal with conflicting interests at workplace level.

There was, however, an appreciable further increase in joint consultation in the 1970s. Thus, there have been at least fifteen surveys in the UK on the current extent and practice of joint consultation (for details see MacInnes, 1985), the evidence of three recent cases being most instructive. In 1978, the Warwick Industrial Relations Research Unit covered 970 establishments in manufacturing industry and found not only that over 40 per cent had joint consultative committees but also that more than 60 per cent of these had been introduced within the last five years (Brown (ed.), 1981: 76–7). The 1980 DE/PSI/SSRC survey investigated over 2,000 establishments and revealed a steady pattern of growth (within the three years prior to the survey, consultative committees had been introduced in 9 per cent of establishments and abandoned in only 1 per cent of cases) (Daniel and Millward, 1983: 132). And in the most recent study (based on 133 manufacturing plants and covering the situation up until 1983), Batstone (1984: 263–70) discovered a series of attempts by management to increase employee involvement, even though most non-union-based consultative committees had been introduced in the 1970s rather than the 1980s.

It is nevertheless relatively easy to account for the principal trends in joint consultation in Great Britain during the present century in terms of changes in both the organizational power of working people and in prevailing values pertaining to social relations at work. But at the micro-level, it is also clear that the nature of joint consultative machinery is a particularly sensitive barometer of the organizational strength of workers and to the values which inform management-worker relations.

This proposition, indeed, was cogently supported in the early research studies associated with the Glacier Metal Company, in which, of course, a series of experiments were undertaken concerning the structure and function of works councils. Thus, in the *Glacier Project Papers*, Brown and Jacques (1965) noted that:

> One phase of our inquiries in our Company led us to the making of an analysis of the sources of power and authority in the industrial situation. We then realized that every industrial company necessarily had, somehow, to produce a series of internal laws to govern its own operations and that, inevitably, these internal company laws received the sanction of the groups that wielded power in each company's separate situation.

More specifically, they diagnosed three social systems (shareholders, customers and employees) which interact with the executive system of the company, and argued that the influence of each waxes and wanes with a change in the environment – for example, a rise of unemployment will weaken the representative system. Similarly, they noted the conflict which often exists between employees (represented by shop stewards) and the management.

Moreover, from an empirical point of view, the association between the demise of the consultative committee and the organizational power of working people has been the subject of a number of studies. Derber (1955), for instance, postulated that three factors affected the status of joint production consultative and advisory committees: union strength, the attitudes of management to personnel work and 'the extent of mutual confidence and goodwill'. Thus, the machinery was used least when unions were weak and when management paid little attention to personnel work. On the other hand, negotiating machinery was prominent when unions were strong, management production-minded and the relationship between senior stewards and top management antagonistic. Finally, advisory machinery was in operation when management was personnel-minded (Derber, 1955: 79–80). Moreover, in the specific instance of the engineering industry, as Marsh (1965) has pointed out, the decline of joint production consultative and advisory committees is directly related to the rise in number and importance of shop stewards. Again, in their study of workers' participation, Clarke, Fatchett and Roberts (1972) found that the greater the degree of unionization, the greater the extent of joint decision-making. Managements in strongly unionized firms were ready to enter into consultation and negotiation with their employees, while in companies with low levels of unionization they tended to look to formal consultation as an alternative to negotiation.

None the less, the relationship between power, values and joint consultation is probably more complex than at first sight appears obvious from the findings of these earlier studies. Thus, to begin with, the climate of values is shaped by members on both sides of industry and, therefore, although a personnel-minded management might be expected to encourage joint consultation, the preferences of workers for particular institutional arrangements are important considerations as well. Again, the fairly subtle relationship between social structural variables (and especially the latent power of workers) and aspects of social consciousness have seldom been satisfactorily developed in this context.

Hence, in a study by the author (Poole, 1969), it was discovered, first, that the organizational strength of workers (and particularly the existence of joint shop stewards' committees) largely determines the *limits* of effective participation by employees at workplace level. But second, it was found that this aspect of latent power is not sufficient to ensure the transformation of joint consultative to negotiational bodies, for the degree of militancy among shop stewards is also of great significance. The status of joint consultative committees would seem, therefore, to depend on a rather subtle relationship between latent power and values in which neither, by itself, is sufficient to ensure a transformation of formal consultative structures. Once again, then, it is the interplay between social structure and social consciousness, between objective and subjective factors, and between latent power and values, which is so crucial to understanding and explaining particular 'participation' practices.

And certainly such propositions are endorsed by recent analyses of the latest phase of growth in the number of joint consultative committees (see, e.g., Ramsay, 1980; MacInnes, 1985). The renaissance of joint consultation can thus be interpreted as an attempt by management to legitimate its authority by emphasizing the common interests of members of the organization. Moreover, 'this represents the way in which managers construct definite social relations of authority with their workforces' or engage, in other words, in the 'negotiation of legitimacy' (MacInnes, 1985: 105). Furthermore, managements are particularly likely to embark upon such a process when: (1) trade unions remain influential at shop-floor level, and (2) economic and other circumstances have ensured that they have to become involved in a series of industrial relations initiatives. rather than being confined to 'reactive' measures to confront the challenge from below.

The above arguments, which are based on data from national surveys, are reinforced by case-study material and particularly that relating to BL cars (Willman and Winch, 1985). After all, following on from the recommendations of the Ryder Report an extensive participation programme had been introduced. But, in the tougher climate from 1978 onwards, much of this machinery fell into disuse. And with the possible exception of the sub-committees in the Metro project, where there was a broadly co-operative and consultative atmosphere, in general, as Willman and Winch (1985: 108) have observed:

> participation acted as a sounding board for managers' ideas. It allowed BL to impress upon union representatives the difficulties and complexities of change and to rehearse ideas which subsequently arose in negotiation. The unions, however, did not find it an effective means to modify management suggestions or proposals.

Hence, while in many unionized plants in the climate of recession, managements developed or re-vivified joint consultative machinery, the actual influence of workers' representatives on these bodies often remained circumscribed.

### Specific committees covering productivity, welfare and safety, the administration of various trusts, funds, and occupational pension schemes

One of the consequences of the development of human relations techniques in modern industry is that in some respects the relationship between management and worker has become more complex. Certainly the range of issues dealt with in many work contexts has grown substantially during the past quarter of a century and will continue to do so for as long as companies take over functions which might otherwise be performed by public bodies and institutions. But this means, of course, that the opportunities for workers' participation in these new areas have been extended as well, and, even if these have only a marginal impact on company policy as a whole, they are not necessarily without interest to the workforce itself.

Individual committees may pre-date the establishment of

personnel functions within the firm. Thus, production and safety committees, which are usually made up of management and workers' representatives, have been a familiar if peripheral part of workplace industrial relations for a great many years. But a host of diverse arrangements only began to emerge as management began to take human relations policies rather more seriously; committees evolved to attend, among other things, to welfare, canteen and transport facilities, accident prevention and the administration of various trusts and funds.

Moreover, there is no doubt that the wider stimulus of the legislature and the underlying power of the workforce in the 1970s have been important in encouraging worker representation on health and safety committees. The Health and Safety at Work Act, 1974 thus contains provisions (brought into force in 1978) which allow for trade unions to appoint safety representatives. And, indeed, in the DE/PSI/SSRC survey, it was found that roughly half of establishments had joint committees dealing with health and safety either specifically or as a part of a wider remit. Again, the connections with the latent power of the workforce were also revealed for such committees were particularly likely where there were recognized trade unions (they were present in 60 per cent of unionized establishments) (Daniel and Millward, 1983: 142).

The role of wider legislation (or the prospects of legislation) and the power of workers are also evident in the experience of participation in occupational pension schemes. Currently nearly 12 million people in the UK belong to some form or other of occupational pension scheme (roughly half the population in regular employment) (Schuller and Hyman, 1983). Usually these funds are managed under a trust and there has been an appreciable increase in recent years in the number of employee trustees. Indeed, there is now extensive participation at board level in the management of pensions and, in a survey by Schuller and Hyman (1983; Hyman and Schuller, 1984), the most common pattern was found to be parity representation. There is no doubt, too, that an important stimulus for the establishment of schemes of this type was the 1976 White Paper on Occupational Pension Schemes, in which parity representation was given official sanction. Furthermore, it is also clear that, in the practical workings of these bodies, the existence of trade union personnel tends to ensure a considerable degree of 'pension negotiation' and contested policies and objectives in the actual meetings themselves (see especially Hyman and Schuller, 1984).

To elaborate on the connection between the power of employees and the genesis of committees of this type is thus unnecessary. After all, we have already seen that human relations policies generally and personnel work more specifically have tended to develop alongside increases in workers' power, and/or the pressure of the legislature. Nevertheless, productivity bargaining and job evaluation are also interesting cases in point and merit more detailed attention.

## Productivity bargaining and job evaluation

In some respects it is paradoxical to include productivity bargaining among managerial efforts to further workers' participation. After all, this form of bargaining offers management the possibility of reclaiming authority over areas which came under the control of particular groups of workers when their latent power markedly increased following certain economic developments in the 1950s and early 1960s. But from the workers' standpoint, certain advantages have accrued from this form of negotiation with management: the scope of some forms of representative participation, for example, has been extended, as has the stature of shop stewards in the plant. And yet productivity bargaining was detrimental to workers' control over a number of shop-floor issues; its net effect being a diminution in workers' participation and control of industry.

Interest in productivity bargaining became very marked in the late 1960s following the important lead given by management at the Esso refinery at Fawley, Southampton. Indeed, between 1967 and 1969 a total of over 4,000 agreements covering over 8 million workers were approved by the Department of Employment and Productivity (Collins, 1970: 86). Essentially, the main aim of such bargains is to ensure large increases in earnings in exchange for a more efficient utilization of labour. To this latter end, major relaxations of job demarcations, the withdrawal of craftsmen's mates, additional forms of shift working, and generally greater freedom for management in the use of its supervisory powers have all been characteristic components of any given productivity 'deal' (Flanders, 1964).

But while necessarily resulting in greater managerial control over the behaviour of workers and workgroups at shop-floor level, these bargains indirectly enhance the power of shop stewards too. Thus, taking the example of the Fawley productivity agreements, major changes in work practices had certain unforeseen consequences from a managerial viewpoint and especially the greater formality and lesser flexibility of the rules governing management-worker relations which prevailed after the agreements, and the growth in shop stewards' influence on union negotiations. In the first place, then, there was a marked disposition on the part of stewards to insist on the *letter* of particular agreements (Flanders, 1964: 199):

The unions were saying in effect 'a bargain is a bargain'. They adopted a measured attitude towards their obligations under the agreements and refused to give anything away they had not signed for. At the same time they were not averse to exploiting any loopholes in the working of agreements, and began to query customary practices accepted without demur before.

The greater formality of workplace labour relations which was consequent upon the introduction of this particular productivity bargain was in fact both a cause and a consequence of shop stewards' power. The existence of such agreements helped to foster the power of shop stewards since workpeople continually sought their advice on the implementation of particular rulings, but equally the stewards themselves were able to insist on such formality given their own bargaining strength. But the power of shop stewards was also heightened by virtue of their influence on union negotiations. Thus, prior to the agreements there was a clear-cut division between the provinces of shop stewards and full-time officials in their negotiations with the Fawley management. And, although the former controlled the distribution of overtime, for example, and in annual wage negotiations their views may have been taken into account, full-time officers undoubtedly controlled the situation from the union side. However, since the agreements had the effect of linking pay with working practices, the effect was, of course, that the stewards began to have far more control over negotiations than had previously been the case. Moreover, because of the differential influence of this particular productivity bargain on individual workgroups, there was clearly a major realignment of forces at shop-floor level and, in the nature of things, workers affected adversely by comparison with their colleagues would seek the help of their stewards in an effort to rectify the situation (Flanders, 1964: 202–3). And this, too, of course, served to promote the standing of shop stewards in relation to the processes of decision-making within the plant.

In many respects, however, it is the factors underlying management's ready countenance of these agreements in the last years of the 1960s, rather than the resulting modifications of workplace labour relations, which are of interest here. For, during the 1950s, most managements had tacitly accepted a great many informal workgroup practices which had effectively extended the workers' frontier of control over production processes and had, by default, presided over the growth of the shop-steward system and domestic bargaining more generally. But in so far as British industry is concerned, it is quite clear that the 1960s witnessed an acute decline in rates of profit and this therefore almost certainly provided the overriding stimulus for an offensive by employers on many hitherto accepted workgroup procedures (Neville, 1973). Indeed, not only did productivity bargaining become important at this time but a number of simultaneous developments, such as measured daywork, reflected the increasing determination of managements to control effectively once more the processes of production at shop-floor level. That they were generally unable to do so, in any significant measure, helped, as we now know, to prepare the ground for the creation of the Industrial Relations Act, and when this in turn was found wanting, when organized labour was prepared to use to the full its considerable powers of numbers and organization under full employment conditions, a new-found willingness among employers and government to involve workers far more in the decision-making processes of the firm was to emerge in the 1970s.

But although interest in productivity bargaining began to wane from the late 1960s, there was probably a slow increase in the 1970s in *job evaluation*. The purpose of this practice is to establish a 'rational' wage structure by involving senior representatives of the workforce in discussions on the overall content of jobs, while reducing sectional shop-steward control and negotiation. And, unlike productivity bargaining, there is no resort 'to detailed written agreements concerning work organization' (Batstone, 1984: 249). The evidence of any trend here is inconsistent and inconclusive, however, since, whereas the Warwick survey (Brown (ed.), 1981) found systematic job evaluation practised for manual workers in 43 per cent of establishments, the DE/PSI/SSRC Survey discovered that only a quarter of establishments had schemes of this type, with only 10 per cent having formal committees involving worker representatives. Moreover, on the basis of the data presented in Batstone's (1984) survey, two-thirds of plants were found to use job evaluation, but few had introduced schemes in recent years. Again, job evaluation appears to have far less of an impact than its more ardent supporters would claim and, above all, does not appear to shift power to a more centralized shop-steward oligarchy or to be associated with less steward control (Batstone, 1984: 251). But what is clear is the link between the existence of job evaluation on the one hand and company size and unionization on the other (see Daniel and Millward, 1983: 146). And this, it should be stressed, is only to be expected from the pattern in the evidence presented so far and in the light of our central theoretical propositions set out in Chapter 2.

## Conclusions

In this chapter we have discovered a complex pattern of forces underlying managerial attempts to foster employee participation. The overall ideology of managerialism is, as we have seen, inconsistent with radical changes in control within the enterprise. But it is conducive, nonetheless, to task-based employee involvement, joint consultation and information sharing. In the climate of labour unrest and full employment in the 1970s, the shift in the underlying balance of power to the workforce was undoubtedly the spring-board for broader encompassing experiments in job enrichment and quality of working life. But these proved to be poorly suited to the economic conditions of the 1980s. Yet it would be incorrect to view managerial initiatives here in straightforwardly cyclical terms. After all, some practices, such as disclosure of information and joint consultation, remained consequential in the latter period. And there was also a substantial increase in profit-sharing and employee shareholding in Britain in the early to mid-1980s. Moreover, and this point cannot be made too strongly, the effects of the economic downturn were uneven, a situation reflected, above all, in the pronounced segmentation of labour which was taking place. This implied, too, that in the new technology industries in particular, a number of independent primary jobs were being created where managements (concerned to attract and retain highly skilled personnel) continued to develop sophisticated practices which linked quality of work-life and profit-sharing in coherent and imaginative 'human resourcing' strategies.

# 4 Workers' initiatives

So far the evidence presented on a variety of experiments in participation has shown consistent support for the view that workers' participation in decision making is linked in a complex way with underlying patterns of power and the values of the disparate groups to the employment relationship. Importantly, too, it has been suggested that there is no consistent tendency for linear or cyclical movements to be experienced across all the types of participation. Indeed, turning to initiatives in participation and control by workers themselves, the following points are worth emphasizing. First, as was observed in Chapter 2, the case for an evolutionary trend in the development of participation machinery is strongest at the level of *institutions* (i.e. in the formal provisions for employee involvement which are arguably more rich and polymorphous than at any previous period in history). Second, *cyclical* movements are most apparent at the so-called 'frontier of control' in actual shop-floor decision-making and in the *types* of programme which became ascendent (radical initiatives are unlikely in periods of economic recession). And thirdly, to reinforce the point to which we have already alluded, there are, at any given historical juncture, variations in pattern both *within* and *between* nations (the one being linked with labour market segmentation and the other with different orientations and commitments of labour in the diverse societies).

## A framework for analysis

Our examination of workers' initiatives in participation and control is first set within the broader backcloth of explanatory forces which underlie the arguments advanced in this study as a whole (see Figure 4.1). Not surprisingly, therefore, the elements identified comprise a series of interlinked structural constraints and subjective meanings which influence, respectively, the latent power of working people and their values towards participation. More specifically, too, latent power is seen to shape the *potential* for workers' participation, and values the *propensity* of working people to seek to advance programmes of this type (see again Figure 4.1).

## Structural constraints

To begin with, then, there can be little doubt that conditions of *economic buoyancy* in the 1960s and 1970s were conducive to considerable interest amongst working people themselves in establishing greater control over shop-floor decision-making and in participating in a wider range of committees covering the overall policies of the enterprise itself. And, of signal importance of course, these circumstances substantially increased workers' *potential* for participation by augmenting their power *vis-à-vis* employers and managements. To be sure, from the vantage point of the mid-to-late 1980s, it is also clear that some initiatives by working people emerge counter-cyclically (and this applies particularly to the growth of producer co-operatives). But compared with the radical fervour of the 1970s (and in contrast with the continuing flow of managerial programmes), the economic recession of recent years has been associated with a decline in the power of organized labour and with a degree of retrenchment on the part of those in employment.

Nevertheless, the straightened economic circumstances of the 1980s have been experienced unevenly by different groups of working people. In part, this is associated with varying locations in the production process and linked with diverse *technologies*. But it also stems from the increasing *segmentation of labour* mentioned in the previous chapter. Indeed, in new technology enterprises and in independent primary sectors of employment, the experiences of groups of working people do not fundamentally differ from that of wider sections of employees in earlier years. And, of course, cohesive *work* or *community* structures can also help to offset some of the problems associated with a declining position of power arising from labour market changes.

## Subjective meanings

Moreover, *propensity* to participation is associated with the values of working people which are set within broader meanings. The origins of values among working people are, of course, central to

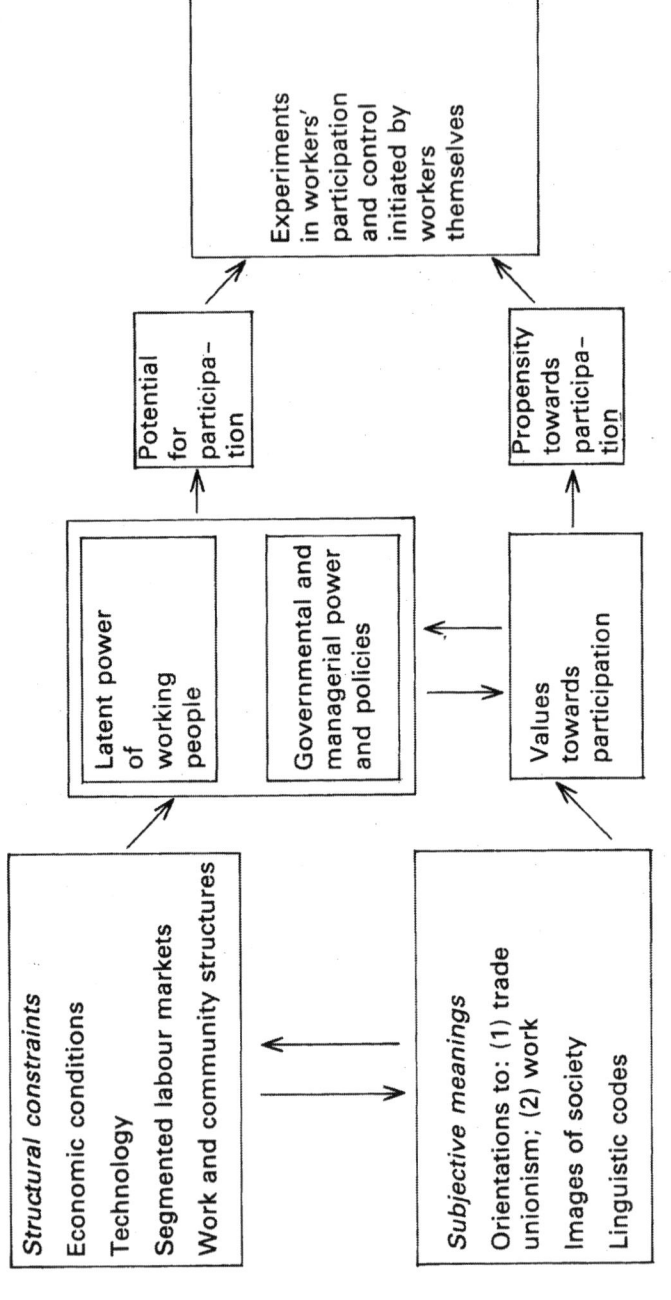

Figure 4.1: **A framework for analysing workers' initiatives**

analyses of the nature of social classes and of their evolution in modern industrial societies. The main controversy surrounding the nature of workers' ideologies and values stems from the work of Marx (1951) and Lenin (1961), both of whom had profound misgivings about the ability of the great majority of working people, at least on the basis of their own efforts alone, to develop any clear understanding of their relation to, and of the workings of, capitalist economic systems. In their view, long hours of work and the division of labour reduced the opportunities for contemplative thought and for other than a fragmented and pragmatic form of consciousness. To be sure, by virtue of considerable workplace deprivation, as well as authoritarian relationships at plant level and the hardships inherent in an uncertain and unplanned economic and political order, working people were aware of their obvious economic and political subordination. But their solution to this dilemma was through 'combination' and the development of a form of 'trade-union consciousness' which enabled them to resist the 'encroachments of capital' and to achieve certain limited ends within the confines of the existing economic system. Moreover, although there were differences of view here (between the so-called optimistic and pessimistic schools of thought: see Hyman, 1971), according to Marx and Lenin, in the absence of an appropriate political party, working-class consciousness would always fall short of a systematic, thoroughgoing critique of a given system of production relations.

Further debates on the nature of working-class consciousness have of course continued apace over the years and, although there is far less research on the effects of the recession than on the pattern in the 1960s and 1970s, in general, investigations into workers' values have been channelled in four principal directions, each having important implications for the orientations of employees to the issue of workers' participation and control. These have been: first, that of workers' attitudes to trade unionism and to the legitimacy accredited to various union activities; second, that of 'orientations' to work which reflect community as much as work influences; third, that concerned with workers' 'images of society', and finally, within educational sociology, that which has focused on linguistic codes and the link these provide between social class, power, and perception.

In so far as workers' attitudes to trade unionism are concerned, the majority of these are clearly consistent with employees seeking to establish a measure of control over decision-making processes at work. Indeed, though circumstantial and situational considerations may well affect the particular pressures that working people will, via their unions, exert upon management, five clusters of attitudes can still be recognized in relation to the appropriate functions of trade unions and, by inference, the members' judgment of legitimate forms of union activity. These can be seen to be 'ideological', 'revolutionary', 'conservative', 'instrumental' and 'political' in nature.

A great many workers are undoubtedly ideologically committed to trade unionism, seeing it as an expression of collective class interest, and emphasizing the 'moral' duty of all workers to belong to an appropriate union. Moreover, their philosophy is most often of a socialist kind and, in the words of Spinrad (1960: 237–44), they view 'work, workplace, workmates and working class' as constituting 'a very meaningful part of the member's life'. It is usual to assume that such an approach to trade unionism reflects a traditional proletarian consciousness which is being continually eroded by the development of collective, instrumental orientations in which concern for pay and other fringe benefits have become paramount. Nevertheless, it is of interest to note that research in Great Britain has shown that a moral commitment to trade unionism is far more frequently held than is generally appreciated: indeed, in a Liverpool study it was the most common perception recorded (Beynon and Blackburn, 1972: 117–22).

This particular conception of unionism should be distinguished, however, from the revolutionary view that unions should be part of the vehicle for overthrowing the capitalist system of production, if necessary by violent means. For here the research evidence overwhelmingly supports the claim of Marx and Lenin that the worker's 'trade-union consciousness' does not as a rule extend to formulations of this type.

Among craft workers, especially, a 'conservative' viewpoint is common, for as Perlman (1949) has argued, union members seek job security and the control of whatever limited employment opportunities are available and value union activities in the promotion of these ends above all. The factors underlying such a disposition are partly economic, partly technical. Thus, by virtue of continual subjection to uncertain employment prospects – especially during periods of economic depression – working-class consciousness has in Perlman's view become shaped by the reality of 'scarcity of opportunities', although only craft workers have been able traditionally to protect themselves from this situation (and then not universally) by controlling employment opportunities, restricting the supply of labour into their particular trade, and by practising what Perlman (1949: 6) has called 'communism of opportunity' among the members of the craft itself.

It is commonly argued, however, that following a sustained and lengthy period of affluence, the development and maintenance of craft practices gradually lose their primary rationale; workers thus tend to become increasingly 'instrumentally oriented', and are prepared therefore to relinquish such controls so long as the economic rewards are considered sufficient for their purposes. But, in so far as workers' attitudes to the primary functions of unionism are concerned, it is important to note that far fewer instrumental approaches have been identified than would be expected if this pattern was now dominant and, indeed, this was true even of the reasons given by a particularly affluent sample of workers for joining trade unions in the first instance (Goldthorpe *et al.*, 1968). To be sure, there may well be different regional, cyclical or international experiences here. In the UK, research conducted in the Midlands has shown more pronounced instrumental commitments than those recorded in the north (see, e.g., Marchington, 1980). The attitudes of trade unionists in different countries vary in terms of degrees of instrumentalism and radicalism (Gallie, 1978, 1983). And, amongst various occupational groups, craft workers consistently have the highest aspirations for control (see Marchington, 1980; Brannen, 1983a).

Indeed, of special interest from our point of view, many workers have been classified as 'political' unionists in the narrow sense of emphasizing, above all, their desire for a greater measure of control over decision-making processes at work in order to ensure greater equity and justice and protection from the arbitrary and capricious exercise of managerial authority. Again, in Great Britain and even in the USA, remarkably strong support for this proposition has been evident in existing research studies (see Rosen and Rosen, 1955; for a review, see Brannen, 1983a).

Clearly, therefore, the majority of these orientations to union activities are consistent with workers seeking extensions in their decision-making power at workplace level. But it is interesting that different types of participation may be expected to be consequent upon these various perceptions. After all, for the 'conservatively minded' craft worker, the main aim is to maintain and if possible to extend *job* control, the question of higher-level decision-making therefore being *potentially* secondary. And while both 'ideological' and to some extent 'political' unionists would be expected to favour rather more ambitious proposals for industrial democracy, the 'revolutionary' unionist, by contrast, would tend to perceive any limited forms of control as scarcely worthwhile and potentially deflecting the activities of workers from their primary goals. 'Instrumentally oriented' unionists might well reject workers' participation in management unless it could be shown to enhance a more effective pursuit of monetary rewards. But, in any event, it is not necessarily reasonable to assume that an emphasis on one particular union function automatically involves the exclusion of others and in sum there is, therefore, a great deal of material on workers' perceptions of unionism which suggests a backcloth of values conducive to a concern for greater participation and control over workplace decision-making processes.

The second line of inquiry on workers' values is addressed to the question of whether employees develop general orientations to work, and if they do so, whether these originate from community rather than factory influences (Goldthorpe *et al.*, 1968). This approach is, of course, ultimately based on the so-called action frame of reference in which special prominence is given to voluntarism rather than determinism in human action and to the ability of particular groups of workers to construct their own meanings and understandings of work roles and relationships independently, say, of the acknowledged constraints of economic and technical variables. And more specifically (Goldthorpe *et al.*, 1968: 184):

> The individuals in the enterprise . . . are not simply a random collection but share rather in certain values and goals to which their involvement may be attributed in the first place, and whose sources must then clearly be sought externally to the enterprise.

Of course an argument of this kind could accommodate the effect of general values and ideologies within particular societies on the incumbents' orientations but, more importantly, it diverts attention to the importance of family and community influences. Where these encourage the pursuit of instrumental goals to the exclusion of other satisfactions, the commitment of workers to participation would then be expected to be minimal. And, indeed, some support for this view is undoubtedly to be found in the first of the affluent-worker studies where, of all occupational groups, only the craftsmen were at all concerned with seeking a greater say in decision-making (Goldthorpe *et al.*, 1968: 109; see also Marchington, 1980; Brannen, 1983a).

But without in any way wishing to become involved in a rather peripheral argument there are, from our point of view, a number of relevant issues raised here. To begin with, the authors of the affluent-worker studies were themselves careful to point out that they regarded their sample as prototypical rather than inevitably typical of the British workforce as a whole. It is quite consistent, then, for certain workers with distinctive and marked instrumental orientations to eschew participation even when the majority of working people seek extensions of their decision-making power. Second, instrumental goals are not necessarily antithetical to the achievement of other conditions such as flexible and more interesting work and greater participation, but rather may be consistent with the pursuit by workers of a number of strategies depending on circumstance and situation (Daniel, 1973). And, above all, when a growth in their latent power enables them to achieve a number of hitherto unattainable goals we may expect equally the so-called 'revolution of rising expectations' to bring certain additional bargaining areas on to the agenda. Moreover, the evidence points more and more to the important interplay between work and community; thus to regard either as the principal source of workers' values is to present only a partial picture (Beynon and Blackburn, 1972: 24; Brannen, 1983a). And finally, it is in any event worth mentioning that communities are themselves shaped by certain structural forces, notably economic and technical, which at the very least extend the range of 'value' options open to working people. Thus it was, of course, precisely the main economic changes of the Keynesian era which facilitated the continuous pursuit of material goals, while a number of technical changes have sharply reduced the potential for the development of local cohesive communities. Thus, with technical advance, the number of workers employed in mining, shipbuilding, textiles and so on (and in their attendant communities) have been abruptly reduced, while with the rapidity of technical change, labour mobility has been at a premium and therefore the opportunities for developing stable communities somewhat restricted. Moreover, economic changes in the post-Second World War period have served to promote the process of urban renewal and its concomitant consequences for family and community relations. In other words, consistent with the view expressed in this study that there is an important reciprocity of influence between objective and subjective variables, it is clear that wider structural factors have affected the fabric of local communities and in turn the attitudes of employees to work roles and relationships. People ultimately shape their own ideas and values but the external constraints on this social choice should never be underestimated.

In any event, the question of workers' orientations and any association of these with assessments of participation ties in closely with the third line of investigation which bears on the issue under review; namely workers' 'images of society'. Now, in the attempt to designate middle-range propositions about human attitudes and behaviour the question of social imagery has been especially significant. The most noticeable statement here was that of Lockwood who, it will be remembered, identified three principal forms of working-class social imagery – traditional-deferential, traditional-proletarian, and privatized – in which social differentiation was seen to be based on prestige, power and money respectively (Lockwood, 1966). Moreover, underlying these variations was a complex inter-relationship between economic, technical and community factors.

Hence, despite a number of subsequent doubts about the validity of these categories (Brown, Curran and Cousins, 1983), the first two images were seen to be encouraged by stable community structures and work relationships. Thus, traditional-deferential imagery accounted not only for a Conservative voting pattern among certain working people, but probably emerged from small scale workplace operations in which close paternalistic ties between employer and employee were enhanced, and which were backed by a clear status hierarchy within restricted local communities. But, by contrast, the traditional-proletarian image was fostered by larger-scale operations in which a clear separation between employer and employee had taken place, by high job involvement among the workers themselves and by homogeneous workers' communities. However, accompanying rapid changes in technology and rising material standards of living, further developments in workers' social imagery are to be expected, characterized by high rates of geographical mobility, increasing 'pecuniary' consciousness and the break-up of extended family and kin networks.

Again, it would not be relevant to enter into the detailed critique and discussion of theoretical and empirical problems raised by this classification but it is worth emphasizing that, if these categories are valid, only *one* would seem consistent with working people pursuing greater participation and control at workplace level. After all, the traditional-deferential image involves the legitimation of an established hierarchical order and the privatized form of consciousness would seem to imply the rejection of participation for two main reasons; first, workers of this kind are dominated by a pecuniary model of class differentiation, and second, because their emphasis is primarily on *extra plant* considerations. And although the traditional-proletarian image involves placing the question of power and its social distribution at the centre point of any wider structural analysis of society (we would therefore expect workers with such an image to be particularly concerned with control issues), this is presumably not only experienced by a small part of the working population, but might even be of *declining* significance if privatized and pecuniary images become increasingly important.

Of course, it may be that such social imagery is quite distinct from the workers' own assessments of the desirability of a greater share in workplace decision-making, but to the extent that there is a connection, it would be difficult to account for the emergence of interest in participation and control in the late 1960s and 1970s. By contrast, however, rising levels of expectation brought about by factors which have stimulated the latent power of working people and which in turn favoured the development of a host of socialist, democratic and libertarian ideals would appear to be far more significant here.

It we turn, then, to a consideration of the evidence on the effects of participation in decision-making on value structures themselves, it is clear first of all that there are dynamic consequences which predispose workers to seek further advances in their decision-making power. Valuable work on the development of linguistic codes, hitherto mainly contained within the study of the sociology of education, is of great relevance in this context. For it has become fairly clear from Bernstein's (1971) work that social class and power intersect at the point of language use. That is to say, the emergence of elaborated codes by which people gain awareness of 'the possibilities inherent in a complex conceptual hierarchy for the organization of experience' (i.e. the capacity to develop truly effective ideologies and values) may well be confined largely to the middle classes precisely because in their own work roles they have a greater ability to manipulate and control events and thereby are able to see connections between them.

And, by contrast, the tendencies to pragmatic forms of consciousness and to more context-specific particularistic forms of judgment by working people (which had of course been commented upon by both Marx and Lenin) may well be the direct consequence of genuine obstacles which prevent them from controlling events within work situations. That is, the denial to working people of 'the cultural capital in the form of symbolic systems through which men and women can extend and change the boundaries of their experience' (Bernstein, 1971: 172) could be amongst the most fundamental and far-reaching effects of current distributions of power and authority at workplace level and may further circumscribe their capacity to develop general forms of 'social imagery' itself. Indeed, if this argument is correct, the more workers participate in decision-making processes, the greater will be their chances of understanding the nature of social class relations and of developing distinct orientations to work. Furthermore, the emergence of diverse forms of social imagery within workers' ranks would also seem to reflect variations in the degree of control over work tasks and over other areas of decision-making. In all, therefore, the question of workers' values and their relationship to a desire for greater control over decisions at workplace and societal levels is exceedingly complex, not least because of a certain circularity implied by our recognition that these attitudes are themselves shaped, in part, by a lack of effective power-sharing among all members of the enterprise.

Table 4.1: **Forms of participation and control initiated by working people**

*Direct participation and control*

1 Control by craft-groups over hours and conditions of work
2 Demarcation and control over 'job rights'
3 Workgroup practices
4 Producer co-operatives

*Indirect participation and control*

1 Workers' control, syndicalism and industrial unionism
2 Guild socialism
3 Shop-steward movements and other plant-based systems of workers' representation
4 Factory occupations, work-ins and takeovers

## Forms of participation initiated by working people

In our examination of some of the forms of participation and control initiated by working people, these considerations will again be raised from time to time. But our main aim is still to demonstrate the inter-relationship between external 'objective' forces and reciprocal responses of workers in accounting for the emergence and the success or otherwise of various efforts to enhance their decision-making powers. For classificatory purposes, it is again useful to retain the distinction between direct and indirect or representative participation here and to summarize the main examples in figurative form (see Table 4.1).

## Direct participation and control

Taking first of all the *direct* forms of participation and control, there are undoubtedly a series of interesting initiatives of working people. Nevertheless, the potential for participation at this level is considerably affected by: (a) changes in technology and the *managerial* control strategies that these encapsulate; and (b) the levels of economic activity and employment. Indeed, the struggle for decision-making responsibility at the so-called 'frontier of control' is a sensitive barometer (as well as important consequence) of wider economic conditions and is clearly subject to cyclical changes associated with shifts in the underlying power of labour and management respectively.

## Control by craft groups over hours and conditions of work

We have of course argued that technology is one of the most important variables to have affected the latent power of working people, but the relationship is fairly complex and involves, in the main, the consideration of four factors; first, the levels of skill required of working people; second, the consequences for managerial structures; third, a recognition that the integration of disparate work processes may lead to the creation of strategically placed workgroups; and, finally, the realization that with the fragmentation and isolation of certain workgroups, the maintenance of external supervision is jeopardized and the establishment of self-governing workteams is a frequent but by no means inevitable result. Now although there are clearly technological constraints of some significance here, the organizational forms developed by working people themselves reflect the dynamic interplay between external conditions such as these and the employees' own definitions of the situations in which they are engaged, as well as the variety of meanings they may attribute to these technical factors and working conditions resulting from them.

Industrial sociologists have commonly argued, of course, that a broad evolutionary trend may be detected in the development of technology, and further that this has had radical consequences for the levels of skill demanded of working people. In the early stages of the industrial revolution, therefore, although large numbers of labourers were required, an equally high premium was still placed on *skilled production work* and hence on craft workers. In an intermediary stage, however, machines began to take over a great many tasks previously performed by skilled workers and the demand therefore became increasingly marked for semi-skilled machine operators and for assembly-line workers. And then in a further stage, in highly automated industries, skilled workers are again essential and form a substantial proportion of the labour force but their work tends to be of a *maintenance* rather than directly productive character.

The opportunities for task-based participation and control practices are of course greatly encouraged at the two extremes of the technical scale, partly because of the difficulties experienced by management in recruiting a skilled workforce but also on account of the expertise of workers in these areas which makes close monitoring and measuring of activities difficult to organize. But in any event managerial structures are also extremely sensitive to technology and loose, 'democratic' styles of decision-making are seemingly encouraged at either end of the scale. Indeed, these so-called 'organic' patterns of managerial control contrast with the tight, authoritarian or 'mechanistic' forms which typify middle ranges of technology and especially assembly-line conditions.

Woodward's (1965) demonstration of such a connection is obviously outstanding in this field, but it is worth mentioning that, notwithstanding these objective constraints within the social organization of work, values are of great importance in this respect as well. An important study in the mining industry by Trist and his colleagues (1963) sheds light on the different ways of organizing work within a given technical system, each of which had radical consequences for workgroup autonomy. Thus, while they discovered, as might be expected, that the middle ranges of the technical scale tended to reduce the opportunities for workgroup control over production processes, the work itself could still be reorganized to reduce the effects of these objective constraints quite substantially.

A third technical factor which enhances the latent power of workgroups and their prospects of influencing managerial decision-making is clearly the increasingly complex integration of tasks brought about by modern technology. As a result, many workers have found themselves strategically placed to exert considerable pressure on employers not only for greater control of a task-based kind but also on the 'wages front'. But again, whether or not workers decide to use the latent power available to them clearly depends on a number of values adhered to by the workgroups concerned.

And finally, within extraction industries and other primary forms of production, it is usual for self-governing workteams to emerge largely free of immediate managerial control. In the mining industry, particularly, then, a whole host of workgroup practices have emerged such as the 'butty' system which left the distribution of wages in the hands of the men, and 'cavilling' in which lots were drawn in a formal ceremony to ensure that each workteam had an equal chance of working in either good or bad mining conditions (Trist *et al.*, 1963: 34).

Skilled workers above all have been the main beneficiaries in this respect, though, to be sure, their relatively favourable position *vis-à-vis* their less-skilled colleagues can be understood partly in terms of the *prior* organization and controls that they were able to develop in the first instance. Many writers have sought to demonstrate parallels between these craft unions and the medieval guilds which protected workers from external commercial competition (Tannenbaum, 1921). Nevertheless, as the Webbs pointed out, there is a fundamental difference between guilds and trade unions in that while under the former system workers sold their labour *directly* to customers, under modern industrial conditions, whatever the level of skill involved, workers serve an employer who stands between producer and customer and who has to extract from this relationship not only the 'wages of management' but also other emoluments for private capital (Webb and Webb, 1902). But even under these more recent structural arrangements in which management has always sought to control working conditions and other aspects of the labour contract whenever possible, many craft groups have successfully opposed these restrictions. Indeed, they have been able at times, especially in the last century, to determine a great many aspects of their working conditions, not least their hours of work (Clegg, 1960).

It is, however, a matter of some speculation whether craft

workers have remained highly skilled because of their ability to control entry into their particular trades and to maintain demarcation lines between them, or whether underlying technical factors have formed the principal source of their power. In the past, the closed character of craft unions was very much consequent upon conscious activities and policies of the workers concerned: indeed, they were difficult to replace precisely because of the 'restrictionist' craft policies they had so successfully pursued (Turner, 1962).

Historically, too, traditional craft practices are being continuously eroded by new technologies, which are in no way neutral in power terms, but rather should be understood as in part the consequence of the attempt by managers to regain decision-making control at shop-floor level. Indeed, without wishing to endorse the de-skilling thesis (Braverman, 1974) (see Chapter 3), there is no doubt that it applies best to the experiences of craft workers during the course of the twentieth century (Martin, 1981; OECD, 1981; Knights, Willmott and Collinson, 1985).

## Demarcation and control over 'job rights'

These points can be further illustrated when we turn to examine the better-known aspects of control by craft unions over technical decision-making processes at work. Indeed, the variety of craft practices involved here is both cause and consequence of the greater participatory role traditionally enjoyed by skilled workers in contrast with their less-skilled colleagues. But it is a practice also restricted by the spread of the new technologies.

Since the advent of industrialism, economic insecurity has been a persistent hazard for working people and, although with rising living standards and social security provisions this danger has been partially allayed in recent times, the increasingly rapid pace of technical change and the economic recession have been sources of further concern. Under such circumstances the desire to control job opportunities has been paramount but, on the whole, only skilled sections of the labour force have been successful in instituting necessary controls. Early practices have focused on the establishment of *job rights* to be defended not only against encroachments by managements but also by 'dilutee' labour. This was achieved, of course, partly through the enforcement of the apprenticeship system, which, by virtue of the long period of training involved, provides a disincentive to membership, and partly by recourse to demarcation. Here, individual crafts ensured that their members performed only certain tasks and did not encroach on the territory of others. Moreover, by insisting on the 'closed shop', i.e. the stipulation that union membership is a *prior* condition of employment, any potential division within the ranks of a particular trade can be satisfactorily overcome. More recently, too, in the 1970s in particular, the 'closed shop' grew appreciably in Britain, to cover approximately 23 per cent of all employees (see Dunn and Gennard, 1984).

Craft workers have thus traditionally sought to control a particular *job territory*. Nevertheless it is worth pointing out at this juncture that demarcation disputes frequently stem from managerial rather than workers' initiatives. In other words, when management seeks changes in work practices which upset the delicate balance of job controls, the main defensive mechanisms of these unions are brought into play. But between craft unions, constant attempts are made to reach agreement over which tasks are the appropriate responsibility of which craft group. Moreover, demarcational controls have usually been interpreted by managements as a prime example of a 'restrictive practice' – one, in other words, which prevents them from ensuring labour flexibility, the direction of particular groups of workers to given tasks and, within the constraints of a given technology, from successfully measuring the work of employees and thus from being able to effect the pace of work, the sequence in which particular activities are carried out, and so on. Again, such demarcational controls have been a major target of productivity bargaining which, as we have seen, represents an attempt by management to extend its own 'frontier of control' over shop-floor decision-making processes. Clearly, therefore, the relationship between technology and the opportunities of workers to exert a measure of job control is a complex issue, for there are important reciprocal influences of workers' organization and values, as well as of the determination of management to prevent such controls over 'on the job decisions' being of a lasting character.

### Workgroup practices

But the controls of craft workers at shop-floor level by no means exhaust all examples of direct participation that have arisen as a result of employees' initiatives because, even under less obviously supportive technical conditions, many working people have struggled to control certain aspects of their immediate working lives.

Certainly the literature in industrial sociology is replete with accounts of workgroup practices, some of which have been consciously designed to reduce alienation effects at workplace level and all of which testify to the complex relationship between the external determinants of human social action and their mediation through socio-cultural values and action.

Of all the workgroup practices which are involved here, however, three main forms are particularly worthy of mention; first, various forms of direct action against machinery and machine processes; second, individual and group practices which modify the experiences of extremely alienating technical environments; and third, control over output which is particularly evident under piecework systems of wage payment.

Undoubtedly the most extreme, if somewhat untypical form of workgroup control here is the direct attempt at machine-breaking and other forms of industrial sabotage. This, as Eldridge (1973) has argued, may be usefully understood as a form of traditional social action in which change is actively opposed. The most colourful instance of all was, of course, provided by the Luddites, but in an endeavour to classify the principal forms of industrial sabotage, Taylor and Walton (1971) have distinguished, in this context, between three main types of motivation. These are: attempts to reduce tension and frustration, to facilitate the work process and to assert some form of direct control. The first two cases involve only a limited measure of restructuring of social relationships and of power, but the final instance embraces the far more ambitious aim of workers' control. Moreover, it is by no means unusual for workers to resort to other, rather more limited, forms of action against machinery, as Coates (1967: 62) for instance, has usefully recalled:

> I was sent to a conveyer-head on the coal face which was rather difficult to operate, since the seam through which the face was running was very thin and rather badly faulted. I arrived to find a lad sitting by the gear-head, wielding a seven-pound hammer. He had stopped the belt from running, and was carefully whacking at the metal tie-rod which joined two long sections of belt together. Raw, I asked him what he was doing. 'Won't that break the belt?' I said. 'What the hell do you think I'm trying to do?' he replied.

But militant direct action of this kind is probably less common than the development of 'solidary' workgroups which are concerned to extend workers' control over immediate work tasks. In mining and steelworking, in particular, a strong awareness of the dependence of the individual on his or her workmates is encouraged by manifestly dangerous conditions and this, in turn, is reflected in a number of controlling practices instituted by the groups concerned. We have already mentioned the 'butty' system and other workgroup practices in mining but among steelworkers there is an interesting form of control exercised over promotion within shop-floor jobs, for in many cases these are not decided upon by management but are determined entirely by the principle of seniority.

Nevertheless, although the existence of such workgroups is undoubtedly dependent on technical processes as well as on the values of the workers themselves, even under relatively unfavourable technical conditions a number of individual and group practices have been recorded which demonstrate the determination of working people to modify even thoroughly alienating work environments. And this can be seen despite the tendency in the middle-range technologies – especially assembly-line industries – for limited task-based participation to be reinforced by especially authoritarian managerial practices. Many informal group systems, well illustrated by Roy (1952; 1954) can be seen to ameliorate some of the tedium and boredom which are apparently inescapable in grossly repetitive work.

However, the best-known instances of workgroup controls which have come more clearly into conflict with managerial goals have undoubtedly been associated with control of output. This has been especially noticeable under 'piecework' systems of wage payment, and indeed, as Eldridge (1973) has shown, the works of Marx, Weber, Taylor and other classical references demonstrate that workers had recourse to such practices in earlier eras. After all, it is obvious that if, by increasing his or her output, a worker would have had his or her 'rate for the job' decreased, he or she has an incentive on 'rational' grounds, to produce no more than would be necessary to prevent such a contingency. But of even greater interest are the strong *workgroup* controls determining norms of output. In these circumstances an individual worker does not make an isolated assessment as to a 'fair day's work' and produce to this level but co-operates with a collective group decision on output. This arrangement, however, is inevitably a major handicap for management who could otherwise use the 'rate-buster' as a yardstick in assessing efforts and earnings of other group members. There is therefore a tendency for such practices to be labelled as 'restrictive', and except in favourable economic circumstances, for management reaction to be hostile.

Nevertheless, it is easy to overstate the prevalence of 'restrictive' practices in British industry. Indeed, in an attempt to discover their frequency, Clarke, Fatchett and Roberts (1972) found that most managements either reported no experience of such difficulties or regarded them as insignificant. It is, however, very important in terms of our understanding of power relations in industry that firms in which a closed shop operated (and this is of course a good indication of the organizational power particularly of skilled workers) were more prone to restrictions of this kind than other firms in the sample. In accordance, therefore, with the main tenets of our argument, it would appear that the *successful* introduction of a number of important workgroup practices aimed at exacting a measure of control over the workplace environment is largely explicable in terms of the latent power of employees themselves.

### Producer co-operatives

Yet, as we have argued, there is no consistent tendency for industrial democracy to follow either a cyclical or evolutionary pattern, a proposition which is clearly sustained by the experience of producer co-operatives. After all, there is, if anything, a likelihood that this form of participation will emerge *counter-cyclically* in: (a) periods of recession; (b) in firms or enterprises in declining sectors of industry; (c) in depressed or periphery economies or regions; and (d) in Third World countries at fairly low levels of development. However, in power terms, the *success* of producer co-operatives is almost certainly enhanced by facilitative legislation (and/or local community support and finance) and by the active pressure of organized labour at grassroots level.

Producer co-operatives, of course, reflect far more ambitious aspirations than the workgroup practices examined so far in this chapter. Indeed, the 'central idea underlying their organization . . . is one whereby labour enterpreneurs, on the basis of one member one vote, form a democratic association or partnership and then either have or use their own capital to productive ends' (Abell, 1983: 73; see also Oakeshott, 1978; Thornley, 1981; Jones and Svejnar, 1982; Bradley and Gelb, 1983b). None the less, there is considerable variability in the types of producer co-operative which have emerged worldwide, and hence, following Abell (1983), it would seem to be useful to distinguish between: (1) 'pure' debt type co-operatives (where property rights and product are vested in the funds of the members or providers of labour); (2) equity-type co-operatives (i.e. involving equity capital); and (3) capital-labour partnerships (see Table 4.2).

Table 4.2: **Types of workers' co-operatives**

|  | Private capital | Socialized capital |
|---|---|---|
| 'Pure' debt co-operatives | *Type I*: Self debt-financed: self-managed (full property rights with labour) Sub-types Egalitarian Non-egalitarian | Collective savings |
|  | *Type II*: External debt-financed: self-managed (full property rights with labour) Sub-type | Socialized debt capital (limited property rights to labour) |
|  | Mixed private and socialized External debt capital | |
|  | *Type III*: Mixed self and external debt finance; self-managed (full property rights with labour) | External debt capital socialized. Industrial capital, collective savings |
| Equity-type co-operatives | *Type IV*: Self equity-managed-financed: self-managed (full property rights with labour) | Collective savings |
|  | *Type V*: External equity-financed; self-managed (full property rights with labour) *Type VI*: Mixed self and external equity finance | Socialized equity-type capital (limited property rights to labour) External equity capital, internal collective savings |
| Capital-labour partnerships | *Type VII*: Capital and labour voting shares; property rights shared between capital and labour | Socialized debt or equity-type capital |

*Source*: Abell (1983: 93)

The most spectacular example of successful producer co-operatives remains the Móndragón group in the Basque province of Spain. Indeed, whereas in 1956 it had only a single industrial enterprise, a consistently impressive period of expansion throughout the 1960s and 1970s ensured that, in 1979, there were seventy (currently eighty) factories with an aggregate employment of 15,672 people. Moreover, there is no doubt that amongst the most important factors associated with the viability of the group have been the strong 'associative spirit' of the region (reflected in community and educational support) and, above all, the existence of a credit co-operative (Caja Laboral Popular) which has provided considerable working capital and long-term funds for investment (see Bradley and Gelb, 1983a).

Elsewhere, however, the record of producer co-operatives has been uneven. Indeed, although co-operative manufacturing enterprises can usually guarantee a far higher degree of moral commitment from the workforce than is typical of the private enterprise company, this is no guarantee of their success. For, in addition, there must be a competent management which, while responsible to the members of the co-operative, is capable of fashioning a comprehensive marketing as well as production strategy. Moreover, a satisfactory method of raising financial capital must be discovered to facilitate investment in new equipment and plant, in a way which does not endanger the co-operative ideal itself.

These conditions have been by no means evident in Britain, where, in the 1970s, there was a major fillip for producer co-operatives stemming from three main developments. First, the Labour government introduced the Industrial Common Ownership Act of 1976, a measure aimed at stimulating co-operative manufacturing industries. Second, it gave financial backing in support of defensive actions by workers whose jobs were placed in jeopardy by factory closures at the *Scottish Daily Express*, the Meriden motorcyle works, and the Kirkby Manufacturing and Engineering enterprises respectively. And third, a series of independent small-scale co-operatives had been initiated especially at Fakenham (Norfolk), Fife and Sunderland. Moreover, in the 1980s, the recession proved to be a major stimulus for local and regional ventures in producer co-operatives (in Wales, for example, the number of workers' co-operatives registered with the Wales Co-operative Development and Training Centre (1984) rose from eleven in 1980 to fifty-nine in 1984) (for further details see Oakeshott, 1978; Bradley and Gelb, 1983b). However, focused support in Britain has been less than in France, where the Confédération Générale des Societies Ouvrières de Production (SCOP) has over 500 affiliates employing 30,000 workers. By contrast, both Job Ownership Limited (JOL) and the Co-operative Development Agency (CDA) have been far less influential.

Moreover, the growth of interest in producer co-operatives (PCs) in the USA has been an important characteristic of the recent period. Indeed, there are two principal supportive legislative strands in America: (1) the Employee Stock Ownership Plan (ESOP), a mechanism for promoting employee ownership; and (2) assistance for declining industries in the 'grey belt' of the industrial North East Corridor (see Bradley and Gelb, 1983b: 68, and also Jones, 1979; Whyte, *et al.*, 1983; Rosen, Klein and Young, 1984). Typically, awards are provided by public rather than state organizations but the success of worker and manager buyouts in the US has been remarkable (of the fifty to sixty buyouts of conventional closing firms in the 1970s, none were known to have failed by 1980) (see Bradley and Gelb, 1983b: 58). Moreover, in some cases, union support (in terms of expertise, lobbying in government and with financial institutions) has been beneficial. For instance, this applies to the role of the Teamsters in the 15–20 ESOPS in trucking, even though this labour organization has preferred to select outside pro-union experts for the board rather than workers themselves.

There is no doubt, too, that in the Third World producer co-operatives have proved to be attractive on ideological grounds. And, in a study of industrial co-operatives in India, Peru and Senegal, Abell and Mahoney (1981) showed that the successful enterprises did not have a distinctly inferior economic performance from other enterprises. More spectacularly, too, in Guyana, the Co-operative Republic Act of 1980 envisages the long-term transformation of both state and private enterprises to worker co-operatives (Poole, 1982a).

In general, however, under-investment and problems over collective savings are a handicap for producer co-operatives. And, as Abell and Mahoney (1981) have observed, the benefits of high labour productivity are usually counterbalanced by low capital productivity. Moreover, although research in producer co-operatives is still not sufficiently rigorous for definite conclusions to be drawn, it would seem that the origins and success of producer co-operatives are linked with adequate supporting mechanisms in the wider power structure of society, in which the legislature and local community and, less commonly, the trade unions are the vital forces.

### Indirect or representative participation

More generally at this point, then, a review of the forms of representative participation initiated by working people brings to light a number of examples based on the highest of human ideals and founded upon a catalogue of embittered struggles. Throughout history, Utopian thinkers have argued passionately the feasibility of other forms of social and economic organization from those which commonly obtain, and have proposed that these be founded on mutual co-operation for the social good, with the respective talents of all men and women being released and developed to the full in an unconstrained and non-exploitive association with their fellows. To be sure, it has also been recognized that in large-scale complex societies with advanced organizational arrangements, some system of representative participation would be necessary to bring these ideals to fruition, but this being so, it has nevertheless been argued that the social distinctions within organizations could be minimal, the possibilities of accountability optimal, and the ratification of any policy decision still be subject to the 'will of the people'. Moreover, in the twentieth century, if technology were deployed to assist in this process, advances in communications systems could promote participatory democracy to a previously unforeseen stage of development.

## Workers' control, syndicalism and industrial unionism

The generic term 'workers' control' has been used to cover a number of different practices but common to them all has been the ideal of replacing 'the capitalist industrial system by a new industrial order in which the industries of the country will be controlled (partly or completely) by associations of the workers employed in those industries' (Pribićević, 1959: 1). Certain proposals therefore are clearly excluded by this definition, notably the suggestion of joint control within a predominantly capitalist industrial order and the relatively limited craft and workgroup practices examined in our earlier sections. None the less, differences of opinion have arisen over the shape of workers' control; thus, while for some this is largely a revolutionary concept designating a system of workers' and soldiers' committees to be used as a basis for social transformation, others have sought more lasting ventures in which the scale of industrial operations has been limited to self-governing and largely headless or *acephalous* organizations to ensure that any representatives are *also* working people. Again, in other formulations, the indispensability of *management* in any advanced industrial order has been argued but attempts have been made to ensure its ultimate accountability to the workers employed in any given concern. And finally, the precise role of state, consumer, and party systems within a given socio-political structure of this kind has been a perennial source of disagreement among those broadly committed to the workers' control movement itself.

Although the late 1960s and early 1970s undoubtedly witnessed a re-awakening of interest in workers' control, the heyday of the movement was considerably earlier, in the years between 1910 and the beginning of the 1920s when a variety of schemes of this type were suggested and implemented. The underlying economic conditions at this time had varied effects. Thus, on the one hand, a war economy fuelled full employment which, in itself, stimulated the power of working people and, by encouraging workplace co-operation and organization, also served to enhance their bargaining strength. But the productive forces in the economy were distorted by the war effort so that, particularly towards the end of hostilities, there were chaotic production difficulties and major shortages of basic commodities, especially severe in Eastern Europe. This situation was thus conducive to the growth of workers' organizations but at the same time provided no real means for satisfying their emerging demands. Moreover, widely shared sympathy for the inevitable victims of the war itself gave rise to widespread mistrust of the political and economic orders which had spawned such a catastrophe. In short, people from many different social orgins were disposed to look favourably on a rich variety of radical and revolutionary movements.

The events leading in 1917 to the success of the Bolshevik Revolution and to the similar but abortive attempt in Germany in 1918 are, of course, historically the most outstanding of the era. Moreover, the very success of the Russian Revolution was seen as in some measure consequent upon the system of councils of soldiers, workers and peasants as a means for transferring all power in the state into the hands of the proletariat. Of course, Marx's concept of 'the dictatorship of the proletariat' has caused a great deal of confusion in this context since it can be interpreted either as a support for authoritarian methods of government, or, in view of Marx's own enthusiasm for the Paris Commune, perhaps more likely, the dictatorship of the proletariat over other classes in society while allowing for democratic methods of organization within the working class itself.

But whatever the correct interpretation, it is interesting to note the long history of the use of councils as organs of revolutionary movements. Around the time of the English Civil War, for example, the levellers' movement was based on an association of soldiers' and citizens' councils. Moreover, in the commune period in the French Revolution, councils of citizens were formed, though to be sure they revolved around working people less than in the case of the Paris Commune of 1871 (Guillebaud, 1928: 5). Soldiers' and workers' councils, too, were formed in many parts of Germany in 1918, while a similar type of organization was adopted by republicans in the Spanish Civil War. Again, to take a more recent example, following the cultural revolution in China, the predominant mode of factory organization was for a time essentially of this character (Wheelwright and McFarlane, 1970).

Of course, although the distinction is not always plain, it is important to differentiate between workers' control systems used as a temporary measure during revolutionary societal transformation, from those envisaged as a permanent aspect of economic and industrial administration. Moreover, examples of the latter kind which may be usefully examined at this point had, as Pribićević (1959: 10–24) has argued, at least three main variants during the 1910s – syndicalism, industrial unionism and guild socialism – although, because the third took a rather unusual position with respect to the role given to consumer interests, we have thought it preferable to include it under a separate heading.

The main aim of both syndicalists and industrial unionists was to organize economic production entirely on industrial lines (Pribićević, 1959: 11):

> The industrial organization would therefore become the foundation of the whole social structure, and industry would be under the full control of the workers' industrial organizations. This was the only way to obtain full economic freedom and equality. State ownership and control of industry was hardly less obnoxious to them than capitalist ownership and control.

Initially, syndicalism appeared to be synonymous with unionism but late in the nineteenth century in France it began to take on a new meaning under the guidance of Pelloutier (Cole, 1972: 235) and then became associated with the idea of producers' control and of a co-operative commonwealth built up from locally strong and self-governing productive units. Moreover, provision was made for conflicting interests among producers to be settled locally in the *Bourse du Travail* (Cole, 1972: 249–50). To be sure, the syndicalist movement was never so strong in Britain as in France but in the 1910s it nevertheless had considerable momentum.

Indeed, this prompted the establishment of an influential journal *Industrial Syndicalist* under the guidance of Tom Mann, at this time the principal exponent of British syndicalism (Pribićević, 1959: 14).

While sharing the common assumptions of producers' control and the undesirability of all forms of bureaucratic state machinery, industrial unionists differed from syndicalists on a number of questions, particularly those directed towards existing trade unions and the use of political parties. Thus, whereas for the syndicalists party politics were considered a waste of time and even inconsistent with their ultimate ends, the industrial unionists thought it necessary to vote into power a socialist party to prevent the machinery of the state (and especially the armed forces) being used against working people. On the day, however, when the socialist party was elected, the industrial unionists planned to lock out the employers and take over industry, and, once this had been achieved, the need for parliamentary political representatives would in their view be ended and the state would therefore wither away (Pribićević, 1959: 14). Moreover, industrial unionists defined the existing unions as reactionary organizations, and, by contrast with the syndicalists, sought quite new union structures outside the existing framework.

Industrial unionism was strongest in the USA, where the Industrial Workers of the World (the 'Wobblies') were effective from 1905 to 1924, directing their efforts towards the combination of the American working class and, ultimately, all wage earners into one trade union which would overthrow the employing classes and establish a workers' commonwealth. They never attracted more than 5 per cent of all trade unionists in America but between 1917 and 1918 their leading members were savagely dealt with in the American courts and the movement as a whole was to throw up a number of labour heroes, none greater than their leading poet Joe Hill whose immortal last words, 'Don't waste time mourning. Organize', are of course legendary (Renshaw, 1967). In Britain, however, industrial unionism was largely confined to the Glasgow area and a number of other Scottish centres and was far less important at this time than the shop-steward movement or, indeed, than syndicalism and guild socialism.

The period from 1910 to the early 1920s thus witnessed some development of workers' control but, in the 1970s, the issue again became a major theme in labour and trade-union circles. This activity had its roots in a number of sources to which we have drawn attention throughout, notably the accretions in workers' power after years of depression and the escalation in the expectations of ordinary people on the fulfilment of 'lower order needs'. And, as a consequence, it is also scarcely surprising that the more radical ideas of this decade were once again to subside when the broader political and economic environment became transformed in the 1980s.

There were thus several schools of thought in the 1970s which bore on the question of workers' control but in terms of ownership, the role of trade unions, the nature of management, and the contemporary organization of industries (increasingly in the hands of supra-national companies), many of the modern theories diverged from previous approaches. Thus, most of the recent proponents of workers' control started with the assumption that the public ownership of the means of production was a necessary prerequisite for democratic industrial relations, but they were, on the whole, opposed to the wholesale ownership of modern industry by working people alone, for such an arrangement was seen to be excessively atomistic in the complex economic system which then prevailed. Moreover, trade unions were credited with a role far more central than that envisaged by industrial unionists. Thus Coates and Topham (1972), in their work *The New Unionism*, urged powerful democratic unions in Great Britain to press for policies of workers' control, so that part of the impetus for such developments would stem from the official labour movement itself. To be sure, in certain cases, the prior democratization of the governing structure of unions might be seen to constitute a necessary preliminary, but workers' control was seldom seen as the alternative to effective trade unionism. Furthermore – and this is the third important departure by modern theorists of workers' control from those of an earlier period – the term 'self-management' was customary in this context. Thus, within a planned economic order it was envisaged that workers would control the general policies of the enterprise but that it would require a democratized managerial structure to bring this into effect. In short, in this conception, the notion of self-governing, acephalous institutions was seen to be incompatible with the large-scale organizations of the modern era. And lastly, recent arguments for workers' control paid regard to a situation in which many companies operate on a multi- or supra-national scale of operations. There was thus a growing recognition that greater inroads into managerial prerogatives would, in these circumstances, have to rely on corresponding alliances between members of the labour movements of the countries affected by these multi-national activities.

To be sure, as has historically been the case with these radical initiatives, in the 1980s, the appreciable change in the power of the industrial classes (brought about by the recession), resulted, as we have said, in a decline of interest in schemes of this type. But the blueprints for new forms of economic and industrial management that were a characteristic of this period had a number of interesting elements which may well resurface in a new era when a further shift in economic and political conditions produces circumstances which are again favourable for organized labour.

### Guild socialism

The theory and practice of guild socialism differed considerably from some of the other examples of workers' control which we have examined in this chapter so far. In some respects it was a more 'idealistic' movement, which was grounded in coherent humanitarian and socialist ideologies and was less a spontaneous outgrowth from the ranks of working people themselves. Moreover, because of the academic sophistication of its leading exponent, G. D. H. Cole, the precise influence of producer, consumer and societal interests within the guild-socialist system was carefully balanced and spelled out. But the guild movement, like many other forms of workers' control, was ultimately to meet the fate common to most of the 'idealistic' practices to have emerged from the womb of a predominantly capitalist economic order and, despite the temporary success of the building guilds in particular, it was not to be a lasting feature of the British industrial landscape.

The guildsmen attempted to marry syndicalism and socialism; thus on the one hand its exponents endeavoured to ensure that a collective state apparatus would not emerge, but on the other they sought to prevent consumer interests being threatened, a possibility, of course, if the means of production are controlled entirely by producers at local levels. Their ideal method for achieving these twin aims was through the development of national guilds and a series of representative bodies at regional and local levels built up from a basis of shop, works and district committees (Pribićević, 1959: 21–4).

Now G. D. H. Cole's (1972) work, *Self-government in Industry*, is, as Corina (1972: xi) has argued, 'essentially a manifesto on the rights of man in industrial society', and it is also the best-developed documentation of the guild socialist philosophy and is self-consciously passionate and idealistic in spirit. 'No movement', wrote Cole (1972: 30) 'can be dangerous unless it is a movement of ideas.' He went on:

> Often as those whose ideals are high have failed because they have not kept their powder dry, it is certain that no amount of dry powder will make a revolution succeed without ideals. Constructive idealism is not only the driving force of every great uprising, it is also the bulwark against reaction.

Guild socialism in fact endeavoured to give workers control of the factories in which they were employed, but the state, in this view, should own the means of production and the guild should control the work of production. Moreover, and this was critical to the theory, political and economic power had to be divided to protect individual freedom while, in addition, consumer interests had to be safeguarded. In other words (Cole, 1972: 38):

> The workers ought to control the normal conduct of industry; but they ought not to regulate the price of commodities at will, to dictate to the consumer what he or she shall consume, or, in short, to exploit the community as the individual profiteer exploits it today.

The guild socialist solution to these joint problems of central control and consumer exploitation was, then, division between the functions of the state as the representative of organized consumers and the trade unions as the representative of the producers. Such a framework would, therefore, give workers considerable influence over general economic, political and social policies. Cole also spelled out the way in which the process of production could be administered at local levels, and did in fact anticipate the existence of managements but argued that they should be controlled by the workers employed in particular establishments. Thus foremen would be elected by ballot of all the workers in their particular shops and a similar procedure would obtain in clerical depart-ments. And finally, the general manager of the works would be selected by the works committee, which was in turn elected section-ally by ballot of the members in each shop (Cole, 1972: 156–210).

But despite the powerful idealism of the guild socialists, their successes were generally short-lived. To be sure, in the 1918–21 period in particular, the miners and railwaymen had adopted modified versions of guild socialism, and the builders and post office workers were fully committed to this philosophy. At the outset, moreover, the building guilds met with a considerable measure of success despite obstruction from government officials and the tactics of 'profiteering employers'. Indeed, building guilds became especially strong in the Manchester area where the municipal authority had been approached with an offer of building 2,000 houses. The quality of work carried out by the guilds was also undeniably good.

The guildsmen thus began to be confident of their ultimate success. They announced that 'the theory of the necessity of capitalism' had 'passed painlessly away' and in all they formed about sixty local building guild committees. The idea also spread to Ireland and to the USA and further attempts were made to form guilds in New Zealand (Reckitt and Bechhofer, 1918). But by 1922 the guild movement had virtually ended and the explanation for this, amply documented by Postgate (1970: 64), lay primarily in economic conditions and the effect that these had on the balance of power between the main industrial classes:

> With the change in industrial conditions, the slump which again had the operative in a position of weakness as against the employer, the fair-weather Parliament and Guild disappeared. The first blow to the Guild was the cessation of the official support given to it by the Ministry of Health, and the abandonment of the Government housing scheme, which gravely affected building as a whole. As trade conditions got worse, the Guild found itself in financial difficulties, as all such experiments in time must, through business inexperience and its capital commitments being too small and its commitments and enterprises too large.

With the benefit of hindsight, G. D. H. Cole was later to re-analyse the experience of the guilds and to trace a number of problems which bear directly on the principal theoretical themes of this study. Thus, with respect to the theory of guild socialism, Cole considered that insufficient attention had been paid to the higher ranges of control in the economic system and especially to the problem of investment. But in so far as the lack of success of the guild movement was concerned, economic conditions apart, there were two further problems; the first, a question of values, and the second, a function of technology. In the first place, then, adherents of the doctrine of workers' control were very divided between the revolutionaries, who, following the success of the Bolshevik Revolution, sought a structural change in society on the Russian model, while the left-wing reformists wanted to build on existing institutions. The result was a great deal of confusion over both the means and the ends of the movement itself. But, in any event, in Cole's view the guild socialists were 'kicking against the pricks', since the development of large-scale organization – which was, of course, brought about by technical changes within the industrial system ' – tended to nullify the prospect of smaller productive operations, envisaged by the leading advocates of this movement. That is to say, the guild socialists' weakness 'was that they never faced the fundamental problems of power and of large-scale organization and planning' (Cole, 1959: viii).

Nevertheless, Cole was optimistic that future changes in technology would provide a much more fertile environment for the construction of new social relationships in industry, since with full automation smaller groups of people would be needed and this would make possible 'a more human kind of factory control'. Moreover, he certainly kept his faith with a particular socialist vision which had provided the ideological basis for his commitment to industrial democracy and, indeed, argued that (Cole, 1959: viii):

> Socialism cannot be soundly built except on a foundation of trust in the capacity of ordinary people to manage their own affairs – which requires methods of management on a scale not so large as to deprive them of all possibility of exercising any real control over what is to be done.

### Shop-steward movements and other plant-based systems of representation

In British industry, the shop-steward system has arguably been the most permanent and durable form of workers' participation using a representative framework. Once again, while economic, technical and governmental factors have had a role to play here, consistent with our own thesis, the *values* of stewards and their constituents can be seen to have been fundamental too, not only in shaping particular orientations to their own duties, but also in their effects on the character of this distinctive and fascinating form of workers' participation in industry.

Of all the flirtations with workers' control in the 1910s and 1920s none was more fruitful than the shop-steward movement, and its subsequent evolution has indeed closely reflected the ebb and flow of economic and technical forces. The first movement was thus primarily associated with the engineers, those archetypal craftsmen who had built on the basis of a major technical power resource to establish a firm position among the aristocracy of labour. But the exigencies of wartime prompted the government to intervene in the munitions industry, to promote labour flexibility, and to pave the way for the 'dilution' of craft skills by employing semi-skilled and female labour. This was achieved via the Treasury Agreement and was to strike at the fundamentals of the engineers' power (Hinton, 1973). In such circumstances, some struggle to preserve the privileges of a craft position was to be expected, but there were also a great many craftsmen – notably J. T. Murphy (1972) – who saw the potential for building an entirely new type of bargaining structure which contained in it the germs of a revolutionary transformation of society.

The First World War had stimulated a growth in union members but, for the most part, union structures remained firmly based on extra-workplace branches. This, however, was a most unsatisfactory arrangement for the engineers affected by the Treasury Agreement and therefore, once they recognized that a struggle against the dilution of craft privilege would be doomed to failure in a war economy, they began 'to break down divisions between craftsmen and less-skilled workers, to develop an industrial policy which united the interests of the two groups and to construct all-grades organization in the workshops' (Hinton, 1972: 3). In short, they realized that it was only through workplace-based organization that sufficient control over the new arrangements could be maintained at workshop level.

But in any power struggle the nature and the direction of any encounter are contingent to some degree on the values of the parties involved. Once their craft position had been challenged, the engineers might have found in the shop-steward system a device merely for maintaining craft privileges by ensuring that, at workshop level, any non-apprenticed workers were kept firmly in check by the skilled workers in the shop concerned. That it took a far more revolutionary course based on the ideal of workers' control was a reflection of the commitment of the participants in this particular struggle. Indeed, the ideological mainspring of the shop-steward system as it gradually evolved at this time was firmly 'based on the theory of class struggle, the abolition of capitalism, the complete re-organization of trade unionism and workers' control of industry'

(Pribićević, 1959: 85). In *The Workers' Committee*, published in 1917 by the Sheffield Workers' Committee, Murphy (1972) advocated means for bringing these principles into effect. The basic unit of organization was the workshop committee composed of shop stewards elected by workers in specific workshops which were to be supplemented by local industrial committees in each district. The next step was to unite all the stewards in each firm by means of works or plant committees and at the same time to establish local workers' committees. And then the final tier was to consist of national industrial committees and the national workers' committee which would presage revolutionary societal change.

But in the eventual evolution of the shop-steward movement, only the preliminary steps of this process were effectively accomplished: although the engineers none the less in this way laid the foundations for a new and lasting organization of the workshop which was distinct from the wider union hierarchy and, in particular, facilitated the collective action of workers in a number of different unions in a given workplace. However, only on the Clyde in 1915–16, and later in Sheffield, did truly effective local workers' committees become established (Pribićević, 1959: Chapter 6).

Moreover, it is obvious, in retrospect, that Murphy's ideas were industrial in character, and that his analysis largely ignored wider political issues. This having been said, it remains paradoxical that, on turning their attention away from industrial organization to political organization following the success of the Bolshevik Revolution, the shop stewards took a crucial step towards the weakening of their main power base at workplace and local levels. But the ultimate demise of the movement occurred later, in 1922, when, with worsening trade conditions, the employers were able to lock out the members of the Amalgamated Engineering Union and to reassert completely the principle of the employers' 'right to manage their establishment' (Pribićević, 1959: 40). However, the early shop-steward movement did at least set the scene for an influential workplace representative structure which was to re-emerge with fresh vigour in the post-Second World War period.

The depression years witnessed a fall in union numbers and the development of a collective bargaining system in which the role of the full-time officer was again supreme. But by the 1950s the phenomenon of wages drift began to be understood: that is to say, full employment and a buoyant economy had meant that, at local levels, workers could obtain higher wage rates than those officially negotiated and the importance of the shop steward in this process of domestic bargaining began to be recognized. Thus, in the 1960s, a steady increase in the number of shop stewards was recorded, to the extent that in 1968 the Royal Commission inquiries suggested that there were probably about 175,000 stewards in British industry and that this represented an increase of about 14 per cent over ten years (McCarthy and Parker, 1968: 15).

Further, there was a substantial growth in the number of shop stewards in the 1970s. Indeed, by the end of the decade, there were estimated to be 250,000 shop stewards in Britain and they were found well beyond the metal handling industries. In manufacturing they are now all but universal in plants with more than 100 workers and both private sector and public sector services witnessed a significant increase in their numbers in the 1970s. Moreover, Terry (1983) has reported further indicators of shop-steward organization that reveal the considerable extent to which senior shop stewards became a characteristic of Britain's industrial relations landscape in the 1970s (see Table 4.3).

Table 4.3: **Shop-steward organization in Britain** (per cent of establishments where a steward is present)

|  | Private manufacturing industry | Local government |
|---|---|---|
| *Manual* | | |
| Recognized senior steward | 74.0 | 70.0 |
| Full-time steward present | 11.7 | 33.0 |
| Regular steward meetings | 36.8 | 50.0 |
| *Non-manual* | | |
| Recognized senior steward | 61.4 | 73.0 |
| Full-time steward present | 2.3 | 17.0 |
| Regular steward meetings | 30.0 | 83.0 |

*Source*: Terry (1983: 69)

To be sure, it would be erroneous to regard the growth of a senior shop-steward system as a recent phenomenon (indeed, there is evidence to suggest that between the 1950s and 1970s the power of joint shop-steward committees and conveners actually declined *vis-à-vis* other members of the steward body – see Batstone, 1984: 95). And it is also possible that, in the 1970s, the development of stop-steward organizations was in part facilitated by management in an attempt to develop adequate procedures for handling disputes at workplace level (see Brown (ed.), 1981; Terry, 1983). But, even in the 1980s, the shop-steward system has remained a robust form of workers' participation in decision-making (Batstone, 1984).

Nevertheless, the decision-making powers of shop stewards at workplace level vary considerably so that although the overall economic climate clearly affects workplace-based union activities, other factors help to explain differences in the degree of influence wielded by shop stewards *per se*; principal among these are technical circumstances and the values of the stewards individually and as a group.

Two technological characteristics have an effect on the workshop organization of stewards, namely the size of the undertaking and the level of skill or knowledge demanded by given technical processes. The strong association between the degree of industrial concentration and the propensity of workers to join unions has been well documented and requires little amplification here. But it is worth remarking again upon the greater propensity of skilled workers than their colleagues to join unions and to participate in decision-making processes at workplace level. Indeed, we have referred earlier to Goldthorpe and his colleagues' (1968) revelation that the majority of craftsmen in their sample sought greater control over decision-making by contrast with most of the less-skilled workers whose enthusiasm for participation was far more muted. Further, skilled workers tend to have better shop-floor organization – the average constituencies of their stewards, the constituencies of senior stewards and the average number of hours expended on union activities all compare favourably with their colleagues in general unions which lack any firm craft basis.

None the less, it is also evident that stewards themselves interpret their duties in a number of ways and that these orientations circumscribe not only what they consider to be legitimate activities but also may affect the range and scope of issues with which they are involved in the bargaining process. In this respect, for example, our own research in the Sheffield region highlighted certain points of difference between the definitions adopted by stewards towards their duties. Broadly speaking, we were able to identify four principal types of steward in this context, namely the 'activist', the 'union man or woman', the 'representative' and the 'dispute solver'. Each of these groups emphasized one aspect of the steward's responsibilities to the comparative neglect of others. Only activists were of the opinion that it was reasonable to promote the interests of their members to the full. The 'union men or women' interpreted their role more in terms of the policing of union agreements; the representatives, on the other hand, recognized their responsibility as spokesmen for the shop, but only in circumstances which concerned their members; and finally, the dispute solvers were essentially management-oriented and understood their obligations in terms of 'smoothing-out' local difficulties and problems (Poole, 1974).

Several subsequent studies on shop stewards have also revealed a complex number of types of orientations with considerable consequences for the *propensity* for active involvement on the part of the stewards themselves. Foremost amongst these remains the work of Batstone, Boraston and Frenkel (1977) who demonstrated that the various shop-steward types could be understood in terms of the extent to which trade union principles were pursued and the degree to which leadership (representative) or delegative responsibilities were assumed. Four types of steward could be identified by this method (leader, nascent leader, cowboy and populist), with the leaders being by far the most active in using the opportunities available to extend the scope, range and level of decision-making influenced by the shop floor (Batstone, Boraston and Frenkel, 1977: 34; see also Terry, 1983; Batstone, 1984).

Naturally, several attempts have been made to map out the range and scope of issues with which shop stewards are concerned at workplace level and these clearly merit consideration at this point. The work of the Royal Commission (McCarthy and Parker, 1968), for instance, included an assessment of the stewards' range of bargaining in British industry and revealed that, while nearly three-quarters of the sample discussed and settled working conditions as a standard practice, this proportion was reduced to just over one-half for wages questions and even less for discussions on hours of work, discipline and employment issues. But these data have been supplemented by evidence from more recent investigations in which the scope of shop stewards' decision-making powers were examined, and in which particular attention has been paid to the areas where a degree of unilateral control is exercised by the stewards involved. Typically, in manufacturing industry, over 70 per cent of managements in Britain report that they are not free to organize the workforce as they wish, and this is of course a good indication of the ability of shop stewards to encroach on so-called managerial prerogatives. But, in addition, the principal areas in which unilateral control is exercised include labour mobility, manning of machines, job demarcation, hampering work study, resistance to dilutees and union demarcation (Evans, 1973; Batstone, Boraston and Frenkel, 1977; Terry, 1983). And this evidence undoubtedly helps to shed light on the precise impact of shop stewards on the decision-making processes of the firm as well as to confirm the still extensive role played by shop stewards in British industry.

## Factory occupations, work-ins and takeovers

> UCS is part of our contemporary history, its story written by workers and their deeds. It is more than that – it is a portent of things to come. Workers will determine the future and in the process will write the most glorious pages in the history of our country. (Reid, 1972)

If the shop-steward movement has proved to the main lasting and influential form of representative participation stemming from workers' initiatives in British industry, undoubtedly the most spectacular development was the wave of factory occupations, work-ins and takeovers which swept much of Western Europe in the late 1960s and early 1970s (Crouch and Pizzorno (eds), 1978a, 1978b). In France, in May and June 1968, the events for a time seemed to herald the revolutionary transformation of French society under workers' control, and in the years following, factory takeovers have been particularly common. Meanwhile, in Great Britain, of course, the events at Upper Clyde Shipyards opened a new chapter in the history of industrial relations in this country.

This special variant of workers' conrol is itself composed of diverse elements, such as factory occupations and sit-ins which are really conflict strategies on the one hand, and, on the other, work-ins and factory takeovers during which, for a period of time, organized groups of workers actually run the factory. And, indeed, the challenge offered to management in its capacity as representative of the owners and the threat to the legitimacy of an existing pattern of control and domination is, of course, especially profound in a situation in which workers are able to demonstrate their ability not only to produce but also to sell particular commodities.

Taking first of all the case of the uprising in France in the spring of 1968, the underlying causes of these events are still open to dispute. Nevertheless, three factors are especially relevant here: first, general economic conditions; second, the political restraints imposed during the Gaullist period; and, third, the value climate of the time which not only rested on strong syndicalist and revolutionary traditions but was also affected by a number of wide-ranging tensions and frustrations of the period.

Since the Second World War, of course, successive French governments have planned to expand the economy at a minimum rate of between 4 and 5 per cent a year (which has been frequently exceeded), but, although in these terms there had been conspicuous success, growth itself had been most uneven. Thus, the bulk of expansion was concentrated in modernizing sectors of the economy and, with the exception of publicly owned industrial enterprises which have been fundamental to the process of development, other public provisions remained sparse. Nowhere was this more evident than in the higher education system where a huge influx of students did not see commensurate increases of facilities and resources. These, then, provided important objective sources of student unrest which were exacerbated by other radicalizing forces of the period (and notably the war in Vietnam), and which were conducive to the growth of anti-capitalist and anti-imperialist ideologies. Furthermore, in a political system which gave little opportunity for redressing these grievances, a number of factors clearly combined to bring the students into open revolt against the regime and to form the catalyst for the general strike and the factory takeovers which followed.

Moreover, despite an impressive and sustained rate of economic growth, the immediate gains of working people were again scarcely compatible with that deemed appropriate after such a period of economic expansion. And these traditional grievances were fused with far more radical elements which furnished the means for the creation of a new social order organized around workers' control. As S. S. Cohen (1969: 251) has argued:

> The traditional protests stemmed from, and were directed against, the failures of the plan *in its own terms*: an archaic and unproductive university system that frustrated the great mass of students in their efforts to prepare for a proper place in the new society; and long hours, low real wage increases, little job security and unacceptable working conditions that belied the promises of ever increasing affluence that the plan made to the mass of workers.
>
> The radical rebellion was a refusal to accept the tight limits the plan proposed for future social changes. The plan, and the political economy it represented, reached the limits of any

idea of radical alterations of authority structures, and any attempt to redistribute power at every level of social organization in order to create fundamentally different social relations.

In Great Britain, attention during this period focused on the UCS work-in, when, for a time in 1971, shop stewards and workers effectively controlled the general policies of the company. The immediate catalyst was the official threat of closure and substantial job losses, but other economic factors were important here too, as was the high level of organization of the Clyde workers and their traditional rejection of capitalism as the most appropriate means of running an economic system. The economic backcloth to the work-in at UCS has been discussed at length by Thompson and Hart (1972: 12):

> That the system of the 'mixed economy' pursued since 1945 was indeed in serious difficulties was a fact universally confessed, though not necessarily in these exact words. It had meant an economy mostly under private ownership run for private profit, but with considerable State backing in loans, subsidies and other forms of assistance, cheap inputs from the nationalized basic industries, free wage bargaining, combined however with a crippling armaments burden and massive financial speculation abroad. By the mid-1960s this was visibly breaking down, with roaring inflation, continual balance of payments crises and industrial stagnation.

The so-called 'lame-duck' policy was of course to be the principal solution offered by the incoming Conservative government in 1970: that is to say, state subsidies to private enterprise would be discontinued and any 'backward and inefficient' industries which had been subjected to substantial neglect and almost non-existent investment in new plant and machinery would as a direct consequence of this be rendered bankrupt. Little if any account would be taken, in the process, of the hardships which would be suffered not only by workers and their families but by dependent communities as a whole, nor was there to be any attempt to apportion blame among the parties involved in such an industry. Other than Rolls Royce, UCS would surely have been one of the more spectacular victims of this policy had it not been for the decisive and sustained actions of the workers concerned. Immediately preceding their collective action to safeguard their livelihood the report by the specialist committee looking into UCS affairs recommended that any continuation of operations 'would be unjustified' and that, more specifically, the workforce should be reduced from 8,500 to 2,500 with what amounted to wage reductions for the remaining employees (Thompson and Hart, 1972: 36–43). Subsequent events are, of course, a milestone in the history of British industrial relations, for not only did the work-in illustrate the great organizational powers of working people, but for a time it successfully challenged the priority of property ownership over workers' rights to employment.

The UCS drama was to be followed by a whole series of occupations and work-ins designed to prevent redundancies, notably at Plessey Alexandria, River Don works, Fisher Bendix and Allis-Chalmers (Gretton, 1972). Moreover, almost all were successful, so much so that this form of workers' action became an established industrial relations practice for the rest of the decade.

Nevertheless, as we have argued, it is important to distinguish between occupations constituted solely as a temporary bargaining strategy and those in which workers have had an opportunity to manage the affairs of their company, if only through the medium of their stewards. To be sure, the occupation or sit-in has many advantages for workers by comparison with the traditional strike weapon. When they are in control of the machinery in the shop, workers can easily prevent 'blacklegging' and the use of white-collar and other staff by management in its attempt to keep up production. Again, the chances are minimized of a direct clash with the police and of unfavourable public reactions, which are an inevitable risk during picket-line activities. But although, with the notable exception of March 1972 in the Manchester area, factory occupations often achieved beneficial results from the workers' point of view, their bearing on the formulation of workers' attitudes to participation and control is somewhat more questionable, in contrast with work-ins which are fundamental in this respect. After all, the UCS experience served, above all, to demonstrate the ability of working people to undertake policy decisions in a self-management framework, and in championing this cause, the Clyde workers were able to provide further grist for the mill of the industrial democrat. Indeed, the significance of this contribution and this form of action towards the goal of greater self-determination by working people could hardly be overestimated. And although, to be sure, accompanying the recession, radical initiatives of this type substantially diminished in the 1980s, an important new category of industrial democracy was still established in the late 1960s and early 1970s for which the Upper Clyde workers were largely responsible.

## Conclusions

It has been our intention in this chapter, then, to examine an extensive range of examples of workers' participation and control which, by contrast with the practices examined earlier, have arisen on the basis of the initiatives of working people. What has been remarkable, of course, is the finding that, despite diversity of origins, of form and of content of these particular schemes, very similar causal elements can be adduced to explain their principal characteristics. And, in particular, we have been able to reinforce once again the main elements of our own model and the more specific derivative argument that a rise in the level of latent power of working people does induce mounting expectations among them in the course of which questions about workers' participation and control attain a new significance. By the same token, too, it is scarcely surprising that, in recent years, despite a number of counter-cyclical developments (and notably, of course, in the growth of producer co-operatives), and the continuing significance of certain representative practices (e.g. the shop-steward system), mass unemployment and the weakening of labour in the 1980s has dramatically reduced the incidence and effectiveness of the most radical types of workers' initiatives.

# 5  Trade unions, their officials, and workers' participation

The leaders of particular labour movements and labour organizations have approached the question of workers' participation and control in markedly different ways. All have tended to support strong plant-based systems of union representation since these help to ensure that agreements are actually honoured at local levels, that non-unionized employees cannot severely impair union activities, and that arbitrary or capricious decisions of management are effectively opposed. But in practice only a rather narrow band of participation or control programmes has attracted the unreserved enthusiasm of officers who, to begin with, have been inclined to reject the majority of schemes initiated by management, largely on the grounds that these serve to duplicate channels of workers' representation and in consequence weaken workers' inclinations to join trade unions and to overcome problems by means of union procedural systems. But, second, in their concern to preserve their own position in the industrial system, trade union officers have frequently looked with suspicion on many of the more ambitious ideas for outright workers' control. Indeed, from time to time they have even resisted particular shop-steward and other plant-based representative systems formally linked to the union structure whenever these have threatened their own decision-making authority within the union hierarchy.

Officials of established labour organizations have an interest therefore in ensuring that workers' participation is clearly integrated into the established union structure. To be sure, many are personally committed to democratic and socialist ideals and at times these have provided an important ideological basis for acknowledging that a greater sharing of power within the ranks of the labour movement would be desirable. But in view of their concern over these matters it is scarcely surprising that their enthusiasm for particular forms of participation has been confined (by and large) to those clearly founded in union structures.

## A framework for analysis: ideology, power and structure

Broadly speaking, it is of course possible to classify the world's labour movements on the basis of their commitment to *instrumentalism* or *radicalism*. The first ideology of labour is linked with collective bargaining and the second with political attempts to transform the employment relationship. These distinctions, in turn, relate to the relative power of trade unions and workers *vis-à-vis* employers and management on the one hand and the state on the other (see Figure 5.1). Moreover, despite the universal preference of union officials for types of industrial democracy grounded in the trade union channel, their impact on actual institutional machinery varies not only in relation to different patterns of ideology and power but also in accordance with the constraints of particular politico-economic structures, economic changes, technology and the degree of democracy obtaining within a given labour union (see again Figure 5.1). For instance, the diverse functions of trade unions under socialism and capitalism clearly influence views on appropriate institutions. Meanwhile, the recession of recent years has inevitably led to a retrenchment on the part of labour with respect to industrial democracy (in Britain this is obvious in the difference between the pre- and post-Bullock eras). By contrast, as we shall see, the new technologies (while posing threats to unions in many cases) have also been the spur to the formulation of different types of agreement involving extensive consultation and information-sharing between management, organized labour and the workforce as a whole.

More especially, however, the attitudes of trade union officials on the question of workers' participation and control would seem to be highly sensitive, both to the general conditions isolated so far in this study and to the degree of democracy obtaining within any given trade union. And this, in turn, depends a great deal on the organization and power of the rank and file and various factional activities amongst internal groupings within the union itself. Indeed, in Great Britain, an analysis of the assessment of leaders of the labour movement of workers' participation and control would in fact reveal a number of distinct alterations of opinion since the First World War. In the early part of this century, differentiation of functions within unions was somewhat more diffuse than is the case today, when trade unions have evolved comparatively 'mature' organizational forms. The growth of general unions from the 1890s onwards had brought to the fore trade union leaders of

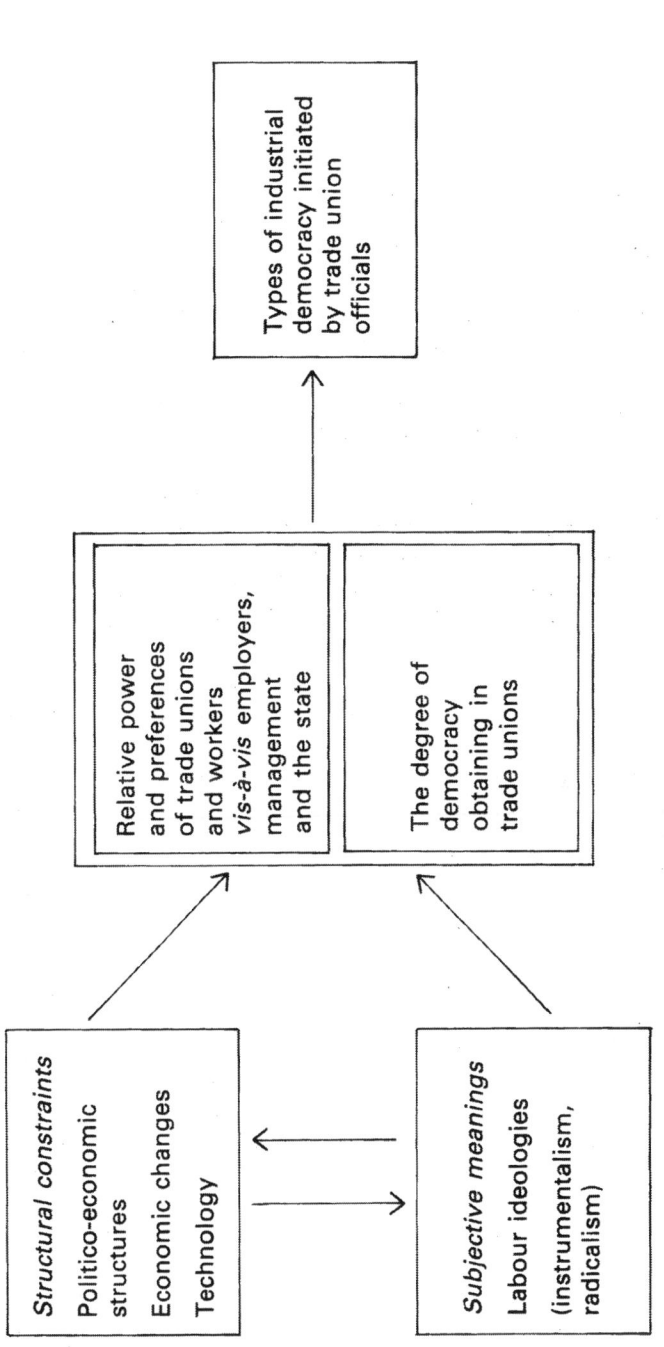

Figure 5.1: **Trade unionism and industrial democracy: a framework for analysis**

an idealistic rather than of an administrative outlook, and although the leaders of craft unions remained solidly 'conservative', other upheavals of the time of course resulted in the emergence of the powerful shop-steward movement. In consequence, as Clegg (1972: 189) has argued:

> During and after the First World War British trade unions were for the most part converted to doctrines of workers' control or joint control which held that in a socialist society industry should be run by unions or by a government. Only if workers ran industry through their own organizations, held the proponents of these doctrines, could 'wage-slavery' be ended.

But the early 1920s witnessed a major retreat from this position. In the first place, with worsening employment conditions trade union officials were preoccupied in traditional bargaining areas and, then, in 1930 a change in emphasis was particularly evident in discussions of the London Passenger Transport Bill. This was a most important test case, for, in introducing the Bill, Herbert Morrison argued that board members in publicly owned industries should be selected on the basis of competence for the job rather than as representatives of the workers concerned. When this view was ultimately upheld it set a major precedent for trade union attitudes to this question in the years to come. Indeed, Morrison's position was officially endorsed by the Trades Union Congress in 1944 in their *Interim Report on Post War Reconstruction* and this very much affected the outcome of discussions on the main nationalization acts after the end of the Second World War.

Of course, in one view, this decision was one of the most unfortunate ever to be taken by the British trade union movement, for although few developments in workers' participation could have been expected in the inter-war years when the unions were severely weakened by adverse economic circumstances, the underlying conditions were undoubtedly propitious at the end of the Second World War. At this time, following their role in that war, the esteem of trade-union officials had reached new heights, union recruitment had risen substantially and a Labour government had been elected on the basis of a deeply felt desire for the introduction of an entirely new social order. In short, although the balance of power between the main industrial relations classes was favourable to extensions in participation, at the value level the birth of indus-trial democracy was sacrificed and displaced by the vision of 'managerialist' thinkers who anticipated the emergence of a meritocratic rather than a democratic industrial social structure.

Naturally, none of this is to suggest that the public sector of the economy is now largely run by persons who easily fit the stereotype of the managerialist thesis, but an important opportunity was undoubtedly missed at this time for developing workers' participation and this, in turn, has affected the attitudes of working people and the public at large to the question of public ownership itself. Indeed, it is clear that the experience of workers in publicly owned industries has not on the whole been significantly different from that of their colleagues in private firms, and this very much reflects the similar decision-making and control structures which obtain under both systems of ownership. Again, the consequent alienation experienced by employees in nationalized firms leads to a general disillusionment and at times fatal agnosticism among working people to the issue of public ownership, and they thereby offer only limited opposition to the more forthright opponents of nationalization itself.

Furthermore, the subordination of the public to the private sector of the economy is perpetuated too by the very composition of most corporation boards. As it happens *neither* democratic *nor* meritocratic criteria have necessarily applied in the appointment of key directors for, as Jenkins (1959) has demonstrated in *Power at the Top*, there is a preponderance of directors of public companies on the majority of these boards and they are, of course, able to ensure that decisions taken in nationalized industries are largely in accord with the interests of privately owned industry. But this state of affairs is to some extent a reflection of the unwillingness of the official labour movement to offer any decisive challenge on the question of control, which is in turn partly consequent upon its general approach to the issue of workers' participation up until the 1960s.

To be sure, at the end of the Second World War public ownership was conceived as co-extensive with certain limited developments in workers' decision-making powers, but in the various nationalization acts this was confined largely to a dual structure of bargaining and consultative committees. Thus, the right of trade unions to negotiate on wages and conditions was secured and so, largely fortuitously, nationalization has been a positive stimulus for unionization especially among white-collar workers. But outside traditional bargaining areas, however, formal *consultation* was apparently considered a sufficient means for involving workers in decision-making processes. This is not to imply, of course, that workers themselves necessarily share these assumptions, as is clear from the demise of formal joint consultation from some nationalized industries, but, for our purposes, it is only important to note the limitations on experiments in workers' participation in the immediate post-Second World War period and to observe that these were in some degree a consequence of the official trade-union position at the time.

But the latter years of the 1960s undoubtedly witnessed a major change in the official view of the labour movement towards industrial democracy, beginning in 1967 with the deliberations of a Labour Party working group headed by Mr Jack Jones of the Transport and General Workers' Union. As it happens, the group was unable to recommend a blueprint for participation to fit all industrial situations and further considered that different issues were involved in the public and private sectors of the economy, but they were at least able to reach certain conclusions on points of principle. These were, first, that workers have the right to determine their economic environments by participating in a widening range of decisions within the firm and that the recognition of that right, and measures to secure it, must be a matter of urgency; second, that workers' participation must be closely identified with the trade-union organization and representation of workers; and third, that industrial democracy must be developed on the basis of a single channel of representation.

These proposals would of course have been favourably received by the progressively minded union official because they envisaged an important extension in the role of workers in affecting decisions in their day-to-day working lives but, at the same time, by virtue of being firmly grounded in the union structure, they offered no major threat to the authority of the officials themselves. And again, although it is patently logical to base the extension of participation on this powerful organizational structure, the preference of union officials for this framework is also consistent with their own particular interests in this matter.

Now these principles were reaffirmed and extended in 1973 in the TUC's interim report on industrial democracy. This report was introduced by Mr Vic Feather who argued that the TUC had an 'emerging and developing policy for giving workers a greater amount of control over the industries in which they worked'. In detail, the official trade-union view was that there should be 50 per cent direct trade-union representation at board level, and to facilitate this, the unions looked for a change in company law which would ensure that an emergent supervisory board could, if the necessity arose, overrule both the board of management and the annual general meeting of shareholders within any privately owned firm. They also sought extensions in industrial democracy within publicly owned enterprises via the union structure although here, by contrast with the TUC proposals of 1944, there was no suggestion that unionists on the board of directors be required to act in an individual capacity only and hence to sever connections with their respective unions. On the contrary, the principle of accountability was a major plank of the new policy.

But why, it may reasonably be asked, did such a change of approach come about? Part of the explanation can doubtless be found in the general shifts of the balance of power and the rising expectations of the period but a principal factor, too, would appear to be the democratization of unions themselves. We have argued at many points in this study that the general interest in participation from the late 1960s onwards was largely consequent upon the growing latent power of working people coupled with a rise in their levels of expectations brought about by a sustained period of 'affluence'. But whether or not union officials were accurately to reflect and even to lead developments along these lines depended greatly on their sensitivity to the wishes of the membership and this in turn was enhanced by the degree of democracy in any given union. Thus, in general, the more accountable the official to the membership the greater his or her enthusiasm for participatory democracy appeared to be, while in more bureaucratically run unions official attitudes to workers' participation remained far more lukewarm.

It has of course long been acknowledged that the prior democratization of unions is an important foundation for building industrial democracy. Thus, as Fletcher (1970: 83) has argued:

> As experienced trade unionists invariably point out whenever 'workers' control' is under discussion, workers have little chance of controlling industry if they cannot control their own unions. Union democracy is therefore one of the prerequisites of industrial democracy.

And as some indication of this, it is scarcely coincidental that union officials who were at the forefront in debates on industrial democracy were also those who were relatively more responsive to democratic pressures within their own organizations. The Transport and General Workers' Union, for example, had, over many years, been plagued by problems of bureaucratic and oligarchic control but, nevertheless, in the late 1960s and early 1970s important structural changes were recorded in its organization, the outcome of which was to involve union activists far more in the decision-making processes of the union. A deliberate policy emerged to include ordinary members in the making of agreements largely by encouraging local collective bargaining, and shop stewards participated formally not only in the final decisions on particular agreements but also in the formulation of union claims. To be sure, these developments were in part a *response* to local initiatives which had been encouraged in turn by the growing latent power of workers at plant level, but the fact that they were positively fostered undoubtedly suggests a sympathetic appreciation of the views and aspirations of the membership, and which was reflected, in turn, in the union's prominence in public discussions about industrial democracy.

Moreover, whatever the correct interpretation it should be stressed that, even in the more recent Trades Union Congress and Labour Party deliberations of the post-Bullock era, the envisaged structure of planning and industrial democracy remains firmly anchored in the official organizations of working people. Hence, as is argued in *Economic Planning and Industrial Democracy* (TUC-Labour Party Liaison Committee, 1982: 10):

> There is a clear and longstanding case for strengthening the rights, status and influence of workers and their unions as part of an extension of democracy throughout society . . . linking planning and industrial democracy will . . . require new rights to enhance the position of trade unionists in day-to-day decision-making at the workplace. . . . Additionally, the new rights to information, consultation and representation . . . will underpin the progress to be made through collective bargaining towards greater influence by trade unionists over decisions at their place of work.

In short, officials of labour movements tend to envisage workers' participation and control in terms of their own organizations and may therefore still be disposed to place obstacles in the way of forms of industrial democracy in which the role of trade unions is limited.

## Types of workers' participation initiated by union officials

Turning, then, to examine the types of participation that have stemmed from the initiatives of trade union officers, it is scarcely surprising that experimentation here has been generally confined to five principal types: collective bargaining, new technology agreements, union segments in enterprises, union ownership and various modes of trade unionism under socialism (see Table 5.1).

Table 5.1: **Forms of participation initiated by union officials**

1 Collective bargaining
2 New technology agreements
3 Union segments in plants
4 Union ownership
5 Trade unionism under socialism

### Collective bargaining

Trade-union participation through collective bargaining in predominantly private enterprise economies is to be distinguished from the relations between trade unions and management in planned economies. The first is typically referred to as a *disjunctive* form of participation (since no harmony of interests is assumed) and the second as *integrative* participation (since unions in planned economies are expected to further the interests of the enterprise as a whole (Rosenstein, 1977; Poole, 1979)). Importantly, too, collective bargaining is as we have seen the principal agency for workers' participation in Australia, Canada, New Zealand, the United Kingdom, and not least the United States (where collective agreements are wide in scope and cover many managerial practices) (Coleman, 1978).

Collective bargaining typically flourishes in pluralist political economies characterized by a low degree of corporatism, the acceptance and recognition of the rights of different interest groups, a spirit of compromise and concession and, above all, adequate material standards to ensure that all parties can gain from collective agreements. And, certainly collective bargaining is best viewed as a *form* of representative participation in decision-making rather than as an entirely different means of seeking to enhance or improve the conditions of working people from those examined in earlier chapters.

In the literature to date, the most influential and sustained theoretical analysis of workers' participation based on collective bargaining was advanced by Clegg (1960) in his now familiar 'new approach' to industrial democracy. Actually his main conclusion – that collective bargaining rather than direct participation was the key to industrial democracy – had been anticipated by the Webbs (1897) more than sixty years previously in their classic work on this subject. But what was more novel about the approach was its relationship with ongoing debates among political scientists about the essential characteristics of democracy. Up to that time, most classical theories of democracy had recognized participation by the people in the processes of government as a centrepiece of any genuine democratic system; but by the mid-1950s, the so-called modern theory of democracy had begun to dominate theoretical work in this area, and here the emphasis was on opposition rather than participation (Schumpeter, 1943). Clegg transposed these terms from the political to the industrial sphere and made the case for a strong and independent oppositional body to management (i.e. the trade unions) since, in his view, this provided the means for developing and sustaining the power of resistance among working people and hence was the mainspring of industrial democracy. But Clegg took the argument further, postulating that workers' participation in *management* was not only irrelevant to the question of industrial democracy but could actually be harmful to workers' interests and to the extension of 'democratic' social relationships in industry, principally because of the problems of role conflict experienced by workers on decision-making bodies, but second because of the inherent danger that they might acquire managerial definitions of the proper functions of the enterprise.

Clegg (1960: 21) thus developed three main principles of industrial democracy: first, that unions must be independent of both state and management; second, that only trade unions can represent the interests of industrial workers; and third, that the ownership of industry is irrelevant to 'good' industrial relations. The main theoretical case against participation was clearly, therefore, a logical consequence of the first principle, since trade unions could not, at least in Clegg's view, operate as an effective opposition if they in any way became part of management, or their activities were shackled by governmental decision.

But the oppositional concept – and, hence, Clegg's more general theory – has been criticized on a number of important counts (see Blumberg, 1968). To begin with, since the main premise rests on a theory of democracy which is not in accord with the way the term has been traditionally understood, it only requires a restatement of classical principles (in which, once again, participation is a crucial component) for there to be many serious semantic objections to the theory. Second, it is quite possible, of course, for there to be democracy in the classical sense without opposition, and this is the case, for example, in smaller trade union branches. Third, 'opposition' itself does not arise in a social vacuum; rather it is located structurally in configurations of interests which characterize specific types of society, and in the absence of these structural divisions the need for organized opposition – to prevent the total domination of one section of society over another – would lose part of its rationale. Fourth, even if we have in mind a definition of democracy based on the modern theory, there are certain major differences between the political and industrial fields in Clegg's formulation, notably that the opposition party in industry (i.e. the trade unions) can never in fact replace management and form a government – they are doomed to the exercise of only a rather negative form of power and, because of this, find difficulties in attracting high-calibre personnel and in gaining widespread public support. And finally, it is in any event rather a dubious policy to countenance merely the existence of organized opposition as a necessary precondition for democratic social relations, for in this formulation the problem of accountability on the part of leaders of any organization to their 'electorate' is simply not catered for at all.

However, although such criticisms are now familiar in the literature, it is at the same time vital to note that Clegg's conception of power rests implicitly on a latent rather than manifest interpretation. In other words, it infers that interests will be accommodated in society largely in proportion to the latent strengths of contending parties or classes. *And here Clegg's arguments are rather more convincing than those of certain of his critics, for while it is clearly nonsense to argue that workers cannot participate in managerial decision-making, to pursue such a strategy at the cost of union organization can leave workers extremely vulnerable in the event of unfavourable economic circumstances or hostile enactments by government.* Moreover, as we have seen, it is precisely when the latent power of workers has increased for some reason or other that participation has been a very common consequence. And, above all, the *strategy* of increasing workers' organizational power which Clegg would appear to favour is by no means unreasonable if one is genuinely seeking an effective form of workers' participation in decision-making.

Certainly, a principal strand of the movement towards industrial democracy in Britain has been through collective bargaining. Hence, in the private sector, three-quarters of manual employees have their pay determined by some sort of arrangement between employers and trade unions. And the bulk of the public sector's workforce is covered by collective bargaining agreements.

Historically, collective bargaining in Britain has evolved from bargaining at the level of the workplace and small firm in the eighteenth and early nineteenth centuries, to district bargaining for the whole industry between the two world wars; and to a mix of industry-wide, company and workplace bargaining since 1945, with the last two types reasserting themselves strongly. Company and workforce bargaining are most typical of industries which operate substantially on piece rates and financial incentives of various kinds. And, in recent years, there have been appreciable changes in the levels at which collective bargaining is conducted. The 1970s witnessed a dramatic increase in establishment or plant-level bargaining (in over half of British firms this became the most important bargaining level for manual workers' pay). But, in the 1980s, there was a decline in establishment-level bargaining and an increase in 'no bargaining'. And, above all, there was an interesting growth in company-level bargaining *above* plant level (in over a quarter of British firms this is the most significant level of bargaining for the pay of manual workers). In the public sector, however, centrally negotiated agreements have remained the dominant bargaining arrangements (see Brown (ed.) 1981; Daniel and Millward, 1983; Batstone, 1984).

Moreover, the shifts in levels of bargaining are undoubtedly linked with changing patterns of power relationships in industry itself. The move to plant level bargaining was thus partly a reflection of the growing power of the shop steward but it was also occasioned by the preference of professional managements to deal with local union representatives rather than to rely on employers' associations. And again this change is clearly intelligible as a cohesive managerial strategy developed in response to the problems which it faced from centrally and locally organized unions in circumstances of major organizational and technological change.

## New technology agreements

At a number of points in this study, we have argued that technology
is an important variable to be taken into account in any comprehensive analysis of workers' participation in industry. Nowhere is
this better revealed than in an assessment of the rise of new technology agreements with which trade unions have been increasingly
involved in the 1970s and 1980s.

Indeed, the so-called micro-electronic revolution has had far-
reaching repercussions for industrial relations. Almost invariably
the introduction of new technologies is accompanied by extensive
consultation, but in some companies new technology agreements
have been signed which involve extensive trade-union involvement
in the implementation (and, sometimes, the planning) process. In
Britain, there have thus been at least eighteen new technology
agreements in the electronics industry. And a typical finding from
research is that disclosure of information to employees increases
substantially following the signing of new technology agreements,
though the overall impact of employees and unions is rather less
than is sometimes supposed (Briefs, Ciborra and Schneider (eds),
1983; NEDO, 1983; Sorge *et al.*, 1983; Ruskin College, 1984).

In other countries where trade unions are influential, too, there
have been many attempts both by union officers themselves and
by managements to increase employee involvement in decision-
making accompanying the introduction of new technologies.
Hence, in Germany, a series of formal agreements (called 'data
agreements') have been negotiated since the early 1970s and, as
Keul (1983: 207) has observed with respect to Norway:

> Data agreements are established at both the local and central
> levels, corresponding to the structure of enterprises as well as
> the arrangements of employer-employee relations in various
> sectors of the economy. The agreements have introduced
> measures and organizational methods for the trade unions to
> deal with data questions. These include data shop stewards,
> data committees, specific educational programmes relating to
> data questions, etc. As a result of this process which has
> spread to most branches of the Norwegian trade union
> movement, the unions now have a set of general action
> patterns related to the introduction and use of new technology.

Indeed, trade unions in most European countries have adopted
strategies for dealing with the new technologies and have sought

access to research and development activities, investment in plants
and companies, the technical organization of production, products,
personnel policy, training and education and the division of labour
(Hingel, 1983).

But of course the ability to participate in new technology agreements and to have an effective influence depends greatly on the
organizational power of the various labour movements. Indeed,
there is evidence to suggest that, even in companies with trade
unions, managements can reduce their impact by ensuring that
decisions are taken at company level and by dividing the loyalties
of different sections of the workforce itself (Davies, 1984).

### Plant-based union segments

But full-time union officials have also been inclined to favour and
to assist in the promotion of union segments at plant level. In the
USA, of course, where industry-wide bargaining is less usual than
in Europe, a great many negotiations have always been carried out
by the members of particular union 'locals' with their respective
employers (Kochan, Katz and Mower, 1984), but early hostility to
unions impeded wholesale international developments along these
lines, and thus the branch, whose members were employed in a
number of firms within a given locality, became the principal basis
of union organization. However, with accretions in the latent
power of working people which have been contingent on economic
and technical change, a power void was created in the channels of
communication in many firms, and this could have been filled by
a number of agencies, including informal workers' organizations,
shop-steward systems, personnel and other paternalistic managerial
practices, and, of course, the one most favoured by the full-time
officer, the plant-based union segment which is formally integrated
into the wider union hierarchy.

In Great Britain, as we have seen, the most common development
in this respect has been the shop-steward system, which owed far
more to the initiatives of local workers than to official union
policies. But in other countries (e.g. Italy and France), officials were
especially anxious to support plant-based representative systems so
long, once again, as these were integrated into the wider union
hierarchy. Thus, in Italy, as in most of Western Europe, much of
the post-Second World War period up until the 1980s witnessed
comparatively 'full' employment, rapid production growth, widespread labour shortages, an advance in real earnings and the

increasing prominence of large corporations. But traditionally here the unions were strong at the centre and comparatively weaker at plant level with the result that collective bargaining was highly centralized and the national or regional multi-employer agreement typical. However, as a consequence of the changing economic climate coupled with the increasing concentration of industry which facilitated the development of plant-based representative systems, such centralized bargaining structures became progressively obsolete and a 'power vacuum' at local levels began to be noticeable. In any event, of course, dependence on a multi-employer collective agreement is a reflection of union weakness since it is clearly a union strategy used like a 'dyke' to ensure that those in more favourable circumstances are able to protect their less well-placed colleagues. But whenever the economic order is more opportune from the standpoint of the labour force, these agreements at best represent a *minimum* level which particular sections of workers can significantly advance through locally based activity.

None the less, immediately after the Second World War, the Italian unions, having no official status within the plant, were in no position to meet the challenge of changing economic circumstances. Moreover, any attempt to rectify this situation was clearly hampered by the existence of 'internal commissions' (works councils) which 'anticipated' locally based union organizations and the widespread attempt by Italian managements to develop paternalistic practices in order to weaken the intent of workers seeking effective union action. But, gradually, leading officials of Italian unions became dissatisfied with the position, and sought to amend it. The first step was a major assault on the 'internal commissions' and here the Confederazione Italiana Sindicati Nazional Dei Lavoratori (CISL) took the lead in 1960 by advocating that unions must have a monopoly of bargaining functions within the plant. Meanwhile, parallel with this development, the three principal unions in Italy began to build 'factory unions'; the CISL set up various plant-based union segments called Sezione Aziendale Sindacale (SAS), the Unione Italiane del Lavoro (UIL) followed suit with their Nuclei Aziendali (NA), and finally, the largest union, the Confederazione Generale Italiana del Lavoro (CGIL), established their Sezione Sindacali di Fabbrica (SSF) (Ross, 1962; Crouch and Pizzorno (eds), 1978a; 1978b). But these were, of course, developed as part of an *official* strategy for, although on the one hand unions have been critical of various managerial practices, they have also at times disapproved of workers' actions (notably factory occupations and takeovers). Once again, then, consistent official support tends to be forthcoming only for those forms of workers' participation and control which are firmly based on the established union structure. And certainly, in Italy's case, the recognition of workplace union segments in the late 1960s and 1970s can be understood in part as an attempt to *re-institutionalize* industrial relations practices during a period of appreciable social and industrial upheaval.

## Union ownership and workers' participation: the case of the Histadrut

But union ownership has also provided trade-union officials with an opportunity to promote participation by their members in the decision-making processes of the firm. The Histadrut (the General Federation of Labour in Israel) is by far the best example of this and highlights very well the central issue of the relationship between latent power, values and the success or otherwise of given forms of workers' participation and control.

Both ideological and economic stimuli may be identified in an analysis of the origins of the extensive arrangements for participation which were originally contemplated in Histadrut-owned plants. Indeed, the Histadrut itself was founded more as a movement than as an institution, and represented a manner of thinking which was directed by a powerful ideology which fused nationalist-Zionist, egalitarian-socialist and general-humanist elements. But, gradually, the first-named ideology became dominant and so, in an attempt to resuscitate egalitarian forms of consciousness, the leaders of the Histadrut sought to develop workers' participation in firms within their jurisdiction. Moreover, this ideological background was augmented by economic pressures which were partly consequent upon general competition from foreign companies and other private firms in Israel but were also conditional on the close relationship between the Histadrut and the state, for it became imperative to increase productivity for nationalistic reasons. Again, in establishing operations in new immigrant areas, the Histadrut had at times failed to take full account of the true economic costs, and this further stimulated the concern for productivity (Rosenstein, 1970; Tabb and Goldfarb, 1970; Dubin and Aharoni, 1981; Histadrut, 1983).

It is worth mentioning, too, that over the years the Histadrut has grown into a mass organization and continues to be very influential in Israel's economy, being responsible for about 23 per cent of employment, 19–25 per cent of the national product and 19 per cent of the country's exports (IDE, 1981a: 239; Histadrut, 1983: 25). Furthermore, although in theory in Histadrut-owned plants all economic activities are ultimately controlled by Hevrat Ovdim (the community of workers), in practice decision-making at the executive level lies largely in the hands of salaried managerial personnel.

In addition to the resolution taken on profit-sharing in 1966 (see Histadrut, 1983), Histadrut firms have adopted four main solutions to the problem of involving workers in decision-making processes: first, workers' committees (which are really plant bargaining committees); second, joint production committees; third, plant councils; and fourth, the joint management programme. Workers' committees and joint production committees have only limited functions since they have no jurisdiction over work assignments and technical matters, over which management has authority, but the plant councils and the joint management programmes have been more ambitious in terms of level, scope and range of decision-making.

Plant councils owe their origins to a resolution passed by the Histadrut Convention in 1956. This provided in each plant for the establishment of a council with representatives of management and workers having equal voting powers, for the authority of the council to encompass all matters pertaining to the enterprise, for the JPCs to be integrated into the plant council, for decisions approved of by two-thirds of the members of each side to be considered binding, and for a twice-yearly general assembly in which management and council members would discuss problems with the workforce as a whole.

Nevertheless, the plant-councils scheme was doomed to failure and by 1961 *all* councils had become inactive and this therefore led to the introduction of the system of joint management. In 1964, a special meeting of the Histadrut council was convened to endorse this programme although it was not until 1968 that this new phase in workers' participation became operational. The scheme provided for participation by Histadrut employees at two levels: first, on central management bodies; and second, in the individual plants. More precisely, one-third of all members of central management bodies were to be workers' representatives, while equal numbers of management and employee representatives were to control plant-level policies.

For all that, the very grave problems experienced in practice by these more ambitious participation programmes require some explanation, particularly in view of the fact that surveys carried out in Israel have suggested that the bulk of rank-and-file employees as well as secretaries of workers' committees are generally enthusiastic about progress along these lines. Indeed, Tabb and Goldfarb (1970: 155–7) reported that 54 per cent of the general workforce and nine out of every ten secretaries they interviewed were in favour of participation, with only 16 per cent of the former and none of the latter being completely antagonistic. However – and this was ultimately to prove decisive in accounting for the demise of the councils in Israel – the attitudes of management were undoubtedly different. For although recently managers have shown increasing co-operation in the system of worker participation (Histadrut, 1983: 26), at the time, only a minority was behind the scheme (although it must be said that on the whole their objections were conceived in terms of its impracticality and they were not generally opposed to participation in principle). In Israel's case, management's ability to subvert the council's operations derived from the structure of power relations at workplace level (Tabb and Goldfarb, 1970: 127):

> The legal right to order managers was not, it seems, enough.
> The managerial group, as one centre of power, had to be won
> over, no less than the worker group. However, the managers
> were not won over because they did not believe that it was
> in their interest or in the interest of the enterprise to involve
> the workers in management. They believed that the workers
> were only concerned with their narrow interests and, therefore,
> were in no position to be concerned with the overall problems
> of the undertaking. The little experience afforded them by the
> enterprise councils convinced them that workers' participation
> in management was a hindrance not a help. Moreover, it was
> the opinion of the managers that 'management is a profession
> and must not be turned over to amateurs'.

The success of the argument deployed by Israel's managers can only be partly understood, however, in terms of their internalization of the main tenets of the 'managerialist' thesis. After all, had there been other competing power centres of any significance, these reforms would presumably have been achieved *despite* managerial hostility. But union ownership can reduce the power of shop-floor workers on two main counts. First and most obvious is that, since the union is both employer and bargaining agent, workers lack an organization designed exclusively to further their particular interests. To be sure, workers' committees (and currently joint management boards) do exist in Histadrut plants, but the loyalty of the secretaries of these committees tends to be divided between firm and members. Equally important, too, with the divorce of ownership from control in Histadrut enterprises, managerial authority must perforce rest almost entirely on technical and professional criteria which are, of course, called into question with every advance in workers' participation. Hence, by contrast with capitalist companies in which unification of interests between owners and top managerial personnel has been the general rule, there are fundamental divisions between policy and executive organs in union-owned firms and, under such circumstances, a hostile managerial reaction to participation would be expected.

In retrospect, then, the proposals for workers' participation in Histadrut enterprises appear flagrantly ill-adapted to the underlying structure of power and values. Managers, who had *de facto* control over decision-making processes, generally failed to identify with the aims of legal owners and were therefore unwilling to accept a curtailment of the primary source of their authority. Thus, the only centres of power which might have been thought likely to insist on such developments were the committee secretaries and the workers, but notwithstanding their general enthusiasm for workers' participation programmes, they were divided and ill-organized: in short, they lacked sufficient latent power to ensure that their interests prevailed against entrenched managerial opposition. The outcome, indeed, was far from the ideal envisaged by the founders of the Histadrut; forms of unorganized conflict, for example, remained endemic, with the consequence that the number of working days lost through stoppages has been higher in Histadrut establishments than in other enterprises in Israel. And this is, of course, just what would be expected when workers are deprived of an effective local channel for resolving their disagreements with management.

More generally, too, the experience of workers' participation in Histadrut enterprises shows the limitations of those participation programmes imposed from above which bear little relation to the underlying structure of power and of values of the interested parties. This theme will be explored further in Chapter 6, but it is one more indication of the problems which inevitably result when an attempt is made to establish effective methods for participation and control on idealistic grounds alone.

## Trade unionism under socialism

The patterns of participation in planned economies linked with the trade unions also merit a brief assessment. To be sure, trade unions in socialist societies have a somewhat ambiguous role, reflecting, in the case of the Soviet Union in particular, an historical compromise at the Tenth Communist Party Congress in March 1921. Indeed, the formative model of trade unionism under socialism was dependent on the view of Lenin and Tomsky that 'allowed for some independence but within the strict confines of broader party and government policies' (Ruble, 1981: 10–11). However, although trade-union involvement in socialist societies tends to be circumscribed by the dominant role of the state in the industrial relations system, there is no doubt that workers' participation has been encouraged in these countries in recent years and that the increasing reliance on markets and local decision-making processes has signally enhanced the involvement of representative organs.

Thus, in the Soviet Union, labour unions (which cover 98 per cent of the workforce) have always had the formal right to participate in job-related grievances and social welfare concerns. And, in the 1960s, those rights were extended to cover the administration of pension and social security systems and the appointment of inspectors by the unions to ensure conformity to health and safety regulations. Elsewhere in Eastern Europe, too, production (or plant or factory) committees have been created or given powers – in Bulgaria, the German Democratic Republic and Hungary. And in Romania, legislation for collective management in 1968, 1971, 1973 and 1978 has produced participation at three levels, the enterprise (workers' council), the 'industrial central' (administrative council) and the economic ministry (industrial college). Moreover, the workers' council (Consiliior Oamenilor Municii, or COM) includes union representatives (Wilczynski, 1983: 106–7). In China, too, the rise of workers' congresses (see Chapter 6) closely parallels the re-emergence of trade unionism (Littler and Lockett, 1983).

But, of course, despite the emergence of 'Solidarity' and other independent trade unions in socialist countries (Singer, 1982; Weschler, 1982; Wilczynski, 1983), the role of the official organs of labour is circumscribed by state and political party policy. Shifts in union and workers' involvement over time do reflect changing ideologies but they are also profoundly affected by the distribution of power in the industrial relations system and by wider politico-economic choices reflected in the relative weights attached to planning and to the use of markets respectively. Indeed, in some respects the importance of taking into account the underlying power of the various parties to the employment relationship in any assessment of the practical workings of participation is exemplified above all by the experience of socialist countries.

# 6 Politics and participation

It has long been obvious to followers of the labour movement that the institution of workers' participation on a permanent basis would not be achieved by industrial action alone. This is because there can be no guarantee of industrial democracy when hostile political parties are in a position to use the machinery of government to subvert specific experiments set up under the auspices of working people themselves. Indeed, there are clearly certain general precepts involved here, notably that locally based actions may be frustrated by state intervention and by the passage of legislation which outlaws such actions, that a hostile government can ensure that a labour movement has a largely defensive approach to all industrial questions including that of participation, and that 'right-wing' dictatorships have usually ensured the emasculation and even destruction of indigenous labour movements and other independent organizations of working people (thereby inhibiting even limited forms of participation via collective-bargaining machinery).

But equally the role of the state in the genesis of durable industrial democracy machinery can be highly positive. Indeed, there are two primary routes to effective workers' participation, the one shaped by the local initiatives of manager, worker and trade unionist, and the other founded on supportive public policies and legal enactments. For Anglo-Saxon scholars, in particular, the first approach has generally been championed, and has been seen to depend on the voluntary agreements of the parties linked with a favourable climate of values and buttressed by the organized power of labour. But the continental European tradition, and the one increasingly favoured by developing countries, has been to rely on strong state involvement, anchored in supportive public policies and ensured in practice by the legislature rather than by the labour movement itself.

In more general terms, the two thrusts of this advance towards industrial democracy have been typically referred to as the *syndicalist* versus *corporatist* dimensions of national industrial democracy systems. However, it must be said that these are by no means mutually exclusive strategies and there are in any event in practice far more complex patterns to be distinguished. Indeed, as Teulings (1984: 244–5) has observed, four distinctive conceptions underlie the main variations here. These are : first, *centralization* versus *decentralization* (i.e. national or company/establishment level); second, *class dominance* (or as we would argue the relative power of the main actors in the industrial relations system); third, *legal* versus *contractual* methods of rule-making; and fourth, *dualism* versus *monism* (i.e. the rules can stem from more than one party or from a single source).

In so far as Europe is concerned, the predominant pattern is for the West German and Dutch systems to be the most corporatist (i.e. they are relatively centralistic, legalistic and monistic); Belgium and Italy have the highest tendencies towards syndicalism; Finland, Denmark and Norway have social democratic structures and powerful trade unions at national level; while in the UK both managerial prerogatives and workers' rights in this area are established via decentralized bargaining procedures and without legally enforceable contracts (see IDE, 1981b; Teulings, 1984).

## A framework for analysis: structure, ideology and power

The origins of these variations are traceable to different strategies by governments (often in periods of national crisis) for accommodating conflicts of interests in the industrial relations sphere. This is depicted in Figure 6.1 in which the diverse national strategic choices for conflict resolution are seen to occur in periods of heightened tension within a society (in turn, arising from economic, technological or social upheavals). Moreover, the choices themselves are in practice taken in a wider context in which the predominant cultural values and ideologies and earlier institutional forms, coupled with the relationships of power between political parties, the state, organized labour and employers, are critical. Finally, various forms of legislative enactments or other modes of institutional construction stem from strategic choices and, in turn, shape the institutional machinery for industrial democracy itself.

Placing these choices in historical perspective, the divergent corporatist and syndicalist strategies in Western Europe stemmed from varied approaches by governments to problems of 'system integration'. After all, accompanying the destruction of the medieval guilds by the industrial revolution it was almost inevitable

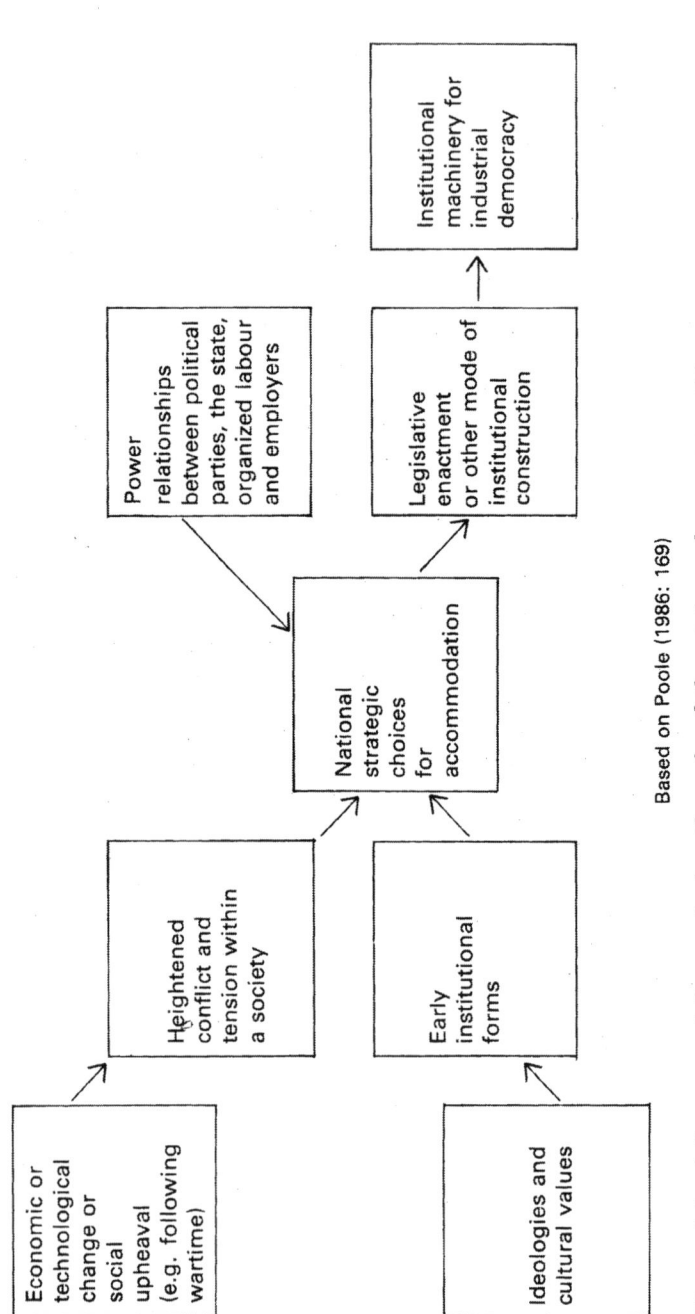

Figure 6.1: **A framework for analysing the role of the state and governments**

Based on Poole (1986: 169)

that the emerging class of propertyless wage earners would seek new forms of collective relationships through labour movements. Governments in the various European nations, however, in practice developed rather different strategies for dealing with this exigency. Indeed, as Bendix (1964) and Rokkan (1970) have observed, they either withheld from workers the freedom of association and the right to combine or they granted the freedom of association but denied the right to combine or they allowed workers' movements both options.

The state in most countries of Western Europe adopted the first policy, while the second was followed in Ireland and the UK and the third in Scandinavia and Switzerland. And, as Sorge (1976: 284) has observed, the predominant pattern was for 'a higher degree of repression to be associated with a higher probability of a legal system of works councils emerging'. Indeed, if the right to form associations was denied to the labour movement, plant-level non-union organizations were likely to develop. And conversely, if collective bargaining emerged in the enterprise, additional legal channels appeared superfluous. More generally, too, when the battle for industrial democracy had to be fought by organized labour against governments *as well as* against employers, 'it became likely that the avenue for industrial democracy would be sought with the help of the state's legal machinery, either by the penetration of the state by workers' movements, or by attempts of the state to placate workers by introducing statutory councils, or by a mixture of both' (Sorge, 1976: 284).

Furthermore, in terms of power, cross-national empirical researches have confirmed that the most effective means of developing industrial democracy are indeed either through legal machinery or by 'mobilization' through trade unionism or by a mixture of both. After an exhaustive analysis of a range of potential causative variables, the Industrial Democracy in Europe Research Group (1979; 1981b) thus concluded that externally promoted support systems based on formal laws or collective bargaining agreements were basic to effective workers' participation and that these two variables together did a better job at predicting influence distribution than 'objective' technological or structural conditions, such as organizational size and level of automation. In short, formal laws or mobilization through trade unions are by far the best means for increasing workers' participation because they rest on the secure foundations of the underlying power and organization of either the state or the labour movement respectively.

## Governmental forms of workers' participation and control

Turning at this point more specifically to assess the main forms of workers' participation and control initiated by governments, it must be emphasized, first of all, that the principal variations are a clear reflection of distinctive political ideologies (for a more detailed analysis see Poole, 1986: Chapter 7). Hence, amongst the types set out in Table 6.1, the various schemes of liberal and social democracy include ventures such as works councils and co-determination; whereas self-management and workers' councils are the product of democratic socialism.

Table 6.1: **Forms of participation initiated by governments**

1 Works councils
2 Co-determination and other 'worker director' schemes
3 Self-management and workers' councils' systems

### Works councils

In Chapter 1 we observed that governments of a great many countries have sought to institute works councils by legislative means, but undoubtedly the best example of intervention along these lines began in Germany prior to the Nazi era, when a succession of orders was enacted which made the establishment of such councils mandatory and so set the main precedent and tradition for other models which were to develop later not only in Germany but also in most other nations in Western Europe. Thus even though we shall return again to the German case in our consideration of co-determination, this example of instituting works-council machinery properly occupies a great deal of our attention here.

For the purposes of our own inquiry, the German legislation in this respect can be best broken up into three historical periods, the first covering the years up to the end of the First World War, the second the revolutionary upheavals following this war, and the third bearing on the decades after the Second World War.

The first germs of enthusiasm for works-council legislation could be detected in Germany as early as the 1830s and 1840s when a period of social unrest was recorded which provided a fertile soil for reformist measures directed at 'overcoming the divisive and negative effects of class antagonism and providing a basis for co-operation between employers and employees' (Shuchman, 1957: 11). Proposals for factory councils gradually filtered through to government levels and, during the Constitutional Convention in Frankfurt in 1848–9, plans for such councils were developed by the Committee on Economics. Even though these were never implemented, they prepared the foundation for workers' participation in decisions relating to personnel and social questions which were to be components of future legislation. In this conception the councils would be empowered 'to mediate disputes between the employer and his employees, to suggest and police factory regulations, to establish and administer health insurance plans, to supervise the morals and education of children employed in the plant, and finally, to select the branch delegates for district, regional and national economic councils'. These proposals, too, were strongly advocated by the 'Fraternity of Labour', even though at this time only a few piecemeal experiments were instituted, but again this initial enthusiasm for the councils was 'engulfed by the tide of conservatism rising at mid-century' (Shuchman, 1957: 12).

Nevertheless, interest in works councils was reawakened in the 1870s in the aftermath of an ideology which was in turn grounded in the ascendancy of two powerful working-class movements (the trade unions and the Social Democratic Party). As Shuchman (1957: 13–14) has argued, the projection of socialist ideals at this time was especially important with respect to workers' participation for they added a new dimension to the ongoing discussions, giving a moral impetus to an idea valued hitherto only as an expedient for uniting different classes during periods of acute and bitter social conflict. It is worth mentioning, too, that Naumann, the founder of the Democratic Party, anticipated the work of the managerialist thinkers as well as Dahrendorf's thesis on the nature of industrial conflict by suggesting that large-scale enterprises would increasingly produce an owning class of *rentiers* who had no direct control and that, in consequence, the primary source of conflict at work would arise progressively from problems of internal organization associated with control over decision-making processes (Shuchman, 1957: 15). And at all events, this controversy helped to fuel an ideological climate which was, by degrees, becoming more favourable to workers' participation in industry.

The first direct legislative action on factory councils in Germany came about in 1891 when the Law for the Protection of Labour provided for factory committees in almost all works employing twenty employees or over. And yet, although much of public opinion would have sustained further evolution along these lines, the balance of power at factory level came to be heavily weighted on the employers' side, and therefore by 1906, notwithstanding the encouragement given to councils by this legislation, only one in ten of the establishments covered by the act had in the event installed a factory committee. Not surprisingly, in this milieu, further inroads into managerial authority were postponed, to be formally sanctioned later when the country was in the throes of the First World War.

As in Britain, this war brought about a number of concessions on the part of the German government to the indigenous labour movement by way of ensuring that industrial production was not jeopardized at a time when the economy generally was strained by a concentration of effort in the military sector. Recognizing these pressures on the administration, the government responded, in part, by means of the Auxiliary Service Act, under which labour service was compulsory for all the adult population. Such a move was obviously most unpopular with the unions, and therefore the government was in a particularly conciliatory mood, being quite prepared, in the process, to countenance further and stronger legislation on works councils. But while these, too, were made compulsory, they were nevertheless bitterly resented by numerous employers who regarded them as an infringement of their decision-making rights. Certainly, in 1918, fines had to be imposed on several employers who had simply refused to comply with the order (Shuchman, 1957: 19). In a general context, then, if such managers are determined to frustrate legislation even during a period of national crisis, there can be no easy passage for such laws in peacetime, unless, that is, the labour movement is soundly organized at local levels and can thereby ensure that laws of this kind are respected.

Further progress for German workers towards a firmer footing in the decision-making structure of the enterprise was furnished by the Works Council Act of 1920. The events leading up to this legislation, however, were revolutionary in character and the Act itself was born out of the ongoing struggles both between capital and labour and (within the ranks of the labour movement) between reformists and revolutionaries. To detail the German Revolution and its aftermath here would be superfluous, but it is worth recording that the law of 1920 clearly reflected the political dominance of the reformists who, by attending to the minutiae of council functions, ensured that the influence of trade-union officials was in no way circumscribed or prejudiced by the Act itself (Guillebaud, 1928: Chapter 1).

The Works Council Act provided, then, for the election of factory councils in all German enterprises with twenty or more employees. A large co-operative element was envisaged here but, aside from this, the councils were endowed with fundamental powers of decision, such as the execution of awards affecting employees as a whole, the making of joint agreements with employers on work rules, the defence of workers' rights of association, the reconciling of certain grievances, and the participation in the administration of works' welfare schemes. None the less, these functions were pale and limited by comparison with those of the independent workers' councils which had been set up by rank-and-file workers as revolutionary and administrative organs.

Moreover, the greatest care was taken in this enactment to prevent councils from encroaching on the responsibilities of trade unions in traditional bargaining areas. Similarly, a number of conciliation boards were requisitioned to control the councils at a higher level and, indeed, management was still accredited with the responsibility for effecting decisions in the enterprise as a whole, so that its executive functions were kept intact. To be sure, at the scheme's inception, many revolutionaries who had served on workers' councils were elected on to the new bodies and were thus able to pursue radical policies, but gradually, with changing conditions and the 'abatement of revolutionary fervour', the electoral processes favoured fewer extremists and, in this way, the struggle to maximize the opportunities available via the councils for the advancement of working people gradually diminished (Guillebaud, 1928: Chapter 3).

The divisions within the ranks of German labour, which were exacerbated by the demarcation between union and council functions, were to prove disastrous for the movement. Certainly, works councils flourished along with unions in the 'fair weather period' of economic boom between 1920 and 1922, but following the German inflation and the ensuing slump and period of high unemployment, the latent power of working people suffered an abrupt demise, and the organizational divisions within the movement itself became an obvious embarrassment. Incredibly, at this juncture, one of the most important functions of works councillors was, thus, the selection of their constituents for dismissal and they, too, not infrequently suffered a similar fate for reasons which are by now familiar (Guillebaud, 1928: 176):

In practice, everything turns on the relative strength of

employers on the one hand, and of organized labour on the other. During 1924 and 1925, the evidence of the intimidation and victimisation of works councillors is so widespread, that it is quite plain that legal provisions, which may be adequate to protect the councillors in times of normal business activity, are largely ineffective when trade is depressed and there is much unemployment.

Moreover, although it would be quite wrong to ascribe the subsequent emergence of the Nazi movement to the weakness of workers' organizations alone, clearly it cannot have helped the opponents of such a creed to have a labour movement, debilitated by economic circumstances, being further enfeebled by the organizational division between trade unions on the one hand and works councils on the other. And, at all events, for labour movements in general, this experience has demonstrated beyond doubt the urgent need to preserve a united oppositional base even during apparently favourable economic circumstances (Guillebaud, 1928: 215):

> There can be no doubt that the existence of the Councils provided the opposition to the official labour movement with what it stood most in need of – a form of organization distinct from that of the Unions. On the one side, this has reacted on the Trade Unions by lessening their control over the forces of labour and giving rise to disharmony and mutual recrimination within the ranks. On the other side, the Councils have often lost through their own actions the backing of the Unions and have exposed themselves to the danger, which to a considerable extent materialised in 1924, of being devoured piecemeal by the employers. Further, the short-sighted exploitation by some of the Councils of their power, in the first two or three years, consolidated the opposition of the employers to their pretensions and helped to bring the whole institution into discredit.

Furthermore – and of significance from our point of view – even in the prosperous years of the early 1920s, works councils were not universally instituted throughout German industry, partly because of the refusal of certain employers to entertain them, but also because the workers themselves by no means viewed them with uniform enthusiasm. And again, the demise of the councils was accelerated as economic and trade conditions worsened. Thus, as a contemporary commentator wrote (Guillebaud, 1928: 244):

Although the Works Councils are universal and compulsory,
in the sense that a Council should be elected in every
establishment above a certain size, there is no penalty attached
to the failure of employees to elect a Works Council, other
than the loss of any privileges that they would have enjoyed
under the Act . . . it is surprising that there should be such
widespread evidence throughout the country of the absence of
Councils where they should exist. It remains true that they
are almost universally to be found in large undertakings, where
employees are numbered by the thousand. But in
establishments with less than 1,000 employees it is becoming
increasingly common to find no works council.

Of course at a number of points in this inquiry we have suggested
that a sizeable workforce is a potential stimulus to combination
and, hence, leads directly to those participation practices which
are usually expressed through the medium of a recognized trade
union. But here we may note too that external constraints which
arise from economic and technical conditions can, in effect,
contribute to the subversion of the letter as well as the spirit of
any law which is not in accord with the delicate balance of power
between the main industrial classes in a given socio-economic
system.

Turning now to the decades following the Second World War,
it is apparent first of all that much of West Germany's present
industrial relations policy has been dominated by co-determination
(to which we will return later), but, none the less, the reformist
mood of this epoch has found expression in the re-introduction of
the works councils system which was forfeited during the Nazi era.
This was accomplished by the Works Constitution Law of 1952
which, if anything, ensured that the new councils spanned a
broader spectrum of issues than those established by the 1920 Act.
At the same time, however, council members are still exhorted to
co-operate with management and cannot, in any event, 'interfere'
in the execution of general policies. This apart, however, a wide
range of general and social functions are entrusted to the councils;
they can conclude plant agreements, supervise the implementation
of laws and decrees, take up employee's grievances and participate
in such matters as working schedules and rest periods, holiday
schemes, accident-prevention measures, piece-work rates and a
great many social issues of this kind. Their influence, however, is
far less marked in other respects, especially on personnel matters

(such as hiring and firing) and economic policy where their role is merely consultative. But by comparison with the earlier period when the unions sought to circumscribe and to restrict the councils' scope, the legislation is far-reaching and extensive and certainly more comprehensive than that envisaged for, say, joint consultative committees in Great Britain.

Moreover, the Works Constitution Act of 1972 made provision for the further strengthening of the powers of works councils in three main ways. First of all, the organizational base of the councils was extended, especially in large companies, by an increase in the number of seats, the creation of more posts releasing councillors from normal duties, the facilitation of union involvement in elections and, above all, the establishment of obligatory central works councils in companies with more than one plant. Second, the influence of works councils over management was substantially enhanced. As Streeck (1984: 400) has observed:

> As far as the substantive rights of works councils in relation to the employer are concerned, the Act entitled works councils to co-determination of all matters relating to *working time* unless regulated by law or industrial agreement. Moreover, it extended co-determination to the setting of *piece rates* and the *design of workplaces* and the *work environment*, and it made it obligatory for an employer to ask the works council in advance for its assent on 'any *engagement, grading, regrading* and *transfer*' of employees. Works councils were given a veto on a number of grounds laid down in the Act. Furthermore, the Act granted works councils an unqualified right to be consulted on an employer's '*manpower planning*'. It obliged the employer to inform the works council on his (or her) plans 'in full and in good time', and it gave the works council a legal right to demand that *vacancies* 'are *notified for internal competition* within the establishment before they are filled'.

And third, the 1972 Act forged stronger links between trade unions and work councils, notably by removing all the legal obstacles that had prevented works councillors taking on union duties, by allowing councillors a right to attend union courses on full pay at the employer's expense and, not least, by extending the rights of *full-time* union officials to take part in works council meetings (Adams and Rummel, 1977; Kennedy, 1978; Streeck, 1984).

The upshot is that there are now close ties between trade unions and works councils. And, as Streeck (1984: 405) has further noted, 'more than ever, industrial unions outside coal and steel use the works council system as the institutional framework and the major source of support for their activities at the workplace and in the enterprise.' Indeed, works councils have increasingly become *de facto* union bodies, with the central works councils even more union-dominated than in the plants and with the facilities available to works councils frequently *exceeding* the legal minimum. In short, the evolution of the works councils in West Germany has latterly been concordant with the underlying structure of power in the industrial relations system, with the legislature paradoxically increasingly involved in fusing the so-called corporatist and syndicalist approaches to industrial democracy itself.

## Co-determination and other 'worker director' schemes

The background and the day-to-day operation of workers' participation in industry organized around works councils and allied machinery thus inevitably bear the stamp of the latent power and values of the main parties concerned. This argument will now be pursued further as we turn to participation at 'board' level where from time to time there has been experimentation on the part of governments. At the outset, however, it must be made clear that debates on this theme have usually been confined to predominantly capitalist economies (the issue of self-management being more apposite under socialist regimes) and that the situation has been confused as a result of the nature of company and corporation law in this respect.

Of course, as Fogarty (1972: 9) has pointed out, participation at board level can take on a number of guises, the following being the most usual: workers' participation in the control of enterprise *without* workers' ownership; workers' ownership of share capital *without* workers' control of enterprises; workers' ownership of share capital and workers' control of enterprise; and workers' ownership of share capital *as a basis* for control over enterprises. And yet, however envisaged, participation at this level gives rise to uncertainties on the issue of accountability, for, in the absence of any special changes in company law, the prime function of the board will remain the protection of shareholders' and creditors' interests (in practice those of private and institutional owners of capital), so that any worker participating at this level must *de jure* take on a role indistinguishable from any other manager or company director. To be sure, a rather different situation may obtain *de facto*, since, in the nature of things, worker directors may well seek to pursue policies which accord more with employee than with shareholder interests, and although worker directors may appear to waver on this matter with the passage of time, they would initially be expected to perceive their functions in a way which deviates from the formal legal situation. Nevertheless, it would seem appropriate for modifications to be made in company law which would relieve the confusion of workers who participate in decisions at board level under current arrangements. Of great value here, too, would be the introduction of new accounting methods based not on profit and loss but on net value added (Fogarty, 1972: 3):

> which is as valid as the present system for ensuring that a company shall maintain its financial stability and avoid the wasteful use of resources, but has the advantage of taking such items as pay or contributions to community services out of the category of costs and expressing them like profit, as shares in the net proceeds of the enterprise.

But whatever the nature of the ultimate solution to the dilemmas inherent in the present formulation of company law and accounting methods in this respect, other fundamental questions remain which are more central to our main themes and it is to these that we now turn.

Interest in co-determination and other worker-director schemes has been aroused especially, of course, by the experiments in West Germany which (together with the Dutch system) have supplied the main European model for legislation to this end. It is therefore helpful at this point to look in some detail at the German experience, paying particular attention to co-determination laws since the Second World War but bearing in mind the important precedent of the 1920 Works Council Act which sanctioned the election of one (or sometimes two) council member(s) to the controlling board of the enterprise (Guillebaud, 1928: 18–19).

During the period immediately after the Second World War, the workers and their trade unions in Germany were without doubt in a very strong position. A great many German managers had been openly discredited for the part they had played during the Nazi era and the principal industrial and commercial capitalists were similarly disgraced because it was appreciated that Hitler could not have come to power without their aid. In many districts, too, workers had on their own initiatives begun to rebuild the economy and had resumed the practice of electing their own works councils. Again, the power of the employers was further circum-scribed by the controls of the occupying allied forces, by the inten-tion to reduce the high concentration of the heavy sector of German industry and by the promise (which was unfulfilled) that previous owners would not be able to regain control of their firms. In short, a power vacuum was created in Germany at this time which was, to say the least, conducive to fresh thinking about the principles and practice of industrial organization in which the question of workers' participation in management loomed large (Spiro, 1958).

But circumstances as propitious as these could have been fore-gone had it not been for certain general ideological and political developments which were unique to West Germany in this period. Indeed, interest in co-determination was strengthened by three philosophical currents of a democratic socialist, religious and liber-tarian variety. The foremost was championed by many members of the Social Democratic Party (SPD) who, as a consequence, sought as a point of principle, to ensure parity for labour in all economic and political bodies (Spiro, 1958: 31). Then again, followers of Roman Catholicism, who were the best organized and most articulate of the Christian groupings which had come together in the Christian Democratic Union (CDU), had strong traditional interest in self-governing bodies and were to be important exponents of co-determination legislation. And finally, there was a measure of support for this development from a number of libertarian reformers among managerial ranks (Hartmann, 1970).

Simultaneously, the ongoing evolution in political institutions, itself in part a reflection of the thinking of the time, contributed further to the already favourable climate. Thus, in both the German Federation of Labour (DGB) and the SPD, co-determination and co-management were a useful rallying cry to accommodate poten-tial dissidents. Similarly, since both leading political parties (the CDU and SPD) were committed to reformist programmes in industry, it was clear that whichever party ultimately came to power, it would inevitably seek legislation with which to promote formal participatory rights for employees at the board level of the enterprise (Shuchman, 1957). For most of the post-war period in West Germany, then, it has been compulsory for workers to be represented on supervisory boards, but the legislation here is complex and its effects by no means uniform throughout West German industry. Thus, until the passage of the 1976 Act, in the coal and iron and steel industries, 50 per cent of the members of supervisory boards were comprised of workers' representatives, while in the rest of West German industry the proportion was of the order of only one in three. Again, while in the aforementioned primary and manufacturing industries, the labour director of the managerial board of the enterprise was also, in essence, a workers' representative, this 'privilege' did not extend on the whole to employees in other sectors of industry (Kennedy, 1978).

Following the Second World War, the first step in the direction of co-determination was taken in 1947 within the confines of a group of steel companies in the Ruhr. These firms were to some extent prompted along this path by the British occupation authorities who were aiming to deconcentrate heavy industry in the area but, in any event, questions of power and its exercise were high on the agenda both in the drafting of the scheme and in its actual operation. As one commentator has argued (Spiro, 1958: 5):

> Political considerations, involving both hindsight and foresight, dominated the birth of the scheme, regardless of whether labour sired it on management, or the other way round. The newly unified German Trade Union Federation consciously made co-determination the main plank in its platform because this seemed the best means for unifying the politically diverse elements among its membership. The legislation which confirmed the procedures then existing in the steel industry and extended them to the iron and coal industries, and the later legislation about wider forms of co-determination for the rest of the economy, and for public services – all this legislation was supported or opposed by people mainly on the basis of their political alignments.

The year 1951 saw the passing of the most notable piece of legislation on co-determination; this applied only to companies engaged in the production of iron and steel and the mining of coal and iron ore, and it was the offspring of a major power struggle. At the time the employers were willing to concede co-determination, but only at plant level on questions of a personnel and social nature, and they objected, furthermore, to giving parity of representation to workers on the supervisory board. In response, the DGB, who wanted equal controlling powers of workers' representatives, organized a referendum among the metal workers, 96 per cent of whom voted for the proposed strike action (Shuchman, 1957: 36). This threat of action alone was to prove successful enough, however, and the first co-determination law (to be supplemented in 1956) was thus inscribed on the Statute Book. But with the CDU in control at the political level, and with the unions becoming progressively less strong and militant in the industrial sphere, the Law on the Constitution of the Enterprise (or Works Constitution Law) of 1952, which made provision for the rest of West German industry, was much less generous to the workers' side: as we have previously mentioned, employees were entitled here to only one-third of the representatives of supervisory boards, and these were nominated by the employers rather than by the trade unions (Shuchman, 1957: Chapter 10).

Legal action in this respect in West Germany has of course been facilitated by the 'double-decker' structure of authority within undertakings. Under this arrangement, there is a clear division between the supervisory board (*Aufsichtsrat*), which consists of shareholders and employee representatives, and the managing board (*Vorstand*), usually made up of commercial, technical and labour directors. This effectively distinguishes, too, between policy and executive organs within the firm. In the coal and iron and steel industries, moreover, the labour director is selected on the basis of nominations made by the metal or mine workers' unions which are then submitted to the works council and supervisory board of the company concerned. Indeed, in some respects, the labour director is, from the employees' point of view, a far more important consequence of co-determination legislation than the worker directors on the supervisory boards (Hartmann, 1970). After all, he or she has administrative responsibility for a whole range of personnel and social policies including recruitment, hiring and firing, employee transfers, education of managerial personnel on human relations practices, pension and insurance funds, wages and salaries, and so on. And although, of course, commercial and technical matters are outside his or her jurisdiction, he or she clearly has ultimate control over many areas of particular interest to shop-floor workers.

Moreover, joint regulation in West Germany received a further fillip when the provisions of the Co-determination Act of 1976 ultimately came to fruition in 1978. Under this legislation (which applies only to companies with 2,000 or more employees), the representation of employees outside the coal and iron and steel industries was increased to parity, but with the proviso that one of the labour representatives had to come from middle management. In addition, the unions were denied the right to appoint labour representatives on to the supervisory boards directly (though some seats were set aside for the representatives of trade unions). Furthermore, although there was provision for a 'labour director' on the management board, appointment was on the same basis as for the rest of the management team (IDE, 1981a; Streeck, 1984: 401–2).

To understand the complex compromise nature of this legislation, the different ideological positions of the interested parties and the intense (and frequently bitter) conflicts at both political and industrial relations systems levels are basic. Indeed, it took about two and a half years until supervisory boards could be 'properly formed and could begin to take up their functions' (Streeck, 1984: 402). There was thus a protracted struggle between the different groups in the ruling SPD-Free Democratic Party (FDP) coalition of the period (the latter opposed what they regarded as excessive union influence on the structure) and between the SPD and the unions (the latter wanting a union-based system). But it was, above all, the reactions of the employers which were the most far-reaching in their industrial relations implications. Some employers thus changed the legal status of their enterprises to ensure that they were outside the provisions of the Act (or split their companies up into smaller, formally separate, firms, or transferred some of their activities to foreign subsidiaries). And, in particular, as Streeck (1984: 402) has documented, 'immediately after the Codetermination Act of 1976 had passed into law, the Federal Association of Employers' Associations (BDA) and a number of major companies challenged its constitutionality in the Federal Constitutional Court.' Moreover, even after the employers' claim had been dismissed, the BDA advised companies to apply the new law as restrictively as possible. This included the establishment of 'quorums for supervisory board decisions that favoured the representatives of the shareholders', the exclusion of 'external labour representatives from supervisory board committees' and the limitation of 'the decision-making powers of supervisory boards in favour of supervisory board committees, the management board and the assembly of stockholders' (Streeck, 1984: 403). However, such moves were followed by extensive litigation, with the Court by and large upholding the position of the unions.

Indeed, given that the final version of the Act was adopted on the unanimous vote of the members of the Bundestag and that the subsequent rulings of the court have been to reinforce its effectiveness, it is likely that the new co-determination legislation will remain for some time on the statute book. But no better illustration could be given of the central tenets of this study that power and the conflicting values of the industrial relations parties are at the root of schemes for extending workers' participation in industry than the intensive and bitter struggles surrounding the passage of the latest enactments on co-determination in West Germany.

Yet the situation with respect to co-determination is somewhat specific to West Germany on account of the rather different role of the trade unions and the diverse institutional history of industrial relations in that country by comparison with, say, Scandinavia or Great Britain. Thus although the underlying power balances between the main industrial relations classes are of decisive importance in accounting for the overall levels of participation, the form of participation is undoubtedly mediated through the values of constituent organized groupings. For example, in 1973 both Norway and Sweden witnessed the enactment of comprehensive legislation on co-determination, but previous researches in both countries have pointed to the fundamental impact of trade unions on the actual operation of any given experiment. Hence, in Norway, despite the fact that worker directors have been authorized to take up positions on the boards of large-scale companies partly or wholly owned by the state for nearly thirty years, Emery and Thorsrud (1974) noted that restrictions were placed on board members by existing trade-union machinery and the consequent tendency for elements of negotiation to be ruled 'out of order' in board-level meetings themselves (see also Thorsrud, 1984).

By the same token, in Sweden a novel attempt to combine co-determination with established trade union practices was contained in the Joint Regulation in Working Life and the Public Employment Acts of 1977. Both pieces of legislation are based on the axioms of freedom of association and collective bargaining and the aforementioned Act in particular ushered in several major legal changes in the Swedish system of industrial relations. First, the principle whereby the employer alone was entitled to organize and assign work and could freely engage or dismiss workers was replaced by a statutory requirement that collective agreements must be concluded in these areas. Second, trade unions now have the priority right of interpretation in the event of disputes arising over such matters as a worker's obligation to perform specific tasks. Third, the position of the unions is also strengthened in areas not covered at present by collective agreements. And fourth, a trade union organization possessing a collective agreement is empowered to veto subcontracting or similar arrangements (Bouvin, 1977; Thorsrud, 1984).

The Scandinavian model of industrial relations, of course, used to mean stable and highly centralized industrial relations with few strikes, a pronounced concern for reform in the quality of working life and strong, usually Social Democratic, governments. Moreover, despite substantial changes in the 1980s, these background conditions were evident in the objectives of the representative systems which included: the sharing of power as a matter of justice, achieving employee influence on company policy and top management, facilitating societal democratization, enhancing a strategy for better resource utilization and attempting to strengthen the unions (Qvale, 1982; Thorsrud, 1984).

However, despite these ideals, the actual practice of co-determination in Scandinavia has been more modest in its accomplishments (see IDE, 1981b; Thorsrud, 1984). To be sure, board members themselves emphasize a number of benefits in co-determination, such as the 'right to be heard', a definite employee influence over managerial personnel policy, the restriction of the action of the board on unpopular measures (e.g. layoffs or closedowns) and the need for boards to take account of the interests of workers. But as Thorsrud (1984: 342) has emphasized:

> The *general conclusion* from the studies of employee
> representation in Norway is that no fundamental change has
> occurred in the functioning of the boards. For workers the most
> important effect has been an extra channel of information
> which unions could use to put political pressure on the board.
> The new supervisory boards are generally seen as unnecessary.
> Management judge them a waste of time. Decision-making has
> not been blocked or hampered, as expected by the members
> representing the owners.

Moreover, the problem of combining co-determination and collective bargaining in a unionized society also arose in Great Britain in the mid-1970s, when over half of the working population was in the fold of the trade union movement. Indeed, in Britain, interest in worker directors was stimulated by two major departures; first, the publication of the Bullock Committee proposals on industrial democracy; and second, a number of experiments in participation in specific nationalized industries or enterprises.

On its return to office in 1974, the Labour government was

committed by its manifesto to a programme of industrial relations reform which included the introduction of legislation on industrial democracy via a single channel of representation (i.e. through the medium of the trade unions). But given the series of major financial and industrial crises which beset the new administration, such legislation was placed low on the scale of parliamentary priorities. However, a private member's bill, sponsored by Mr Giles Radice, appeared to be heading for the statute book and hence, in order to defuse a difficult political situation, a committee of inquiry (under the chairmanship of Lord Bullock) was appointed to report on the most appropriate means of introducing industrial democracy based on the trade-union channel. Clearly, therefore, the genesis of the proposals of the Bullock Committee of Inquiry were structured by the realities of power in British industry and society and reflected the pre-eminence of the trade union movement during the period in question.

The committee itself reported early in 1977 but a seemingly unbridgeable division of opinion emerged between the academics and trade unionists who signed the majority report and the industrialists who favoured more limited co-determination proposals. Thus while the majority expressed a preference for a single-tier board structure, based on a $2X + Y$ formula, which would give shareholders and trade unionists equal representation together with a smaller 'Y' group of impartial members, the minority advocated a two-tier structure with employee representatives comprising one-third of the members of supervisory board of enterprises exclusive of banks and other financial institutions. To be sure, both groups considered that the proposals should cover only firms employing over 2,000 workpeople but there were again differences on the mechanics of the electoral processes. Thus the majority report envisaged a situation whereby all employees (whether trade unionists or otherwise) would initially vote on whether an industrial democracy programme should be established, but then, in the event of an affirmative decision, a Joint Representative Committee of the unions in the enterprise would decide upon the trade-union membership of the board by itself. In contrast, the minority expressed their opposition to non-unionists being disenfranchised in such a manner and hence proposed a lower-level employee participation council with all factory employees voting in the election of actual worker directors (Bullock Committee of Inquiry, 1977).

The publication of the Bullock Committee proposals was a signal for implacable opposition from all leading employers' associations and city organizations, however, and in the light of divisions of view amongst the trade unions and the accession to power of a Conservative administration in 1979 the legislation never came to fruition.

But we have also noted that in seeking to extend public ownership, governments can prepare a fertile ground for the growth of industrial democracy. And although, in the British context, traditionally, the main aim of nationalization on the industrial relations front has been to secure consultative and collective bargaining rights for employees, in the 1960s and 1970s this was extended to encompass more radical proposals for workers' participation at boardroom level. Thus, during the 1960s, a limited worker director scheme was established in the steel industry and, in the 1970s, not only was the National Enterprise Board charged with encouraging employee participation (and in British Leyland, for example, a major scheme was introduced), but also in the Coal Board there were once extensive discussions with the unions on the future of that industry and in the Post Office an experiment took place to establish comprehensive co-determination facilities along the lines of the Bullock Committee proposals.

None the less, research on the worker director programmes in the steel industry and in the Post Office amply demonstrate that the power relations between management and the workforce are of the utmost significance in shaping the actual operation of the individual experiments. Indeed, in the steel case, the co-determination proposals were timid because: first, the boards had only advisory functions; second, worker directors were to act in a personal capacity; and third, although nominated by the trade unions, the corporation ratified the appointments. To be sure, the scheme was ultimately modified to strengthen the trade-union links of the worker directors, but management tended to use the proposals as a means of overcoming resistance of the workforce to a major restructuring of the industry. And, without the backing of shop-floor power, 'no scheme for participation can hope for more than a marginal impact upon the life chances of workers' (Brannen *et al.*, 1976: 209; see also Brannen, 1983a, 1983b).

In the Post Office case, the co-determination structure was more directly linked with the trade unions than in the steel industry. As we have noted, this worker director scheme was based on a Bullock-style 2X + Y formula, and, as a consequence, the union nominees 'had a clearly structured role as representatives of worker and union interests'. Moreover, this situation led them 'to challenge management on many issues'. And, again, their links with well-organized unions meant that they had active constituencies (Batstone, Ferner and Terry, 1983: 87). Nevertheless, in practice this influence was counterbalanced by the strategies of management and the divisions amongst the worker directors themselves. In particular, management curtailed the influence of the worker directors by holding informal meetings, keeping issues away from the board, inhibiting the floating of ideas and challenging the contributions of the union nominees (Batstone, Ferner and Terry, 1983). Finally, in the harsher economic and political climate of the 1980s, the whole scheme was ultimately abandoned.

## Self-management and workers' councils

No study of workers' participation and control would, of course, be complete without some reference to self-management and, above all, to the Yugoslav system, for, although this is not a unique experiment in that workers' councils have been established administratively at various times in a number of other nations (and notably Poland, Czechoslovakia and Algeria), it clearly supplies us with a general model from which certain conclusions about the operation of self-management systems may be drawn. Furthermore, since a great many investigations have now been carried out within Yugoslav factories, we have far more systematic information on the day-to-day workings of the scheme upon which to rely than is readily available for the other countries. But in order to illustrate the principal themes of the present study, it is pertinent to review the relevant material on the self-management system under three main headings: first, the background conditions; second, the principal legislation on the scheme itself; and third, its actual operation at enterprise level.

In contrast with co-determination, self-management is not founded on the premise of the potential unity of different class interests but upon the prior abolition of economic classes by means of the expropriation of individual capital holdings. In Yugoslavia, this move followed the Second World War when, although the system of agriculture was left in private hands, all existing industries were taken into public ownership. To begin with, during the so-called administrative period, the authorities set out to organize their economy on the Soviet model and, with this aim in view, they drew up a massive central plan which was designed to achieve rapid economic development via a system of production targets for individual enterprises. Indeed, targets for between 16,000 and 20,000 commodities were set out in minute detail (Riddell, 1968).

The ensuing clash with Soviet leaders precipitated a shift in Yugoslav thinking on these matters, and in the resulting ideological controversy on the future of socialism, interest revolved around the classical writings of Marx and Lenin on the ultimate 'withering away of the state' and this in turn led to intense criticism of state-dominated, bureaucratic forms of socialism. Again, Yugoslavia was in fact expelled from the Cominform in 1948 and then faced an economic blockade from Eastern European countries – two further circumstances which were to stimulate new ideas about the principles of economic administration.

Nevertheless, if the prior abolition of private capital provided a necessary condition for the creation of a thoroughgoing self-management system and if this was precipitated by the emergence of fresh ideologies brought on by the break with Russia, there were yet other aspects of Yugoslav culture which, as Riddell has argued, tended to militate against 'the permanent establishment of a centralized state on the Soviet model' (Riddell, 1968: 51). Thus, to begin with, although the country had been overrun by Axis forces, the partisans had succeeded in regaining parts of this terri-tory without the immediate assistance of the Red Army and, in liberated areas, where autonomous administrative units were in operation, the idea of self-management became by no means foreign to ordinary people. Second, many of the communist leaders in Yugoslavia had become acquainted with anarcho-syndicalist ideas while fighting with Republican forces in the Spanish Civil War and this experience, too, kindled an ideology in which self-government was a principal component. And finally, since Yugo-slavia was, in any event, made up of a number of contrasting and heterogeneous regions, it was hardly conceivable that such diversity could be easily united under the aegis of a centralized nation state. This unique cultural configuration was thus an ideal framework for the development of ideologies in which democratic and socialist ideals were given approximately equal weight.

Now, in statutory terms, the Law on the Management of State Economic Enterprises, passed in 1950, laid the foundations for the present system of administration in Yugoslav factories. In detail, the principal organs established by the Act were: first, the workers' council; second, the management board; and third, the enterprise director. In each workplace, a workers' council elected by the entire labour force was to be given overall responsibility for policy and entrusted with the legal obligation to determine the general economic activity of the works. The council itself would be of a range of between fifteen and 120 members, according to the size of establishment, and it in turn elected its own executive committee (the management board) to carry out policy and to settle a number of personnel and economic matters. Finally, the director was to be charged with responsibility for day-to-day administration of policies which stemmed from the decisions of the workers' council. Moreover, his or her own appointment and its termination was also to depend on the initiatives of the workers' councillors, albeit with the sanction of the commune people's committee (the decentralized political wing brought into being by the Yugoslav authorities) (ILO, 1962; Sturmthal, 1964).

To be sure, since its inception, this Act has been supplemented and revised on many occasions and the formal character of Yugoslav enterprises has been modified accordingly. But two changes of particular note have accompanied these legal changes, namely, direct participation has come to the fore as a supplement to the representative system and, at the same time, even greater autonomy is now being exercised in individual plants than was conceded by the initial legislation. Thus, in an attempt to promote the ordinary workers' involvement in decision-making, workers' councils were extended to middle management levels and, in 1961, so-called 'economic units' were spawned in an effort to ensure greater freedom of decision on the shop floor. Enterprise autonomy has been encouraged, too, by later measures, not least by the legislation of 1969, which carefully avoided any detailed provision for the organization of management at factory level.

Moreover, the Yugoslavian authorities have sought to overcome the problems arising from the increasing power of senior management at the expense of the workers' councils by a further major restructuring aimed once again at involving the shop-floor worker far more in the processes of industrial decision-making. Thus the framework of self-management institutions was altered in a new constitution approved by the Federal Assembly in 1974, its principal aim being to redefine the enterprise as an Association of Labour each of which would be composed of a number of 'Basic Organizations of Associated Labour' or BOALs (Stephen, 1976–7; IDE, 1981a). These, in turn, were to be founded on groupings of workers seen to have similar interests and who contributed to the production of marketable output. Moreover, in an attempt to bring self-management to as low a level as possible, each BOAL was permitted to produce for the market *outside* its own 'enterprise', to elect its own workers' council and to subdivide its activities via a series of workers' meetings. Again, two further changes introduced by the constitution were the creation of workers' assemblies as the principal decision-making bodies of BOALs and the establishment of a special system of workers' control (including a commission of workers' control to supervise all self-management and administrative activities) (see IDE, 1981a: 230).

Any summary of the main characteristics of the councils' system in Yugoslavia, therefore, must of necessity recognize the pains which have been taken to distinguish between state and social ownership of production and should thence go on to describe the ideal-typical economic system there as follows. First, there is self-government in the sense that the process of management is formally based on democratic majority rule; second, a policy of income-sharing operates; third, the economy is decentralized and the deployment of resources depends on market mechanisms; fourth, employees have a right to use the assets of the enterprise but do not personally own the firms in which they work; and finally, there is 'freedom of employment' in the sense that there is no state direction of labour (Vanek, 1970: Chapter 1). And as Vanek (1970: 397) has also pointed out, although such principles are incompatible with control and management by capital, they need not be socialist either:

> In fact, the distinction between labor-managed and non-labor-managed is far more significant than the distinction between socialist and non-socialist. While the former involves a whole way of life bearing on every hour of a man's entire day, the latter, from an individual's point of view, may not mean much more than a different distribution of wealth and income.

But how successful, it may reasonably be asked, is the Yugoslav self-management system and to what extent are the legal provisions constrained by the day-to-day realities of decision-making power in industry? It is important first of all to present a balanced view of the gains and losses to Yugoslav workers of the self-management system. Moreover, to place its achievements in a comparative perspective, it is worth examining some of the central findings of the Industrial Democracy in Europe (IDE) Research Group (1979; 1981b) on the Yugoslav experience. To begin with, then, in terms of formal provisions for participation, what the group termed the representative peaked pattern (i.e. where representative bodies have greater *de jure* influence than any other group), was found to be specific to Yugoslavia. Furthermore, with respect to the actual distribution of influence, Yugoslavia was the principal exception to the general pattern of top management control. Indeed, whereas in most countries the influence of workers and representative bodies was found to decrease and that of top management to increase as one moves from short-term to long-term decisions, this pattern did not apply in the case of Yugoslavia. And again, as far as involvement of workers and representative bodies was concerned, the Yugoslav experience was found to be untypical of Europe as a whole. As the IDE (1979: 289) researchers recorded:

> In Yugoslavia, workers' involvement in short term decisions is only slightly higher than in some other countries (and lower than Denmark), but their involvement in medium and long term decisions is very much higher than in any other country. These characteristics suggest that while the technical division of labour is the most important factor determining the involvement of workers in short term decisions, institutional legislation prevails in determining their involvement in medium and long term decisions.

But there are a number of further important consequences for industrial relations of the operation of the Yugoslavian self-management system. To begin with, although major regional inequalities of income remain in Yugoslavia, social-class variations in material standards of living are typically less by comparison with those current in the West and, indeed, in predominantly capitalist societies as a whole. This, too, is of particular significance in a market economy because the 'distortion-effect' of really large disparities of income and wealth on production priorities are correspondingly reduced because a sizeable percentage of firms are not engaged solely in producing for consumption by the rich. Again, while there is good reason to believe that, on technical and commercial questions, the views of workers and their representatives have been of only limited consequence, over a range of personnel and social issues (including hiring and firing, working conditions, fringe benefits and even wages) their influence has been noticeably more pronounced. And, above all, since the remuneration of all employees is open to discussion and debate, the disparity of income between higher managerial staff on the one hand and unskilled labourers on the other is seldom of an order of more than approximately three or four to one. In addition, the practice of rotation of membership has given large numbers of workers the opportunity to experience office-holding on workers' council and management boards: indeed, between 1950 and the early 1960s, well over a million people served in these capacities. Finally, although women and semi-skilled workers have had disproportionately unfavourable treatment in this respect, the chances for widespread participation are clearly extensive and appear especially so by comparison with those available to workers in any other West European country (see Pateman, 1970; Rus, 1984).

On the debit side, however, there is no doubt that the influence of both trade unions and strike activity have both appreciably expanded in the 1970s and 1980s. Over 90 per cent of Yugoslavia's industrial workforce is unionized and the trade unions not only conclude social compacts with governments, but also have strong 'middle' range geographical associations. Moreover, in the enterprise, they have acquired the functions of proposing candidates for all self-management and administrative organs, safeguarding the new system of workers' control, and criticism and initiatives with respect to self-management agreements (IDE, 1981a; Zukin, 1981; Wilczynski, 1983). Again, so far as industrial conflict is concerned, the first known strikes in Yugoslavia under socialism took place in 1958, a further 1,000 work stoppages were recorded up to 1969, and from 1973, more than 200 occurred in Slovenia alone (Wilczynski, 1983; see also Rus, 1984). There is no doubt, then, that self-management has not ensured that workers will not seek further means of representation outside the enterprise or that they will forego strike action completely.

But if we turn finally to assess the prospects for self-management in socialist societies generally, there is no doubt that, in power terms, the role of the state and the degree of central regulation of the economy by government are the decisive factors affecting the extent of any evolution towards industrial democracy. As Wilczynski (1983) has observed, there are at least four main types of state-industry relations in the economically advanced socialist countries: (1) the Stalinist command model of the Soviet Union between 1928 and 1962; (2) reformed, centralized directive planning (as in the German Democratic Republic and the USSR at present); (3) moderately revisionist planned socialism (Bulgaria, Czechoslovakia); and (4) market socialism (Hungary, Yugoslavia). And it is almost invariably the case that moves towards market socialism tend to be consistent with a growing power of representative bodies of workers (as well as of management) and that, conversely, it is the more centrally regulated economies that have highly integrative, formal participatory structures but hardly any genuine workers' self-management. To be sure, throughout Eastern Europe legislation on industrial democracy was implemented in the 1970s but the provisions varied substantially in type and were closely connected with the role of the state in the industrial relations system as a whole. In Romania, for example, the 'collective management' and workers' councils machinery established by legislation in 1968, 1971, 1973 and 1978 was more ambitious than the proposals for expanding the powers of plant or factory committees in Bulgaria, the German Democratic Republic and the USSR.

The same general argument may be applied to the experiences of Third World socialist countries. Typically, in many of these emergent nations, the state has been active in fostering industrial democracy (this is certainly the case, for instance, in Algeria and Guyana). Moreover, as the recent Chinese experience reveals, the moves towards market socialism have been accompanied by an extensive role given to so-called workers' congresses. Currently these exist in 95 per cent of the big and medium-sized enterprises with formal powers that include the discussion, examination and initiation of production targets and plans, the formulation and administration of enterprise policies on labour protection and welfare, and a new capacity to elect factory management (Ng, 1984). In short, amongst developed and developing socialist countries, power and values remain basic to understanding the development and practical operation of industrial democracy but it is the role of the state (as employer and overall economic planner), rather than factory-level management, the workers themselves or the trade unions, that is crucial to the ultimate shape of the institutional machinery that actually unfolds.

# 7 Conclusions and prospects

In introducing this volume we declared our intention to review the material pertaining to a highly interesting and significant subject in a somewhat novel light. With this end in view, we directed our attention both to our explanatory analysis of workers' participation and control and to the fundamental question of the exercise of power in industry and in society at large. It is now opportune to restate those conclusions to which we attach special significance and to assess the implications of our findings for the issues of power and participation.

It has been our main contention that workers' participation in decision-making may be best understood as one index of the exercise of power in industrial life. But to explain its genesis and, indeed, to account for the success or otherwise of the actual operation of any arrangement designed for this purpose, it is essential to examine those components of industrial life which underpin variations in the power of the main social classes, parties and groups and which encourage, too, the formation of values specific to industrial participation. In the first place, then, we elucidated those forces (economic, technological and governmental – i.e. political) which seemed to be especially salient to the underlying power of the industrial relations parties. And, in the second, we emphasized those values which made intelligible the otherwise erratic and inconsistent variations in types of participation arising from roughly similar balances of power. But equally central to our own understanding of the operation of workers' participation and control in industry was the realization that values favourable to these developments could not, in isolation, ensure the lasting success of any of the schemes under consideration. Furthermore, such values were not in our view confined to individual responses to specific social situations but had other origins as well. Indeed, many emanated from more comprehensive ideologies or from political actions, while others sprang from the practice of participation and from a rise in the level of power among workers themselves.

The validity of these propositions was established by an examination of a rich and interesting array of practices and programmes for extending workers' participation and control of decision-making processes. Moreover, this analysis was facilitated by a classification which replaced 'rule of thumb' categories by ones which differentiated between the initiators of the programmes in question.

Armed with this framework, we began by examining the variegated forms of participation stemming from managerial initiatives. Here we observed that, on balance, certain changes in managerial ideologies had worked against the expansion of participation, for although traditional-ownership sentiments had been progressively abandoned they had been replaced by the idea that management has an expertise indispensable to the efficient organization of industry. This indeed has now become the main source of legitimacy of managerial authority. Furthermore, such a view, which is encompassed in the managerialist thesis and finds more specific expression in the assertion that modern managers are highly professional, technically proficient and largely non-propertied, clearly represents a fundamental obstacle to any fully-fledged system of workers' participation and control. Nevertheless, it has been in the interests of many efficiency-conscious employers to relinquish some of their decision-making prerogatives (especially where these are restricted to those of foremen and other lower-managerial personnel) in return for higher output and productivity, acceptance of change, flexible working arrangements and relatively conflict-free industrial relations. Moreover, in our view – and despite the far from favourable political and economic circumstances of the 1980s – such developments are almost certain to expand in the years ahead, partly because of the competitive advantages to be gained by introducing experiments of this nature, but also because, particularly in independent primary sectors of the labour market, employees themselves are still likely to demand greater control over decision-making processes at shop-floor level. And, indeed, there is no question that in the changed patterns of power relationships over the past few years, management has proved to be a principal initiator of participatory programmes that have included joint consultation, quality circles and a major extension of profit-sharing and employee shareholding.

The discussion was given new direction at this juncture as we examined a wide range of participation and control practices which have emerged from the ranks of working people. These again varied greatly in scope from limited workgroup practices to those more ambitious programmes in which workers' control was a means for transforming an entire social order. But, somewhat remarkably, and despite the very diverse origins and ideals which precipitated them, the success or otherwise of these practices could be seen to depend in great measure on the same basic forces of latent power and values among the parties concerned. Moreover, although workers' initiatives declined somewhat in the 1980s (certainly this was so by comparison with the idealism and imagination of the experiments in the late 1960s and 1970s), this did not apply universally for the producer co-operative movement developed counter-cyclically in response to the problems engendered by the economic recession itself.

We then examined the role of the trade-union officer and noted that only a narrow band of participation practices had as a rule attracted unreserved enthusiasm from this source. To be sure, whenever these have been rooted in the union structure, officials have supported them, but those initiatives of managements and workers which have failed to relate to union organization have met with some suspicion. Naturally, of course, all trade-union officials have not reacted in this way, for those with a strong personal commitment to socialist and democratic ideologies and those who are subject to democratic pressures in the internal organization of their union have usually been more positive in this respect. But typically union officers have sought to extend workers' influence through collective bargaining and, in the UK, once the Bullock era was eclipsed by a change of government and by a worsening economic climate, concerted pressure for reform from the TUC receded.

Finally, in Chapter 6 we turned to an examination of the function of governments and political parties in this regard. Here we examined the contribution which could be made by legislation in this field. And although we noted that statutory provisions can themselves be understood as specific responses to contemporary conditions and that their success may be seen ultimately to hinge on those key elements which have been identified in this study, at the same time the legislative route to participation is undoubtedly fundamental. Indeed, international researches suggest that, alongside trade union action, it is the most effective means of extending workers' influence and involvement in decision-making.

From a specialist viewpoint, then, we have touched on many themes which are currently important in industrial sociology and industrial relations. We hope that our discussions on power will have added a certain measure of conceptual clarity to the arguments here and that we have provided a framework by means of which to make intelligible a number of otherwise disparate themes, studies and experiments. Again, on the question of industrial democracy, our approach differs from that of those who, in criticizing the untenable position that workers cannot participate in management, in their turn have advanced somewhat Utopian opinions about the genesis of effective participation, and in so doing have failed to recognize that it is precisely by augmenting the latent and oppositional power of workers (and stimulating values conducive to experiments of this kind) that progress can be made towards the establishment of workers' participation in decision-making at every level.

Moreover, in terms of the debates on long-term trends in industrial democracy and, in particular, whether these have a linear and evolutionary or a cyclical character, our position is again somewhat distinctive. To begin with, then, the case for an evolutionary approach seems to us to be best supported at the level of institutions for, in most cases, even in the relatively unfavourable climate of the 1980s, legislative-backed bodies have typically remained intact. The term favourable conjunctures is preferred to the notion of cycles (for these seem to imply a too rhythmic sequence of change), but in terms of actual workers' influence and involvement there is in our view force in this alternative interpretation of the historical record in a number of key respects. Certainly this pattern applies to most workers' initiatives, and particularly to those on-the-job controls which are vulnerable to managerial counter-offensives during periods of economic downturn. On the other hand, the favourable conjunctures case is not supported entirely even amongst the workers' initiatives, for some types of development (and notably, as we have seen, the producer-co-operative movement) appear to emerge *counter-cyclically*.

Furthermore – and of far-reaching importance so far as our own position is concerned – we have noted that the appreciable segmentation of work activities in the 1970s and 1980s made the debates on workers' participation far more complex than had earlier been the case. For there is no question that in expanding enterprises, where a skilled or knowledge-based labour remained scarce, management continued to mount a series of human resourcing programmes which included a substantial degree of employee participation. By contrast, in highly competitive labour markets, and, above all, in those firms which have borne the main brunt of the recession, the underlying conjuncture of circumstances was indeed unfavourable for employee participation. And, in these contexts, it was scarcely surprising that the workers' enthusiasm for developing new initiatives appreciably declined and, in many cases, managements sought to end those union and workgroup controls which had impeded their capacity to organize the production processes in ways which maximized efficiency (measured in terms of profitability). Moreover, in enterprises between these two extremes, managements found it possible to extend a number of practices (notably joint consultation and profit-sharing). In short, in the light of the experiences of the 1980s, it is in our view essential to develop a complex and sophisticated theoretical position to understand the main developments and, without undue equivocation, to advance a case which does not rely exclusively on a simplistic evolutionary or cyclical interpretation of long-term trends and movements.

But throughout this study we have also attempted to satisfy the interests of the general reader, and to this end it would seem reasonable here to assess some of the prospects ahead: first, by an estimate of the probable success of those schemes which are being suggested at present; second, by an analysis of those changes which might be efficacious in this respect; and finally, by relating these to the social and political climate of our time.

In contemporary political debates five classes of industrial democracy are frequently advocated: (1) producer or worker co-operatives; (2) the extension of collective bargaining; (3) board-level representation either based on works councils or trade unions; (4) shop-floor level forms of participation; and (5) profit-sharing and share ownership. In the light of the evidence presented above, can these proposals be expected to meet with any major success?

A concern for refashioning the social structure of industry upon the basis of worker or producer co-operatives is undoubtedly an imaginative proposition. There is little doubt, too, that under such conditions a cohesive and harmonious work environment would be facilitated and that flexibility, higher productivity and output would be additional accompaniments. Moreover, in political terms, producer co-operatives appear as an attractive alternative to the traditional capitalist enterprise with its endemic class antagonisms and to the state-run corporation with its seemingly intractable problems of bureaucracy. Again, other champions of co-operatives, such as Mr Peter Jay (1977), have noted a further potential economic advantage of transcending the difficulty of combining full employment with collective bargaining without intolerable inflationary pressures.

But workable schemes for co-operative manufacture depend upon a comprehensive programme of support. Indeed, there is a real danger that the foundering of a few isolated experiments will bring the whole institution into discredit, and this is unnecessary since the problems encountered by producer co-operatives are increasingly understood. Indeed, there are four main pitfalls: (1) the absence of an obvious power base to carry these enterprises through difficult economic periods; (2) the lack of a competent management; (3) the major problem of obtaining capital to finance new ventures; and (4) the increasing social tensions which arise when these operations increase in scale.

To achieve feasibility, then, a fundamental and far-reaching decentralist campaign would be required involving the participation of both government and the members of existing, successful producer co-operatives. To be sure, in Great Britain, legislative provisions have encouraged the expansion of co-operative manufacture, governments have continued to offer their assistance to specific co-operatives and the Manpower Services Commission and other bodies have looked with favour on co-operative work projects. Again, members of the Industrial Common Ownership Movement (in which the Scott Bader commonwealth is a key participant) have assisted fellow co-operatives over organizational problems, while an offshoot, Industrial Common Ownership Finance, has received small-scale assistance from government. But despite the worthiness of these endeavours, they still only scratch the surface of the problem. By way of contrast, a fully-fledged movement would enable managerial skills and talent to be effectively transmitted and pooled, it would facilitate a comprehensive banking structure (with or without workers' contributions), and it would permit a network of interlinked co-operatives (as opposed to a few concentrated combines) that would help to avoid the deleterious social consequences of excessive scale of enterprise. Similarly, the problems of surviving in a market economy could at least be partially resolved by backing successful ventures, ideas and projects and transferring part of their development to those co-operatives where demand for a particular product was dwindling. But, in the absence of economic collapse, and without a comprehensive programme such as we have just described, the dice will continue to be loaded against co-operative manufacturing and hence ensure that it remains a peripheral feature on the industrial landscape.

As a consequence, in any highly unionized society, there are many who regard the optimum method of extending the influence of worker representatives over decision-making processes in the firm as being through the expansion of collective bargaining. After all, this is so clearly consistent with the existing structure of power and values at enterprise and industry levels. But, on the debit side, the economic and social problems inherent in the nature of collective bargaining are undoubtedly severe. After all, the individual worker (as distinct from his or her trade union representative) frequently exerts little influence over collective bargaining agreements, and, in contrast with worker co-operatives, the formulation of ever more extensive regulations covering a host of workplace practices almost invariably results in deleterious consequences for industrial efficiency and the related willingness to work flexibly and intelligently in the light of specific problems arising in the work environment itself. In short, for better or for worse, the extension of collective bargaining encourages further an already pervasive zero-sum power consciousness (where the gains of one party or group are seen as inescapably involving losses for another), rather than a non-zero-sum conception of facilitating conditions, in which, during the course of productive activity, all members of the enterprise are able to develop to the full their capacities of sensibility and intellect in an unconstrained association with their colleagues.

Turning, then, more specifically to board-level representation, this will almost certainly become a universal characteristic of West European industry in the forthcoming years, but its success or otherwise will still turn as much upon the latent power of constituent parties to industry as upon the legal niceties of any EEC provisions themselves. However, without a measure of compulsion in this field it is almost certain that managerial hostility to participation at this level will impede other than piecemeal moves in this direction. Equally, in highly unionized countries, without the support of unions, representatives on boards of directors will tend to be constrained and ineffective. Interestingly, therefore, although in Great Britain the Bullock Committee proposals are currently not seriously debated, the strategy of basing board-level representation on a single channel of representation is clearly consistent with the grain of power in the wider society, and this could forestall a situation where, say, a structure based on works councils was boycotted by the unions concerned. By the same token, however, an openly hostile atmosphere between management and the workforce is unlikely to be abated by legislation of this type but rather, as in the Post Office experiment, would tend to result in an outcrop of informal managerial meetings designed to by-pass official procedures.

And yet, in both collective bargaining and board-level representation, the position of the ordinary worker would seem of limited consequence. However, there are signposts as disparate as the devolution of power in Yugoslavian enterprises and the job enrichment programmes of Sweden and the USA that lasting developments may be effected in shop-floor-level participation as well. After all, these experiments often involve only a slight adaptation in the formal structure of authority in the firm and, at present, they offer no serious challenge to existing collective bargaining machinery. Moreover, in a number of advanced new technology firms, in which high skills and knowledge are at a premium, direct forms of employee participation are not only being routinely introduced, but have high prospects of at least a limited success.

Recently, too, the debates on industrial democracy have been extended to encompass employee financial participation in the firms in which they are employed. Certainly the 1980s witnessed an appreciable expansion in profit-sharing and share ownership schemes in Britain that were encouraged not least by the provisions of the relevant Finance Acts. Moreover, in terms of the endorsement of schemes by ordinary workers, there has been a surprisingly high degree of success. And there is no question that, in the long march towards industrial democracy, the issue of participation in ownership (which the shareholding schemes inevitably raise) is as far-reaching in importance as involvement in decision-making processes themselves.

But any progress towards industrial democracy will also of course hinge greatly upon a series of economic, technical and political variables which decisively influence the balance of power in industry, and upon the constellation of values prevalent at any given place or time. More generally, therefore, it is our considered view that economic buoyancy and full-employment are still vital guardians of workers' rights to decision-making. More specifically, too, on the question of values, the contribution of legislation in the field of attitude formation and change could be considerable, and yet values could perhaps be more susceptible to other influences. If, for instance, humanistic doctrines were to gain general currency, the consequent elevation of the minimum conditions deemed tolerable at work could, in the most favourable circumstances, serve as an insistent pressure for the equalization of rights in the workplace. Furthermore, the maintenance and enhancement of a high material standard of living, being generally conducive to rising expectations for autonomy, creativity and involvement, could further stimulate this demand. And if participation were to be demonstrably effective, it would be received with enthusiasm from many additional quarters.

It is conceivable, too, that the sharing of industrial power will similarly induce a long-overdue change in the organization of industrial society and pave the way for a far more satisfying post-industrial culture than would seem to be feasible at present. Representation of the views of rank-and-file workers at local and higher levels of industry, coupled with public accountability from those in control of key sectors of the economy, could, indeed, herald a new era characterized by an upsurge of creative energy and positive thinking. Moreover, the contributions of ordinary people with detailed experience of the operation of industry could be an invaluable asset in overall economic planning; public funds could be made available for new projects employing advanced technologies and arising from local as well as national discussions about what should be produced within any given social order. And this would not only ensure a sound and expanding economy, but would also assist the solution of environmental and regional problems while offering new opportunities for experimenting in democratic methods of management and control. Furthermore, there is in work, as well as in wider social life, a fundamental tension between the forces of creativity and control which must be synthesized in favour of the former if some of the most intractable problems of conflict are to be resolved. The path towards a future which promises the realization of creative human potentialities may, therefore, be strewn with major obstacles but it remains a vital goal for those who, despite adverse economic and political conditions, have continued incessantly to strive to eradicate permanently antagonisms which have disfigured productive activities since the dawn of industry itself, and which should have no part whatsoever in those truly humanitarian societies which should be the birthright of all progressive, visionary and democratic people.

# Bibliography

Abbott, S. (1973), *Employee Participation*, Old Queen Street Paper, London, Conservative Research Department.

Abell, P. (1983), 'The viability of industrial producer co-operation', in C. Crouch and F. A. Heller (eds), *International Yearbook of Organizational Democracy*, vol. 1., Chichester, Wiley, pp. 73–103.

Abell, P. and Mahoney, N. (1981), *The Potential of Small Scale Producer Co-operatives in Developing Countries*, London, The International Co-operative Alliance.

Adams, H. C. (1891–2), 'An interpretation of the social movements of our time', *International Journal of Ethics*, 2, pp. 32–50.

Adams, R. J. and Rummel, C. H. (1977), 'Workers' participation in management in West Germany – impact of the worker, the enterprise and the trade union', *Industrial Relations Journal*, 8 (1), pp. 4–22.

Albrecht, S. L. (1981), 'Preconditions for increased workers' influence: factors in the Swedish case', *Sociology of Work and Occupations*, 8, pp. 252–72.

Almond, G. A. and Verba, S. (1965), *The Civic Culture*, Boston, Little Brown.

Andreski, S. L. (1954), *Military Organization and Society*, London, Routledge & Kegan Paul.

Armstrong, R. and Marchington, M. (1982), 'Shop stewards and employee involvement: a variety of views', *Employee Relations*, 4(4), pp. 3–48.

Bain, G. S. (1970), *The Growth of White-collar Unionism*, London, Oxford University Press.

Balfour, C. (ed.) (1973), *Participation in Industry*, London, Croom Helm.

Banks, J. A. (1970), *Marxist Sociology in Action*, London, Faber & Faber.

Barakat, H. (1969), 'Alienation: a process of encounter between utopia and reality', *British Journal of Sociology*, 20, pp. 1–10.

Bate, P. and Mangham, I. (1981), *Exploring Participation*, New York, Wiley.

Batstone, E. (1984), *Working Order*, Oxford, Blackwell.

Batstone, E., Boraston, I. and Frenkel, S. (1977), *Shop Stewards in Action*, Oxford, Blackwell.

Batstone, E., Ferner, A. and Terry, M. (1983), *Unions on the Board*, Oxford, Blackwell.

Bendix, R. (1956), *Work and Authority in Industry*, Berkeley and Los Angeles, University of California Press.

Bendix, R. (1964), *Nation-Building and Citizenship*, New York, Wiley.

Bendix, R. and Lipset, S. M. (ed) (1967), *Class, Status and Power*, London, Routledge & Kegan Paul.

Ben-Porat, A. (1980), 'Reply to Professor Shirom', *Industrial Relations*, 19, pp. 236–7.

Benson, J. (1982), 'Worker involvement: an analysis of the SECV working parties – a reply', *Journal of Industrial Relations*, 24, pp. 583–8.

Bernstein, B. (1971), *Class, Codes and Control*, London, Routledge & Kegan Paul.

Bevan, A. (1952), *In Place of Fear*, London, Heinemann.

Beynon, H. and Blackburn, R. M. (1972), *Perceptions of Work*, Cambridge, Cambridge University Press.

Bierstedt, R. (1950), 'An analysis of social power', *American Sociological Review*, 15, pp. 730–8.

*BIM Management News* (1985), 'Minister presents participation awards to top companies', February, p. 3.

Blackburn, R. K. and Cockburn, A. (1967), *The Incompatibles*, Harmondsworth, Penguin.

Blackler, F. H. M. and Brown, C. A. (1980), *Whatever Happened to Shell's New Philosophy of Management?*, Aldershot, Saxon House.

Blauner, R. (1964), *Alienation and Freedom*, Chicago, University of Chicago Press.

Blum, F. H. (1968), *Work and Community*, London, Routledge & Kegan Paul.

Blumberg, P. (1968), *Industrial Democracy: The Sociology of Participation*, London, Constable.

Boehmer, H. von (1977), 'The new co-determination act 1976 in West Germany', *Personnel Management*, 9, pp. 42–6.

Bottomore, T. B. (1964), *Elites and Society*, Harmondsworth, Penguin.

Bottomore, T. B. (1970), 'Comment on Dr Pašić's paper', in M. J. Broekmeyer (ed.), *Yugoslav Workers' Self-management*, Dordrecht, Reidel, pp. 30–2.

Bottomore, T. B. and Rubel, M. (eds) (1963), *Karl Marx: Selected Writings in Sociology and Social Psychology*, Harmondsworth, Penguin.

Bouvin, A. (1977), 'New Swedish legislation on democracy at the workplace', *International Labour Review*, 115, pp. 131–41.

Bradley, K. (1980), 'A comparative analysis of producer co-operatives', *British Journal of Industrial Relations*, 18, pp. 155–68.

Bradley, K. and Gelb, A. (1981), 'Motivation and control in the Móndragón experiment', *British Journal of Industrial Relations*, 19, pp. 211–13.

Bradley, K. and Gelb, A. (1982), 'The replication and sustainability of the Móndragón experiment', *British Journal of Industrial Relations*, 20, pp. 20–33.

Bradley, K. and Gelb, A. (1983a), *Co-operation at Work: The Móndragón Experience*, London, Heinemann.

Bradley, K. and Gelb, A. (1983b), *Worker Capitalism: The New Industrial Relations*, London, Heinemann.

Brannen, P. (1983a), *Authority and Participation in Industry*, London, Batsford.

Brannen, P. (1983b), 'Worker directors: an approach to analysis', in C. Crouch and F. A. Heller (eds), *International Yearbook of Organizational Democracy*, vol. 1, Chichester, Wiley, pp. 121–38.

Brannen, P., Batstone, E., Fatchett, D. and White, P. (1976), *The Worker Directors*, London, Hutchinson.

Braverman, H. (1974), *Labor and Monopoly Capital*, New York, Monthly Review Press.

Briefs, U., Ciborra, C. and Schneider, L. (eds) (1983), *Systems Design For, With and By the Users*, Amsterdam, North Holland Publishing Co.

Brittan, S. (1985), 'Profit sharing: the link with jobs', *Financial Times*, 25 February, p. 16.

Broekmeyer, M. J. (ed.) (1970), *Yugoslav Workers' Self-management*, Dordrecht, Reidel.

Brown, R. K., Curran, M. M. and Cousins, J. (1983), *Changing Attitudes to Employment*, London, Department of Employment.

Brown, W. (ed.) (1981), *The Changing Contours of British Industrial Relations*, Oxford, Blackwell.

Brown, W. and Jacques, E. (1965), *Glacier Project Papers*, London, Heinemann.

Bull, P. E. (1981), 'Industrial relations attitudes and worker participation', *Journal of Industrial Relations*, 23, pp. 268–73.

Bullock Committee of Inquiry (1977), *Report on Industrial Democracy*, London, HMSO.

Carr, E. H. (1966), *The Bolshevik Revolution*, Harmondsworth, Penguin.

Cartwright, D. and Zander, A. (eds) (1959), *Group Dynamics*, London, Tavistock.

Cassidy, B. (1973), *Workers on the Board*, London, Conservative Political Centre.

Chamberlain, N. W. (1951), *Collective Bargaining*, New York, McGraw-Hill.

Chell, E. (1980), 'Worker directors on the board: 4 case studies', *Employee Relations*, 2(6), pp. 1–39.

Child, J. (1969), *The Business Enterprise in Modern Industrial Society*, London, Collier-Macmillan.

Child, J. (ed.) (1973), *Man and Organization*, London, Allen & Unwin.

Church, R. A. (1971), 'Profit sharing and labour relations in England in the nineteenth century', *International Review of Social History*, 14, pp. 2–16.

Clark, D. G. (1966), *The Industrial Manager: His Background and Career Pattern*, London, Business Publications.

Clarke, R. O., Fatchett, D. J. and Roberts, B. C. (1972), *Workers' Participation in Management in Britain*, London, Heinemann.

Clegg, H. A. (1960), *A New Approach to Industrial Democracy*, Oxford, Blackwell.

Clegg, H. A. (1972), *The System of Industrial Relations in Great Britain*, Oxford, Blackwell.

Clegg, H. A. (1979), *The Changing System of Industrial Relations in Great Britain*, Oxford, Blackwell.

Clegg, I. (1971), *Workers' Self-management in Algeria*, London, Allen Lane.

Coates, K. (1967), 'Wage slaves', in R. K. Blackburn and A. Cockburn, *The Incompatibles*, Harmondsworth, Penguin, pp. 56–92.

Coates, K. (ed.) (1976), *The New Worker Co-operatives*, Nottingham, Spokesman.

Coates, K. and Topham, T. (1970), *Workers' Control*, London, Owen.

Coates, K. and Topham, T. (1972), *The New Unionism*, London, Owen.

Coates, K., Topham, T. and Barratt-Brown, M. (1970), *Trade Union Register*, London, Merlin.

Coch, L. and French, J. R. P. Jnr (1959), 'Overcoming resistance to change', in D. Cartwright and A. Zander (eds), *Group Dynamics*, London, Tavistock, pp. 257–79.

Cohen, S. (ed.) (1971), *Images of Deviance*, Harmondsworth, Penguin.

Cohen, S.S. (1969), *Modern Capitalist Planning*, London, Weidenfeld & Nicolson.

Cole, G. D. H. (1959), Foreword to B. Pribićević, *The Shop Stewards' Movement and Workers' Control*, Oxford, Blackwell, pp. v–viii.

Cole, G. D. H. (1972), *Self-government in Industry*, London, Hutchinson.

Coleman, R. J. (1978), 'Employee participation in the US enterprise', *British Journal of Industrial Relations*, 16, pp. 175–94.

Collins, R. (1970), 'Trends in productivity bargaining', in K. Coates, T. Topham and M. Barratt-Brown (eds), *Trade Union Register*, London, Merlin, pp. 86–108.

Copeman, G. (1958), *The Challenge of Employee Shareholding*, London, Business Publications.

Copeman, G. (1975), *Employee Share Ownership and Industrial Stability*, London, Institute of Personnel Management.

Cordova, E. (1982), 'Workers' participation in decisions within enterprises: recent trends and problems', *International Labour Review*, 121, pp. 125–40.

Corina, J. (1972), Introduction to G. D. H. Cole, *Self-government in Industry*, London, Hutchinson.

Cotgrove, S. F. (1967), *The Science of Society*, London, Allen & Unwin.

Cotgrove, S. F., Dunham, J. and Vamplew, C. (1971), *The Nylon Spinners*, London, Allen & Unwin.

Creigh, S., Donaldson, N. and Hawthorn, E. (1981), 'A stake in the firm: employee financial involvement in Britain', *Employment Gazette*, 89, 5, pp. 229–36.

Cressey, P., Eldridge, J., MacInnes, J. and Norris, G. (1981), 'Participation prospects: some Scottish evidence', *Employment Gazette*, 89, 3, pp. 117–23.

Cronin, J. E. (1979), *Industrial Conflict in Modern Britain*, London, Croom Helm.

Crouch, C. and Heller, F. (eds) (1983), *Organizational Democracy and Political Processes*, Chichester, Wiley.

Crouch, C. and Pizzorno, A. (eds) (1978a), *The Resurgence of Class Conflict in Western Europe Since 1968, vol. 1, National Studies*, London, Macmillan.

Crouch, C. and Pizzorno, A. (eds) (1978b), *The Resurgence of Class Conflict in Western Europe Since 1968, vol. 2, Comparative Analyses*, London, Macmillan.

Dahl, R. (1961), *Who Governs? Democracy and Power in an American City*, New Haven, Conn., Yale University Press.

Dahrendorf, R. (1959), *Class and Class Conflict in Industrial Society*, London, Routledge & Kegan Paul.

Daly, K. (n.d.), *Participation: The Next Industrial Revolution*, London, Conservative Trade Unionists.

Daniel, W. W. (1969), 'Industrial behaviour and orientation to work – a critique', *Journal of Management Studies*, 6, pp. 366–75.

Daniel, W. W. (1973), 'Understanding employee behaviour in its context: illustrations from productivity bargaining', in J. Child (ed.), *Man and Organization*, London, Allen & Unwin, pp. 39–62.

Daniel, W. W. and McIntosh, N. (1972), *The Right to Manage?*, London, MacDonald.

Daniel, W. W. and Millward, N. (1983), *Workplace Industrial Relations in Britain*, London, Heinemann.

Davies, A. (1984), 'The management/union relationship in the introduction of new technology', in N. Piercy, (ed.), *The Management Implications of New Information Technology*, London, Croom Helm, pp. 172–85.

Davis, K. and Moore, W. E. (1945), 'Some principles of stratification', *American Sociological Review*, 10, pp. 242–9.

Davis, L. E. and Cherns, A. B. (eds) (1975a), *The Quality of Working Life*, vol. 1, London, Collier-Macmillan.

Davis, L. E. and Cherns, A. B. (eds) (1975b), *The Quality of Working Life*, vol. 2, London, Collier-Macmillan.

Dawe, A. (1970), 'The two sociologies', *British Journal of Sociology*, 21, pp. 207–18.

De Marquez, V. B. (1981), 'Politics, bureaucracy and industrial democracy: a comparative framework for the analysis of worker control in Latin America', *Sociology of Work and Occupations*, 8, pp. 165–80.

Department of Employment (1983), 'Workers' involvement in a changing world', *Employment Gazette*, 91, pp. 102–4.

Derber, M. (1955), *Labor-Management Relations at the Plant Level under Industry-Wide Bargaining*, Wisconsin, University of Illinois Press, 1955.

Derrick, P. and Phipps, J. F. (1969), *Co-operation and Control*, London, Longmans.

Deutsch, S. (1981), 'Work environment reform and industrial democracy', *Sociology of Work and Occupations*, 8, pp. 180–94.

Dickson, J. (1981), 'The relation of direct and indirect participation', *Industrial Relations Journal*, 12(4), pp. 27–35.

Dickson, J. (1982), 'Participation: an organizational bandaid?', *Employee Relations*, 4(1), pp. 12–16.

Dore, R. P. (1973), *British Factory – Japanese Factory*, London, Allen & Unwin.

Douglas, D. (1972), *Transitional Economic Systems*, New York, Monthly Review Press.

Dowling, M., Goodman, J., Gotting, D. and Hyman, J. (1981), 'Employee participation: survey evidence from the North West', *Employment Gazette*, 89, 4, pp. 265–71.

Dubin, R. and Aharoni, Y. (1981), 'Ideology and reality: work and pay in Israel', *Industrial Relations*, 20, pp. 18–35.

Dunlop, J. T. (1958), *Industrial Relations Systems*, New York, Holt.

Dunn, S. and Gennard, J. (1984), *The Closed Shop in British Industry*, London, Macmillan.

Edwards, C. (1983), 'Power and decision making in the workplace: a study in the coal mining industry', *Industrial Relations Journal*, 14(1), pp. 50–69.

Eldridge, J. E. T. (1973), *Sociology and Industrial Life*, London, Nelson.

Elliott, J. (1984), *Conflict or Co-operation?: The Growth of Industrial Democracy* (2nd ed), London, Kogan Page.

Emery, F. E. and Thorsrud, E. (1974), *Form and Content in Industrial Democracy*, London, Tavistock.

Estrin, S. (1984), *Self-management: Economic Theory and Yugoslav Practice*, Cambridge, Cambridge University Press.

Evans, E. O. (1973), 'Cheap at twice the price?', in M. Warner (ed.), *The Sociology of the Workplace*, London, Allen & Unwin, pp. 82–115.

Financial Times (1976), 'Demand for board parity approved by unions', 9 September, p. 10.

Financial Times (1977a), 4 January.

Financial Times (1977b), 'Government seeks full public debate on Bullock Report', 24 January, p. 1.

Financial Times (1977c), 'Worker directors for top policy boards', 27 January, pp. 24–5.

Financial Times (1985), 'Ford go-ahead for worker participation', 6 March, p. 11.

Flanders, A. (1964), *The Fawley Productivity Agreements*, London, Faber & Faber.

Flanders, A. (1967), *Collective Bargaining – Prescription for Change*, London, Faber & Faber.

Flanders, A. (1970), *Management and Unions*, London, Faber & Faber.

Flanders, A., Pomeranz, R. and Woodward, J. (1968), *Experiment in Industrial Democracy*, London, Faber & Faber.

Fletcher, R. (1970), 'Trade union democracy – structural factors', in K. Coates, T. Topham and M. Barratt-Brown (eds), *Trade Union Register*, London, Merlin, pp. 73–85.

Fogarty, M. P. (1972), 'Company and corporation reform and worker participation: the state of the debate', *British Journal of Industrial Relations*, 10, pp. 1–11.

Ford, R. N. (1969), *Motivation Through the Work Itself*, New York, American Management Association.

Fox, A. (1971), *A Sociology of Work in Industry*, London, Collier-Macmillan.

Fox, A. (1985), *History and Heritage*, London, Allen & Unwin.

French, J. R. P. Jnr, Israel, J. and As, D. (1960), 'An experiment on participation in a Norwegian factory', *Human Relations*, 13, pp. 3–19.

Friedrich, C. J. (1950), *Constitutional Government and Democracy*, Boston, Ginn.

Galbraith, J. K. (1968), *The New Industrial State*, Harmondsworth, Penguin.

Gallie, D. (1978), *In Search of the New Working Class*, Cambridge, Cambridge University Press.

Gallie, D. (1983), *Social Inequality and Class Radicalism in France and Britain*, Cambridge, Cambridge University Press.

Giddens, A. (1968), ' "Power" in the recent writings of Talcott Parsons', *Sociology*, 2, pp. 257–72.

Goldthorpe, J. H., Lockwood, D., Bechhofer, F. and Platt, J. (1968), *The Affluent Worker: Industrial Attitudes and Behaviour*, Cambridge, Cambridge University Press.

Goodman, J., Dowling, M., Gotting, D. and Hyman, J. (1982), 'Approaches to employee participation', *Employment Gazette*, 90, 7, pp. 301–10.

Gordon, R., Edwards, R. and Reich, M. (1983), *Labour Market Segmentation*, Cambridge, Cambridge University Press.

Gorfin, C. C. (1969), 'The suggestion scheme', *British Journal of Industrial Relations*, 7, pp. 368–84.

Gretton, J. (1972), 'To sit or not to sit', *New Society*, 20, 15 June, pp. 564–6.

*Guardian* (1973), *Report on the TUC Annual Congress*, September.

Guillebaud, C. W. (1928), *The Works Council*, Cambridge, Cambridge University Press.

Halmos, P. (ed.) (1964), *The Development of Industrial Societies*, Sociological Review Monograph no. 8, Keele, Staffs, University of Keele.

Halsey, A. H. and Trow, M. A. (1971), *The British Academics*, London, Faber & Faber.

Hansard (1985), 'Employee involvement', 28 January, pp. 537–50.

Hanson, C. and Rathkey, P. (1984), 'Industrial democracy: a post-Bullock shopfloor view', *British Journal of Industrial Relations*, 22, pp. 154–68.

Harrison, R. (1960), 'Retreat from industrial democracy', *New Left Review*, 4. pp. 32–7.

Hartmann, H. (1970), 'Codetermination in West Germany', *Industrial Relations*, 9, pp. 137–47.

Hawes, W. R. and Brookes, C. C. P. (1980), 'Change and renewal: joint consultation in industry', *Employment Gazette*, 88, 4, pp. 353–61.

Hawes, W. R. and Smith, P. (1981), 'Employee involvement outside manufacturing', *Employment Gazette*, 89, 6, pp. 265–71.

Hayes, R. H. (1981), 'Why Japanese factories work', *Harvard Business Review*, July-August, pp. 57–66.

Heller, F. A., Wilders, M., Abell, P. and Warner, M. (1979), *What Do the British Want from Participation and Industrial Democracy?*, London, Anglo-German Foundation.

Herzberg, F., Mausner, B. and Snyderman, B. (1959), *The Motivation to Work*, New York, Wiley.

Hespe, G. and Little, A. (1971), 'Some aspects of employee participation', in P. B. Warr (ed.), *Psychology at Work*, Harmondsworth, Penguin, pp. 322–46.

Héthy, L. (1981), 'Trade unions, shop stewards and participation in Hungary', *International Labour Review*, 120, pp. 491–503.

Hingel, A. J. (1983), 'The challenge of new technology for European unions – a comparative approach', in U. Briefs, C. Ciborra and L. Schneider (eds), *Systems Design For, With, and By the Users*, Amsterdam, North Holland Publishing Co., pp. 195–206.

Hinton, J. (1972), Introduction to J. T. Murphy, *The Workers' Committee*, London, Pluto Press.

Hinton, J. (1973), *The First Shop Stewards' Movement*, London, Allen & Unwin.

Histadrut (1983), *Histadrut – General Federation of Labour in Israel*, Tel Aviv, Histadrut.

Holter, H. (1965), 'Attitudes towards employee participation in company decision making processes', *Human Relations*, 18, pp. 297–322.

Horner, J. (1974), *Studies in Industrial Democracy*, London, Gollancz.

Hunter, F. (1953), *Community Power Structure: A Study of Decision Makers*, Chapel Hill, University of North Carolina Press.

Hussey, R. and Marsh, A. I. (1983), *Disclosure of Information and Employee Reporting*, Aldershot, Gower.

Hyman, J. and Schuller, T. (1982), 'Employee participation: the pension trustee experience', *Employee Relations*, 4(5), pp. 6–12.

Hyman, J. and Schuller, T. (1984), 'Occupational pension schemes and collective bargaining', *British Journal of Industrial Relations*, 22, pp. 289–310.

Hyman, R. (1971), *Marxism and the Sociology of Trade Unionism*, London, Pluto Press.

Industrial Democracy in Europe (IDE) International Research Group (1979), 'Participation: formal rules, influence, and involvement', *Industrial Relations*, 18, pp. 273–94.

Industrial Democracy in Europe (IDE) International Research Group (1981a), *European Industrial Relations*, Oxford, Clarendon Press.

Industrial Democracy in Europe (IDE) International Research Group (1981b), *Industrial Democracy in Europe*, Oxford, Clarendon Press.

International Labour Office (1962), *Workers' Management in Yugoslavia*, Geneva, International Labour Office.

International Labour Office (1976), *Workers' Participation in Decisions Within Undertakings*, International Labour Office.

Jain, H. C. (ed.) (1980), *Worker Participation: Success and Problems*, New York, Praeger.

Jay, P. (1977), 'St George and Mondragon', *The Times*, 7 April, p. 23.

Jenkins, C. (1959), *Power at the Top*, London, MacGibbon & Kee.

Jenkins, D. (1974), *Job Power*, London, Heinemann.

Jones, D. C. (1979), 'US producer co-operatives: the record to date', *Industrial Relations*, 18, pp. 342–57.

Jones, D. C. (1980), 'Producer co-operatives in industrialised western economies', *British Journal of Industrial Relations*, 18, pp. 141–54.

Jones, D. C. and Svejnar, J. (1982), *Participatory and Self-managed Firms*, Lexington, Mass., D. C. Heath & Co.

Jones, J. (1973), 'Unions on the board', *New Statesman*, 6 July, pp. 3–4.

Joyce, P. and Woods, A. (1984a), 'Joint consultation in Britain: results of a survey during the recession', *Employee Relations*, 6/3, pp. 2–7.

Joyce, P. and Woods, A. (1984b), 'Joint consultation in Britain: towards an explanation', *Employee Relations*, 6(2), pp. 2–8.

Kamušič, M. (1970), 'Economic efficiency and workers' selfmanagement', in M. J. Broekmeyer (ed.), *Yugoslav Workers' Selfmanagement*, Dordrecht, Reidel, pp. 76–116.

Kelly, J. E. and Clegg, C. W. (eds) (1982), *Autonomy and Control at the Workplace*, London, Croom Helm.

Kelsall, R. K. (1955), *Higher Civil Servants in Britain*, London, Routledge & Kegan Paul.

Kennedy, T. (1978), *European Labour Relations*, London, Associated Business Programmes.

Kenny, G. K. (1984), 'Who gains? A case analysis of employee ownership and managerial prerogatives', *International Journal of Manpower*, 5(4), pp. 11–18.

Kester, G. (1980), *Transition to workers' self management: its dynamics in the decolonising economy of Malta*, Research report series no. 7, The Hague, Institute of Social Studies.

Keul, V. (1983), 'Trade union planning and control of new technology', in U. Briefs, C. Ciborra and L. Schneider (eds), *Systems Design, For, With, and By the Users*, Amsterdam, North Holland Publishing Co., pp. 207–18.

Knight, I. B. (1979), *Company Organisation and Worker Participation: A Survey of Attitudes and Practices in Industrial Democracy with Special Emphasis on the Prospects for Employee Directors*, OPCS, London, HMSO.

Knights, D., Willmott, H. and Collinson, D. (eds) (1985), *Job Redesign*, Aldershot, Gower.

Kochan, T. A., Katz, H. C. and Mower, N. R. (1984), *Worker Participation in American Unions*, Kalamazoo, Michigan, W. E. Upjohn Institute for Employment Research.

Kolaja, J. (1960), *A Polish Factory*, Lexington, University of Kentucky Press.

Kolaja, J. (1965), *Workers' Councils*, London, Tavistock.

Kuhne, R. J. (1980), *Co-determination in Business: Workers' Representation in the Boardroom*, New York, Praeger.

Labour Party (1967), *Industrial Democracy*, London, Labour Party.

Labour Party (1968), *The Community and the Company*, London, Labour Party.

Labour Party (1974), *The Community and the Company*, London, Labour Party.

Labour Party (1980), *Workers' Co-operatives*, London, Labour Party.

*Labour Weekly* (1973), 'Industrial democracy', 8 June.

Lammers, C. J. (1967), 'Power and participation in decision making in formal undertakings', *American Journal of Sociology*, 73, pp. 201–16.

Lansbury, R. D. (ed.) (1980), *Democracy in the Workplace*, Melbourne, Longman.

Lansbury, R. D. and Prideau, G. J. (1981), 'Worker participation in management: the Australian experience', *International Institute for Labour Studies*, Geneva, ILO.

Lenin, V.I. (1961), 'What is to be done?', *Collected Works*, Moscow, Foreign Languages Publishing House.

Leonard, J. (1965), *Co-operative, Co-partnership Productive Societies*, Leicester, Co-operative Productive Federation.

Lesieur, F. G. (1958), *The Scanlon Plan*, New York, Wiley.

Lewis, J. S. (1948), *Partnership for All*, London, Kerr-Cross.

Lewis, J. S. (1954), *Fairer Shares*, London, Staples.

Liberal Party (1973), *Evidence and Memorandum on EEC Proposals on Supervisory Boards and Worker Participation*, London, Liberal Party.

Liberal Party (1985), *Liberal Party Policy Briefing*, London, Liberal Party.

Likert. R. (1961), *New Patterns in Management*, New York, McGraw-Hill.

Littler, C. R. and Lockett, M. (1983), 'The significance of trade unions in China', *Industrial Relations Journal*, 14(4), pp. 31–42.

Lockwood, D. (1964), 'The distribution of power in industrial society: a comment', in P. Halmos (ed.), *The Development of Industrial Societies*, Keele, Staffs, University of Keele.

Lockwood, D. (1966), 'Sources of variation in working class images of society', *Sociological Review*, 14, pp. 249–67.

Long, R. J. (1980), 'Job attitudes and organizational performance under employee ownership', *Academy of Management Journal*, 23, pp. 726–37.

Long, R. J. (1982), 'Worker ownership and job attitudes: a field study', *Industrial Relations*, 21, pp. 196–215.

Loveridge, R. (1980), 'What is participation? A review of the literature and some methodological problems', *British Journal of Industrial Relations*, 23, pp. 297–317.

Loveridge, R. and Mok, A. L. (1979), *Theories of Labour Market Segmentation*, The Hague, Martinus Nijhoff.

McArthur, A. A. (1984), *The Community Business Movement in Scotland*, Glasgow University, Centre for Urban and Regional Research.

Macbeath, I. (1975), *Power Sharing in Industry*, Essex, Gower Press.

McCarthy, W. E. J. (1967), 'The role of shop stewards in British industrial relations', Research Paper 1, Royal Commission on Trade Unions and Employers' Associations, London, HMSO.

McCarthy, W. E. J. and Parker, S. R. (1968), 'Shop stewards and workshop relations', Research Paper 10, Royal Commission on Trade Unions and Employers' Associations, London, HMSO.

McGregor, D. (1960), *The Human Side of Enterprise*, New York, McGraw-Hill.

MacInnes, J. (1985), 'Conjuring up consultation: the role and extent of joint consultation in post-war private manufacturing industry', *British Journal of Industrial Relations*, 23, pp. 95–113.

Mandel, E. (1973), 'Workers' control and workers' councils', *International*, 2, pp. 1–17.

Marchington, M. (1980), *Responses to Participation at Work*, Farnborough, Gower.

Marchington, M. (1984), 'Participating through the recession', *Employee Relations*, 6(5), pp. 17–20.

Marchington, M. and Armstrong, R. (1981a), 'A case for consultation', *Employee Relations*, 3(1), pp. 10–16.

Marchington, M. and Armstrong, R. (1981b), 'Employee participation: problems for the shop steward', *Industrial Relations Journal*, 12(1), pp. 46–61.

Marchington, M. and Armstrong, R. (1984), 'Employee participation: some problems for some shop stewards', *Industrial Relations Journal*, 15(1), pp. 68–81.

Marcuse, H. (1954), *Reason and Revolution*, London, Routledge & Kegan Paul.

Marsh, A. I. (1965), *Industrial Relations in Engineering*, Oxford, Pergamon.

Marsh, A.I. (1982), *Employee Relations Policy and Decision Making*, London, CBI and Gower.

Marsh, A. I. and Hussey, R. (1979), *Company Secretary's Review – Survey of Employee Reports*, Croydon, Tolley.

Martin, R. (1981), *New Technology and Industrial Relations in Fleet Street*, Oxford, Clarendon Press.

Marx, K. (1946), *Capital: A Critical Analysis of Capitalist Production*, London, Allen & Unwin.

Marx, K. (1951), *Value, Price and Profit*, London, Allen & Unwin.

Marx, K. (1963), *Selected Writings in Sociology and Social Philosophy*, ed. T. B. Bottomore and M. Rubel, Harmondsworth, Penguin.

Maslow, A. H. (1954), *Motivation and Personality*, New York, Harper & Row.

Mattick, P. (1969), *Marx and Keynes*, London, Merlin.

Meadows, D. H., Meadows, D. L., Randers, J. and Behrens, W. W. (1972), *The Limits to Growth*, London, Earth Island.

Mechanic, D. (1962–3), 'Sources of power of lower participants in complex organizations', *Administrative Science Quarterly*, 7, pp. 349–64.

Meidner, R. (1981), 'Collective asset formation through wage earner funds', *International Labour Review*, 120, pp. 303–17.

Mills, C. W. (1956), *The Power Elite*, New York, Oxford University Press.

Mills, C. W. (1958), 'The structure of power in American society', *British Journal of Sociology*, 9, pp. 29–41.

Mills, C. W. (1959), *The Sociological Imagination*, New York, Oxford University Press.

Modiano, P. and Dimoldenbery, S. (1981), 'Internal relationships in industrial co-operatives', *Employee Relations*, 3(4), pp. 13–16.

Monaj, J. (1981), 'Workers' participation in decisions within undertakings', *International Labour Office*, Geneva, ILO.

Morse, M. C. and Reimer, E. (1956), 'Experimental change in a major organizational variable', *Journal of Abnormal and Social Psychology*, 52, pp. 120–9.

Murphy, J. T. (1972), *The Workers' Committee*, London, Pluto Press.

Musgrove, F. (1963), *The Migratory Elite*, London, Heinemann.

National Economic Development Office (1983), *The Introduction of New Technology*, London, NEDO.

National Institute of Industrial Psychology (1952), *Joint Consultation in British Industry*, London, Staples.

Neville, P. (1973), 'Productivity bargaining', Sheffield University, unpublished undergraduate dissertation.

Ng, S.-H. (1984), 'One brand of workplace democracy: the workers' congress in the Chinese enterprise', *Journal of Industrial Relations*, 26, pp. 56–75.

Nichols, T. (1969), *Ownership, Control and Ideology*, London, Allen & Unwin.

Nightingale, D. V. (1981), 'Work, formal participation and employee outcomes', *Sociology of Work and Occupations*, 8, pp. 277–96.

Oakeshott, R. (1978), *The Case for Workers' Co-ops*, London, Routledge & Kegan Paul.

Obradovic, J. (1970), 'Participation and work attitudes in Yugoslavia', *Industrial Relations*, 2, pp. 161–9.

O'Connor, R. and Kelly, P. (1980), *A Study of Industrial Workers' Co-operatives*, Dublin, Economic & Social Research Institute.

Olsen, M. E. (1970), *Power in Societies*, London, Macmillan.

Organization for Economic Co-operation and Development (OECD) (1981), *Microelectronics, Productivity and Employment*, Paris, OECD.

Otley, C. B. (1973), 'The educational background of British army officers', *Sociology*, 7, pp. 191–209.

Owen, G. (1977), 'The case for co-operatives', *Financial Times*, 29 April.

Parsons, T. (1960), *Structure and Process in Modern Societies*, Chicago, Free Press.

Parsons, T. (1963), 'On the concept of influence', *Public Opinion Quarterly*, 27, pp. 37–62.

Parsons, T. (1967), 'On the concept of political power', in R. Bendix and S. M. Lipset (eds), *Class, Status and Power*, London, Routledge & Kegan Paul, pp. 240–65.

Pateman, C. (1970), *Participation and Democratic Theory*, Cambridge, Cambridge University Press.

Pateman, C. (1983), 'Some reflections on *Participation and Democratic Theory*', in C. Crouch and F. A. Heller (eds), *International Yearbook of Organizational Democracy*, vol. 1, Chichester, Wiley, pp. 107–20.

Paul, L. (1964), *The Deployment and Remuneration of the Clergy*, London, Church Information Office.

Paul, W. J. and Robertson, K. B. (1970), *Job Enrichment and Employee Motivation*, London, Gower.

Peel, J. (1979), *The Real Power Game*, London, McGraw-Hill.

Perlman, M. (1958), *Labor Union Theories in America*, Illinios, Row Peterson.

Perlman, S. (1949), *A Theory of the Labor Movement*, New York, Kelley.

Pettigrew, A. M. (1985), *The Awakening Giant*, Oxford, Blackwell.

Philips (1968), *Work Structuring: A Summary of Experiences at Philips*, Eindhoven, Philips.

Pipkorn, J. (1984), 'Employee participation in the European community: progress and pitfalls', in B. Wilpert and A. Sorge (eds), *International Yearbook of Organizational Democracy*, vol. 2, Chichester, Wiley, pp. 49–70.

Polsby, N. W. (1960), 'How to study community power: the pluralist alternative', *Journal of Politics*, 22, pp. 478–84.

Poole, M. J. F. (1969), 'A power approach to workers' participation in decision making', Sheffield University, unpublished PhD dissertation.

Poole, M. J. F. (1974), 'Towards a sociology of shop stewards', *Sociological Review*, 22, pp. 57–82.

Poole, M. J. F. (1979), 'Industrial democracy: a comparative analysis', *Industrial Relations*, 18, pp. 262–72.

Poole, M. J. F. (1980), 'Industrial democracy and managers: an explanatory and critical perspective', *Journal of Industrial Relations*, 22, pp. 54–72.

Poole, M. J. F. (1981a), 'Industrial democracy in comparative perspective', in R. Mansfield and M. J. F. Poole (eds), *International Perspectives on Management and Organization*, Aldershot, Gower, pp. 23–38.

Poole, M. J. F. (1981b), *Theories of Trade Unionism: A Sociology of Industrial Relations*, London, Routledge & Kegan Paul.

Poole, M. J. F. (1982a), 'Personnel management in Third World countries', *Personnel Review*, 11(4), pp. 37–43.

Poole, M. J. F. (1982b), 'Theories of industrial democracy: the emerging synthesis', *Sociological Review*, 30, pp. 181–207.

Poole, M. J. F. (1984), 'New technology and industrial relations', in N. Piercy (ed.), *The Management Implications of New Information Technology*, London, Croom Helm, pp. 143–60.

Poole, M. J. F. (1986), *Industrial Relations: Origins and Patterns of National Diversity*, London, Routledge & Kegan Paul.

Poole, M. J. F., Mansfield, R., Blyton, P. R. and Frost, P. E. (1981), *Managers in Focus*, Farnborough, Gower.

Postgate, R. (1923), *The Builders' History*, London, National Federation of Building Trades Operatives.

Postgate, R. (1970), 'Builder guilds: a second view', in K. Coates and T. Topham (eds), *Workers' Control*, London, Panther, pp. 60–4.

Pribićević, B. (1959), *The Shop Stewards' Movement and Workers' Control*, Oxford, Blackwell.

Pryke, R. (1971), *Public Enterprise in Practice*, London, MacGibbon & Kee.

Purcell, T. (1960), *Blue Collar Man*, Cambridge, Mass., Harvard University Press.

Qvale, T. U. (1982), *Bedriftsdemokratiet i Norge*, AI-dok 102/82 (Oslo).

Ramsay, H. (1976), 'Participation: the shop-floor view', *British Journal of Industrial Relations*, 14, pp. 128–41.

Ramsay, H. (1977), 'Cycles of control', *Sociology*, 11, pp. 481–506.

Ramsay, H. (1980), 'Phantom participation: patterns of power and conflict', *Industrial Relations Journal*, 11(3), pp. 46–59.

Ramsay, H. (1983), 'Evolution or cycle? Worker participation in the 1970s and 1980s', in C. Crouch and F. A. Heller (eds), *International Yearbook of Organizational Democracy*, vol. 1, Chichester, Wiley, pp. 203–25.

Reckitt, M. B. and Bechhofer, C. E. (1918), *The Meaning of National Guilds*, London, Palmer.

Rees, W. D. (1963), 'The practical functions of joint consultation, considered historically and in the light of recent experiences in South Wales', London University, unpublished MSc dissertation.

Reid, J. (1972), Foreword to W. Thompson and F. Hart, *The UCS Work-In*, London, Lawrence & Wishart, pp. 7–8.

Remus, J. (1983), 'Financial participation of employees: an attempted classification and major trends', *International Labour Review*, 122, pp. 1–21.

Renshaw, P. (1967), *The Wobblies*, London, Eyre & Spottiswoode.

Rice, A. K. (1958), *Productivity and Social Organization*, London, Tavistock.

Riddell, D. S. (1968), 'Social self-government: the background of theory and practice in Yugoslav socialism', *British Journal of Sociology*, 19, pp. 47–75.

Robbins, J. R. (1982), 'The co-operative alternative: the revival of a democratic ideal in industry', *Journal of Industrial Relations*, 24, pp. 3–18.

Roberts, E. (1972), *Workers' Control*, London, Allen & Unwin.

Robson, M.P. (1981), 'Worker participation in the UK', *Management Bibliography and Review*, 7, Bradford, MCB.

Roethlisberger, F. J. and Dixon, W. J. (1939), *Management and the Worker*, Cambridge, Mass., Harvard University Press.

Rokkan, S. (1970), *Citizens, Elections, Parties: Approaches to the Comparative Study of the Process of Political Development*, Oslo, Universitetsforlaget.

Rosen, C., Klein, K. and Young, K. (1984), *Employee Ownership in America*, Lexington, Lexington Books.

Rosen, H. and Rosen, R. A. H. (1955), *The Union Member Speaks*, Englewood Cliffs, New Jersey, Prentice-Hall.

Rosenberg, R. D. and Rosenstein, E. (1981), 'Operationalising workers' participation: a comparison of Yugoslavia and the USA', *Industrial Relations Journal*, 12(2), pp. 46–52.

Rosenstein, E. (1970). 'Histadrut's search for a participation program', *Industrial Relations*, 9, pp. 170–86.

Rosenstein, E. (1977), 'Workers' participation in management: problematic issues in the Israeli system', *Industrial Relations Journal*, 8(2), pp. 55–69.

Ross, A. M. (1962), 'Prosperity and labour relations in western Europe: Italy and France', *Industrial and Labor Relations Review*, 16, pp. 63–85.

Rothschild-Whitt, J. (1981), 'There's more than one way to run a democratic enterprise: self-management from the Netherlands', *Sociology of Work and Occupations*, 8, pp. 201–23.

Roy, D. (1952), 'Quota restriction and goldbricking in a machine shop', *American Journal of Sociology*, 57, pp. 427–42.

Roy, D. (1954), 'Efficiency and the "fix": informal inter-group relations in piecework machine shops', *American Journal of Sociology*, 60, pp. 255–66.

Rubery, J., Tarling, R. and Wilkinson, F. (1984), 'Industrial relations issues in the 1980s: an economic analysis', in M. Poole, W. Brown, J. Rubery, K. Sisson, R. Tarling and F. Wilkinson, *Industrial Relations in the Future*, London, Routledge & Kegan Paul, pp. 95–137.

Ruble, B. A. (1981), *Soviet Trade Unions*, Cambridge, Cambridge University Press.

Rus, V. (1970), 'Influence structure in Yugoslav enterprises', *Industrial Relations*, 9, pp. 148–60.

Rus, V. (1984), 'Yugoslav self-management – 30 years later', in B. Wilpert and A. Sorge (eds), *International Yearbook of Organizational Democracy*, vol. 2, Chichester, Wiley, pp. 371–89.

Ruskin College (1984), *Workers and New Technology: Disclosure and Use of Company Information*, Oxford, Ruskin College.

Sadler, R. J. (1982), 'Employee representatives on boards of directors: limiting directors' fiduciary duties', *Journal of Industrial Relations*, 24, pp. 282–90.

Sallis, H. (1965), 'Joint consultation and meetings of primary working groups in power stations', *British Journal of Industrial Relations*, 3, pp. 328–44.

Savall, H. (1981), *Work and People: An Economic Evaluation of Job Enrichment*, Oxford, Clarendon Press.

Sawtell, R. (1968), *Sharing our Industrial Future*, London, Industrial Society.

Sayles, L. R. (1958), *The Behavior of Industrial Work Groups*, New York, Wiley.

Scanlon, H., 'Workers' control and the threat of the international combines', in K. Coates, T. Topham and M. Barratt-Brown (eds), *Trade Union Register*, London, Merlin, pp. 45–52.

Schrank, R. (ed.) (1984), *Industrial Democracy at Sea*, Cambridge, Mass., MIT Press.

Schregle, J. (1970), 'Forms of participation in management', *Industrial Relations*, 9, pp. 117–22.

Schuller, T. and Henderson, S. (1980), 'Worker representation and the articulation of training needs', *Industrial Relations Journal*, 11(2), pp. 49–57.

Schuller, T. and Hyman, J. (1983), 'Pensions: the voluntary growth of participation', *Industrial Relations Journal*, 14(1), pp. 70–9.

Schumpeter, J. A. (1943), *Capitalism, Socialism and Democracy*, London, Allen & Unwin.

Scott, W. H., Banks, J. A., Halsey, A. H. and Lupton, T. (1956), *Technical Change and Industrial Relations*, Liverpool, Liverpool University Press.

Scott, W. H., Mumford, E., McGivering, I. C. and Kirkby, J. M. (1963), *Coal and Conflict*, Liverpool, Liverpool University Press.

Seibel, H. D. and Damachi, U. G. (1982), *Self Management in Yugoslavia and the Developing World*, London, Macmillan.

Sheehan, B. (1981), *Employee Financial Participation*, Canberra, Australian Government Public Service.

Shirom, A. (1980), 'Political parties and democracy in the Histadrut', *Industrial Relations*, 19, pp. 231–5.

Shuchman, A. (1957), *Co-determination, Labor's Middle Way in Germany*, Washington, Public Affairs Press.

Silver, M. L. (1981), 'Worker management: a power-dialectic framework', *Sociology of Work and Occupations*, 8, pp. 145–64.

Simon, H. A. (1953), 'Notes on the observation and measurement of political power', *Journal of Politics*, 15, pp. 500–16.

Singer, D. (1982), *The Road to Gdansk*, New York, Monthly Review Press.

Singleton, F. and Topham, T. (1968), *Workers' Control in Yugoslavia*, London, Fabian Society.

Sloman, M. and Barr, R. (1981), 'Opportunities for co-operatives in the 1980s', *Employee Relations*, 3(2), p. 2.

Social Democratic Party (n.d.), *Industrial Democracy*, Fourth Policy Document on Industrial Relations, London, SDP.

Sorge, A. (1976), 'The evolution of industrial democracy in the countries of the European Community', *British Journal of Industrial Relations*, 14, pp. 274–94.

Sorge, A., Hartmann, G., Warner, M. and Nicholas, I. (1983), *Microelectronics and Manpower in Manufacturing*, Aldershot, Gower.

Spillane, R., Findlay, A. W. and Borthwick, K. (1982), 'Perceptions of worker participation: the influence of job status and political affiliation', *Journal of Industrial Relations*, 24, pp. 19–32.

Spinrad, W. (1960), 'Correlates of trade union participation: a summary of the literature', *American Sociological Review*, 25, pp. 237–44.

Spiro, H. J. (1958), *The Politics of German Co-determination*, Cambridge, Mass., Harvard University Press.

Spriggs, J. and Armstrong, R. (1982), 'KME: the life of a co-operative', *Employee Relations*, 4(1), pp. 17–22.

Stephen, F. H. (1976–7), 'Yugoslav self-management 1945–74', *Industrial Relations Journal*, 7, pp. 56–65.

Stephen, F. H. (1982), *The Performance of Labor-Managed Firms*, New York, St Martin's Press.

Stephenson, T. (1981), 'Co-operative democracy and employee involvement', *Industrial Relations Journal*, 12(5), pp. 55–65.

Stern, R. M., Wood, K. H. and Hammer, T. H. (1979), *Employee Ownership in Plant Shutdowns*, Kalamazoo, Michigan, W. E. Upjohn Institute for Employment Research.

Strauss, G. (1979), 'Workers' participation: symposium introduction', *Industrial Relations*, 18, pp. 247–61.

Strauss, G. (1984), 'Industrial relations: time for change', *Industrial Relations*, 23, pp. 1–15.

Streeck, W. (1984), 'Co-determination: the fourth decade' in B. Wilpert and A. Sorge (eds), *International Yearbook of Organizational Democracy*, vol. 2, Chichester, Wiley, pp. 391–422.

Sturmthal, A. (1964), *Workers' Councils*, Cambridge, Mass., Harvard University Press.

Supek, R. (1970), 'Problems and perspectives of workers' selfmanagement in Yugoslavia', in M. J. Broekmeyer (ed.), *Yugoslav Workers' Self-management*, Dordrecht, Reidel, pp. 216–41.

Tabb, J. Y. and Goldfarb, A. (1970), *Workers' Participation in Management*, Oxford, Pergamon.

Tannenbaum, F. (1921), *The Labor Movement*, New York, Putnam.

Taylor, L. and Walton, P. (1971), 'Industrial sabotage: motives and meanings', in S. Cohen (ed.), *Images of Deviance*, Harmondsworth, Penguin, pp. 219–45.

Teicher, J. (1982), 'Worker involvement: an analysis of the SECV working parties – a comment', *Journal of Industrial Relations*, 24, pp. 578–82.

Terry, M. (1983), 'Shop steward development and management strategies', in G. S. Bain (ed.), *Industrial Relations in Britain*, Oxford, Blackwell, pp. 67–91.

Teulings, A. W. M. (1984), 'The social, cultural and political setting of industrial democracy', in B. Wilpert and A. Sorge (eds), *International Yearbook of Organizational Democracy*, vol. 2, Chichester, Wiley, pp. 233–56.

Thompson, W. and Hart, F. (1972), *The UCS Work-in*, London, Lawrence & Wishart.

Thornley, J. (1981), *Workers' Co-operatives: Jobs and Dreams*, London, Heinemann.

Thorsrud, E. (1980), 'The changing structure of work organization', in G. Kanawaty (ed.), *Managing and Developing New Forms of Work Organization*, Geneva, International Labour Office, pp. 3–32.

Thorsrud, E. (1984), 'The Scandinavian model: strategies of organizational democratization in Norway', in B. Wilpert and A. Sorge (eds), *International Yearbook of Organizational Democracy*, vol. 2, Chichester, Wiley, pp. 337–70.

Thorsrud, E. and Emery, F. E. (1969), *Form and Content in Industrial Democracy*, London, Tavistock.

Thorsrud, E. and Emery, F. E. (1970), 'Industrial democracy in Norway', *Industrial Relations*, 9, pp. 187–96.

Tinbergen, J. (1970), 'Does self-management approach the optimum order?', in M. J. Broekmeyer (ed.), *Yugoslav Workers' Self-management*, Dordrecht, Reidel.

Toscano, D. (1981), 'Labor-management co-operation and the West German system of co-determination', *Industrial Relations Journal*, 12(6), pp. 57–67.

Trade Union Congress (1944), *Interim Report on Post War Reconstruction*, London, TUC.

Trade Union Congress (TUC)-Labour Party Liaison Committee (1982), *Economic Planning and Industrial Democracy: The Framework for Full Employment*, London, Labour Party.

Trist, E. L., Higgin, G. W., Murray, H. and Pollock, A. B. (1963), *Organizational Choice*, London, Tavistock.

Turner, H. A. (1962), *Trade Union Growth, Structure and Policy*, London, Allen & Unwin.

Undy, R. and Martin, R. (1984), *Ballots and Trade Union Democracy*, Oxford, Blackwell.

Vanek, J. (1970), *The General Theory of Labor-Managed Economies*, Cornell, Cornell University Press.

Vanek, J. (1972), *The Economics of Workers' Management: A Yugoslav Case Study*, London, Allen & Unwin.

Vaughan, E. (1980), 'Industrial democracy: consensus and confusion', *Industrial Relations Journal*, 11(1), pp. 50–6.

Vaughan, E. (1983), 'Structure and strategy in the case for worker participation', *Journal of Industrial Relations*, 25, pp. 317–26.

Verba, S. (1961), *Small Groups and Political Behaviour*, Princeton, New Jersey, Princeton University Press.

Vidaković, Z. (1970), 'The function of the trade unions in the process of establishing the structure of Yugoslav society on a basis of workers' self-management', in M. J. Broekmeyer (ed.), *Yugoslav Workers' Self-management*, Dordrecht, Reidel, pp. 42–60.

Wajcman, J. (1983), *Women in Control: Dilemmas of a Workers' Co-operative*, Milton Keynes, Open University Press.

Walder, A. (1981), 'Participative management and worker control in China', *Sociology of Work and Occupations*, 8, pp. 224–52.

Wales Co-operative Development and Training Centre (1984), *Annual Report 1983–4*, Cardiff, WCDTC.

Wallas, G. (1912), 'On syndicalism', Sociological Society: Annual Meeting, *Sociological Review*, 5, pp. 247–57.

Walton, R. E. (1975), 'Criteria for quality of working life', in L. E. Davis and A. B. Cherns, *The Quality of Working Life*, vol. 1, London, Collier-MacMillan, pp. 91–104.

Warner, M. (ed.) (1973), *The Sociology of the Workplace*, London, Allen & Unwin.

Warner, M. (1982a), 'Work democracy: towards a 3-dimensional approach', *Journal of Industrial Relations*, 24, pp. 215–26.

Warner, M. (1982b), 'Worker participation and employee influence: a study of managers and shop stewards', *Industrial Relations Journal*, 13(4), pp. 18–25.

Warner, M. (1984a), 'Organizational democracy – the history of an idea', in B. Wilpert and A. Sorge (eds), *International Yearbook of Organizational Democracy*, vol. 2, Chichester, Wiley, pp. 5–21.

Warner, M. (1984b), *Organizations and Experiments*, Chichester, Wiley.

Warner, M. (1984c), 'The impact of new technology on participative institutions and employee involvement', in N. Piercy (ed.), *The*

*Management Implications of New Information Technology*, London, Croom Helm, pp. 161–71.

Warr, P. B. (ed.) (1971), *Psychology at Work*, Harmondsworth, Penguin.

Webb, S. and Webb, B. (1897), *Industrial Democracy*, London, Longmans.

Webb, S. and Webb, B. (1902), *A History of Trade Unionism*, London, Longmans, Green.

Webb, S. and Webb, B. (1932), *Methods of Social Study*, London, Longmans, Green.

Weber, M. (1968), *Economy and Society*, New York, Bedminster Press.

Weschler, L. (1982), *Solidarity*, New York, Fireside.

Wheelwright, E. L. and McFarlane, B. (1970), *The Chinese Road to Socialism*, New York, Monthly Review Press.

Whyte, W. F., Hammer, T. H., Meek, C. B., Nelson, R. and Stern, R. N. (1983), *Worker Participation and Ownership: Co-operative Strategies for Strengthening Local Economies*, Ithaca, New York, Institute of Labour Relations Press.

Wilczynski, J. (1983), *Comparative Industrial Relations*, London, Macmillan.

Wilkinson, T. (1983), 'Positive policies on employee involvement', *Employee Relations*, 5(3), pp. 2–4.

Willman, P. and Gospel, H. (1983), 'The role of codes in labour relations: the case of disclosure', *Industrial Relations Journal*, 14(4), pp. 76–82.

Willman, P. and Winch, G., in collaboration with Francis, A. and Snell, M. (1985), *Innovation and Management Control*, Cambridge, Cambridge University Press.

Wilson, N. and Coyne, J. (1981), 'Worker co-operatives and the promotion of co-operative development in Britain', *Industrial Relations Journal*, 12(2), pp. 30–45.

Wintour, P. (1977), 'The Social Contract's last stand', *New Statesman*, 7 January, pp. 3–5.

Wolfinger, R. E. (1960), 'Reputation and reality in the study of community power', *American Sociological Review*, 25, pp. 636–44.

Woodward, J. (ed.) (1965), *Industrial Organization: Theory and Practice*, London, Oxford University Press.

Woodworth, W. (1981), 'Forms of employee ownership and workers' control', *Sociology of Work and Occupations*, 8, pp. 195–200.

Worsley, P. (1964), 'The distribution of power in industrial society', in P. Halmos (ed.), *The Development of Industrial Societies*, University of Keele.

Wrong, D. H. (1968), 'Some problems in defining social power', *American Journal of Sociology*, 73, pp. 673–81.

Zukin, S. (1981), 'The representation of working-class interests in socialist society: Yugoslav labour unions', *Politics and Society*, 10, pp. 281–316.

# Author index

# Subject index